Caesar Tondini

The Pope of Rome and the popes of the Oriental Orthodox Church

An essay on monarchy in the church, with special reference to Russia

Caesar Tondini

The Pope of Rome and the popes of the Oriental Orthodox Church
An essay on monarchy in the church, with special reference to Russia

ISBN/EAN: 9783742835611

Manufactured in Europe, USA, Canada, Australia, Japa

Cover: Foto ©Lupo / pixelio.de

Manufactured and distributed by brebook publishing software (www.brebook.com)

Caesar Tondini

The Pope of Rome and the popes of the Oriental Orthodox Church

THE
POPE OF ROME
AND THE
POPES OF THE ORIENTAL ORTHODOX CHURCH.

LONDON: PRINTED BY
SPOTTISWOODE AND CO., NEW-STREET SQUARE
AND PARLIAMENT STREET

ÉTUDES SUR LA QUESTION RELIGIEUSE DE RUSSIE.
DEUXIÈME ÉTUDE.

THE
POPE OF ROME
AND THE
POPES OF THE ORIENTAL ORTHODOX CHURCH:

AN ESSAY ON MONARCHY IN THE CHURCH,

WITH SPECIAL REFERENCE TO

RUSSIA,

FROM ORIGINAL DOCUMENTS, RUSSIAN AND GREEK.

BY THE

REV. CÆSAREUS TONDINI,

BARNABITE.

LONDON:
LONGMANS, GREEN, AND CO.
1871.

NIHIL OBSTAT.

        Thomas F. Knox, Cong. Orat.,
              Censor deputatus.

IMPRIMATUR.

        ✠ HENRICUS EDUARDUS,
              Archiep. Westmonast.

Die 5 Julii, 1871.

TO

CHARLES DU GARD MAKEPEACE, ESQ.
M.A. LOND.

DEAR SIR,

Authority in the Church has formed the topic of frequent conversations between us during my sojourn in London.

I beg to dedicate to you this 'Essay' on the same subject.

I can hardly better acknowledge your many tokens of friendship than by thus causing you to become better acquainted with my religion,—the source of true happiness and of incomparable blessings.

I remain, DEAR SIR,
Yours affectionately,
CÆS. TONDINI,
Barnabite.

PARIS: 64 RUE DE MONCEAU.
July 16, 1871.

CONTENTS.

INTRODUCTION, pp. 1-9.

Progress of infidelity—Impotency of Protestantism to resist it—The State Churches—Probable disestablishment of that of England—What will follow?—Apprehensions for the religious future of England—Manifestations of sympathy towards the Oriental Orthodox Church—Attempts at union with her—Consequences of this reunion if realised—On the contest about the procession of the Holy Ghost, pp. 1-5, text and *note*. Reason of this work—The discussion confined to the *government* of the Oriental Orthodox Church—Division of the work—Why we shall speak more especially of Russia—Statistics of the Oriental Orthodox Church pp. 5-9, *note*.

CHAPTER I.

THE ORIENTAL ORTHODOX CHURCH IS ACTUALLY SO GOVERNED AS NOT TO ALLOW OF HER BEING CONSISTENT WITH HER OWN DOCTRINE CONCERNING THE RIGHTS OF BISHOPS IN THE GOVERNMENT OF THE CHURCH, pp. 10-115.

Doctrine of the Oriental Orthodox Church concerning her *government*—The Church ought to be governed by *bishops*, pp. 10-13.

(A) ORTHODOX CHURCH OF THE RUSSIAN EMPIRE.

This Church is administered through the Holy Synod of St. Petersburg—The Synod likened by the Russians to a Council, pp. 13, 14. (Statutes of the Synod, or the 'Spiritual Regulation,' p. 15, *note*). The Synod composed of men taken 'from the different ranks of the ecclesiastical hierarchy'—Reasons which suggested such composition, pp. 15-17. Original minority of bishops—Early remarks against it—The number of the bishops successively increased—How this modification was carried out—The present composition of the Synod—Remarks, pp. 17-20.
Contests as to the Russian Church being really governed by the Tsar, pp. 21, 22.

History of the Establishment of the Synod—The State Colleges created by Peter the Great in 1718, p. 22. Peter's fear of conscience—Ukase (*in extenso*) for the establishment of the Synod, pp. 22–25—The Synod a State College like the others—Why and when its original name of 'Spiritual College' was changed into that of 'Most Holy Synod,' pp. 25–26—The 'Appendix' to the 'Spiritual Regulation'—Synod's jurisdiction fixed by the Tsar—Ukase (*in extenso*) for the creation of the Chief Procurator of the Synod, pp. 26–28.

Remarks on Peter's proceeding—His mere style an outrage to the Russian bishops—Abdication by them of their personal dignity, pp. 28–30. Document sent to Voltaire concerning the establishment of the Synod—Attempt at opposition to the despotism of Peter—(Voltaire's history of Peter the Great—WRITING FORBIDDEN TO RUSSIAN MONKS). Peter's and Luther's 'So I will,' pp. 30–36, text and *notes*. Abdication by the Russian bishops of their right of being rulers of the Church—Peter's crafty policy in bringing about the establishment of the Synod—The Orthodox Church, through want of external unity, resembles political society—Application to her, by Peter, of the theory of 'accomplished facts'—Of the recognition, by the Oriental Patriarchs, of Peter's Holy Synod, *two years and eight months after its establishment*, pp. 36–39. Voltaire's judgment of Peter's design confirmed by that of the Protestant historians of Peter, pp. 39–40 and *note*.

Oath taken by the members of the Synod (*in extenso*), pp. 40–41 and *note*. The Tsar acknowledged by them upon oath as '*supreme judge of the Synod*'—Remarks upon this oath, pp. 42–43 and *note*.

'*Instruction*' *of the Chief Procurator of the Synod*—It is identical with that of the General Procurator of the Senate—Quotations from this single yet two-faced Instruction—Duties of the Chief Procurator of the Synod (the same, respectively, as those of the General Procurator of the Senate)—The Tsar just as much the judge of the Synod as he is the judge of the Senate, pp. 43–46. Other quotations from the same two-faced Instruction—Remarks, pp. 46–48.

The administrative and legislative powers of the Russian Church both in the hands of the Tsar—Synod and Senate both termed 'governing,' and in what sense, p. 48. Synod a mere organ or instrument, through which the Tsar *acts*—Testimony of the Russian jurists, Mikhailoff and Speranski, pp. 48–50—Testimony of the Russian Code of Laws—Synod and Ministries compared—The *administrative* power belongs, in its entire extent, to the Tsar, pp. 51–53. Definition of the *legislative* power by Blackstone and Stephen, pp. 53–54. The Russian Code on the composition, explanation, and completion of the laws, pp. 54–56.

The Tsars and the Ecclesiastical Canons—Division of canons into dogmatical and disciplinary—The *Kormchaia Kniga*—Canons admitted by the Oriental Orthodox Church—How Peter the Great acted with respect to them, pp. 56–62 and *notes*—(The divorce of the Grand-Duke Con-

stantine Paulovich, brother of Alexander I., and the 35th canon of
St. Basilius the Great, pp. 61–62, *note*.)

The Bishops in their relations to the Synod—The 'Spiritual Regulation' on
the Russian bishops' submission to the Synod—Contradiction with the
Orthodox doctrine, pp. 62–64 and *note*. In what sense the Synod is
the 'supreme power' for the bishops—Rite for the election and consecration of bishops. Limits to their obedience to the Synod—Quotations from
the oath taken by them—The Tsar the source of the Synod's jurisdiction;
his will the test of the moral obligation of its prescriptions—The 'Statute
of the Ecclesiastical Consistories,' pp. 64–68. Quotations from it,
showing prodigious extent of the bishops' submission to the Synod—
Comparison with the Catholic bishops' submission to the Pope, pp. 68–73.
The Secretary of the Ecclesiastical Consistories—His functions and
duties, pp. 73, 74.

*The enslavement of the Russian Church by the Tsar, not a mere fact but a
kind of dogma for her*—Complete distinction between the civil and
ecclesiastical powers, each moving in its own sphere, pp. 74–75, and *note*.
Principles laid down in the 'Spiritual Regulation'—Peter the Great's
opinion on the matter, pp. 76–77. Catherine II.'s declaration that
'sovereigns are invested with the supreme authority in the Church,'
p. 77. The Tsar, in the 'Act of Succession' of Paul I., and the Pope
St. Leo, in the Russian liturgy, both called 'Head of the Church'—How
this title is explained by each of them, pp. 78–81. Ukases of Paul I.'s
successors, p. 81.

The Russian Catechisms—The three principal catechisms, pp. 81–82—Catechism of Peter the Great—Its *orthodoxy* judged by Protestants, pp.
82–83 and *note*. Explanation of the fifth commandment in Peter's
Catechism—(Of the different division of the Ten Commandments in the
Catholic and in the Oriental Orthodox Church) pp. 84–86 and *note*.
Catechism of Platon, metropolitan of Moscow—Bacmeister's judgment of
its *orthodoxy*—Extracts from it, pp. 86–90. Doctrine *virtually* contained
in these two catechisms—Aphorisms concerning the power of the Tsar,
pp. 90–92. (Of the note appended to Art. 42 of the Russian Code of Laws
concerning the title of 'Head of the Church' applied to the Tsar, p. 91,
note). The Church totally deprived of her right of self-government—
Catechism of Mgr. Filaret—Striking omissions in it—The episcopal
office reduced to the bare administration of sacraments and the teaching
of the word of God, pp. 92–94.

Marks of servility exhibited in the liturgical books of the Russian Church—
The imperial family's names in huge capital letters—Formula of appro-
bation of the liturgical books—Remarks, pp. 95–97—Extracts from the
'Rite for the election and consecration of a Bishop'—Of the election of
bishops in the Russian Church, pp. 97–101—The office of Orthodoxy—
Anathema against those who deny that THE GIFTS OF THE HOLY GHOST
ARE POURED OUT UPON ORTHODOX SOVEREIGNS, pp. 101–108—Tacitus'

'Praisers the worst kind of enemies' applied to the praisers of the Russian Church, as regards the consequences of their praises, pp. 101-103.

Prescription of the Criminal Code concerning the REVELATION OF THE SECRET OF CONFESSION—Arguments for quieting the conscience of priests: 'Tell it to the Church' in Matt. xviii. 15-17, pp. 104-106.

Peter the Great's 'I am your patriarch'—Account of the fact printed at St. Petersburg, pp. 106-107.

Questions to English Protestant divines—Remarks on the behaviour of the rest of the Oriental Orthodox Church with regard to the State Church of Russia, pp. 107-109.

(B) ORTHODOX CHURCH OF THE KINGDOM OF GREECE.

The King proclaimed in the Council of Nauplia (1833) 'Head of the Church' with regard to her administration—Of the royal delegate attached to the Synod of Athens, pp. 109-111.

(C) ORTHODOX CHURCH OF THE TURKISH EMPIRE.

Judgment of Dean Stanley—Right solemnly conferred by this Church on the Sultan of finally settling disputes among Patriarchs—Address of thanksgiving to the Sultan in 1853, pp. 111-115. Conclusion of the first Chapter, p. 115.

CHAPTER II.

THE ORIENTAL ORTHODOX CHURCH IS REALLY DIVIDED INTO SEVERAL SEPARATE AND INDEPENDENT CHURCHES AND EVEN PAPACIES, WHILST CATHOLICS ADMIT ONLY ONE CHURCH AND ONE POPE, pp. 115-144.

Misconceptions of the Catholic doctrine concerning the Pope—Real and imaginary Catholicism—Instance taken from the 'Orthodox Doctrine of the Oriental Church,' by the Archimandrite Makary, pp. 115-117. Of the invisible and *visible* portions of the Church—The latter needs *visible governors*—In what different sense the title of 'Head of the Church' is applied to Jesus Christ, and in what to men—How perfectly the 'Orthodox Confession' and the 'Catechism of the Council of Trent' both agree in stating that difference of meaning—The Pope, called 'Head of the Church' in the 'Catechism of the Council of Trent,' in the very same sense in which the bishops are called 'Heads of the Church' in the 'Orthodox Confession'—Accordingly, the question is one of the Church's form of government, pp. 117-122.

Of *unity*, as a mark of the true Church of Jesus Christ—How far the Oriental Orthodox Church agrees with Protestants in the explanation of the mark of *unity*—Consequences, pp. 122-124.

The Oriental Orthodox Church divided into several Papacies—What the Pope is with regard to the *government* of the Church—Three powers of the Pope of Rome: the doctrinal power, the power of order, and the power of *jurisdiction*—How distinct and separate these powers are—That which, with regard to the *government* of the Church, makes the Pope to be Pope is the last, or the power of jurisdiction, pp. 125-128.

Jurisdiction of the Tsar compared to that of the Pope—Whether the Tsar is bound by the canons of his Church. '*Faith* alone preserves him within the bounds of holy justice'—Extract from Schnitzler, and remarks on his statements—Nicholas Tourgeneff on the Pope—Effects of the episcopal consecration, pp. 128-133.

What the Tsar is in Russia, the King of Greece is in his kingdom, pp. 133-134. Of the Concordat of the Hellenic Church with the Church of Constantinople in 1852, p. 134, *note*.

Of the Œcumenical Councils considered as limiting the jurisdiction of the Tsar and of the King of Greece—Who has power authoritatively to assemble such a Council? question still pending—Instance taken from the recent convocation of an Œcumenical Council by the Patriarch of Constantinople—The number of Œcumenical Councils of the Oriental Orthodox Church apparently fixed for ever—The seven pillars of the House of Wisdom and the seven Seals—No such Councils can be held without the consent of the Tsar and of the King of Greece—Their behaviour concerning the canons of the seven past Œcumenical Councils admitted by them, a pledge of a similar line of conduct with regard to future canons of any future Œcumenical Council, pp. 135-138.

Of the four Oriental Patriarchs—They cannot be considered separately as Popes; they constitute together a sort of oligarchy—Development of the Roman papacy compared to that of the patriarchal dignity—*Reconsecration of Patriarchs for the* SECOND *and even the* THIRD *time*—'*A double grace required to be Patriarch*'—(Did not the Oriental Orthodox Church create a NEW DOGMA in 1672?)—The oligarchy formed by the Oriental Patriarchs taken as a whole—The Patriarch of Constantinople professing to be entrusted by God 'With the care of all the Churches,' pp. 138-142 and *notes*.

Conclusion of the Second Chapter—Enslavement, as a first fruit, borne by the denial of the Church's external unity of government, as a mark of the true Church of Jesus Christ, pp. 141-144.

CHAPTER III.

THE ORIENTAL ORTHODOX CHURCH IS LIABLE TO ANY REVOLUTION, JUST AS CIVIL SOCIETIES ARE, pp. 145-160.

What we mean by revolution—Theory of revolutions—By what they are originated—The Oriental Orthodox Church more powerless against them than civil societies ordinarily are—Revolutions from within and from without, pp. 145–147.

Peter the Great's reformation a revolution from without, viz., from the civil power—Extract from the 'Spiritual Regulation'—The Oriental Orthodox Church unable to oppose any such revolution, pp. 147–150.

The proclamation of the independence of the Hellenic Church in 1833, as an instance of revolution from within—Of the recognition of her independence by the Patriarch of Constantinople, *seventeen years after it had been proclaimed*—The 'Synodical Volume'—Refutation of it by the Archimandrite Pharmakides—Extracts from this refutation—Principles laid down in it—The seed and the previous apology of all possible revolutions are both to be found in it, pp. 150–154. The lessons of the Archimandrite Pharmakides reduced to practice by Prince Cousa in Roumania, and by the Bulgarian Orthodox Church, pp. 154–155.

The chief authorities of the Oriental Orthodox Church of human institution—What men have made men can destroy—Whether it is not a duty for this Church to conform herself to the tendency of the times, and constitute herself a republic—An *Orthodox ecclesiastical republic* not beyond the limits of possibility, pp. 155–157. What would follow if the cherished dream of Russian patriots should be realised, pp. 157–158. The Oriental Orthodox Church unable finally to settle disputes of jurisdiction—To what her episcopal jurisdiction is reduced—Catholicism or revolution, pp. 158–160.

CHAPTER IV.

THE ROMAN PAPACY, pp. 161–181.

The Church in a perfect sense the *Society of God*—Her founder is Jesus Christ—He must have told her who ought to be entrusted with the supreme government in the Church, pp. 160–161.

How can we know Jesus Christ's will on that point?—Of the best form of government, pp. 161–163. Patent fact which can lead us to discover Jesus Christ's will: *there has* ALWAYS *been in the Church some authority superior to that of simple bishops*—An authority appointed by Jesus Christ must have existed from the time of Jesus Christ.

Application of this principle to the chief authorities of the Oriental Orthodox Church—The patriarchates of Alexandria and of Antioch alone might in this respect advance some claim to a divine origin—Their history is connected with that of St. Peter—Both unfit for a *Catholic* or 'universal' Church—The Church's conduct towards them to be listened to, pp. 163–166.

The only authority fit for a *Catholic* (*universal*) Church, leading us back to Jesus Christ, and spoken of in the Church as coming from Jesus Christ, is the Pope of Rome—Whether this authority is able to preserve the

Church from enslavement—May revolutions threaten the Catholic Church?
—Is the jurisdiction of the Bishops in this Church effectually supported?
—How the episcopal authority is strengthened by that of the Pope—
Extract from the dogmatical constitution, 'de Ecclesia,' issued by the
Vatican Council (July 18, 1870), pp. 166–170.

Limits to the Pope's authority and power of jurisdiction stated by St. Bernard—Illustration taken from civil Governments, pp. 171–172. Of the
Pope's abuses of power—The increased number of rulers too often increases the amount of human passions, preventing the right exercise of
the supreme authority—Pope's infallibility and impeccability, their distinctness—Abuses of power in a Pope are possible—Saints have acknowledged, and Popes have confessed them—Extract from St. Leonard du Porto-
Maurizio concerning the Popes at the universal judgment, pp. 172–174.
(Father Newman on the Pope, p. 175, *note*). Nobody has more constantly and more effectually protested against the Pope's abuses of power
than the Popes themselves—How?—The conduct of the Popes and that
of the *Reformer* of Wittemberg—Jesus Christ mutilated by Luther, pp.
175–176.

What is good for the Church—Fatalism and filial confidence in God—
Always some need of reform in the Catholic Church—How this is connected with the return of the Oriental Orthodox Church to Catholic unity,
pp. 176–178. (The Barnabite Father Schouvaloff and the *Association of
Prayers* for the return of the Oriental Orthodox Church to Catholic unity,
p. 178 *note*.)

Of the most sure and powerful means to bring about the most perfect reform in the Catholic Church—Reform and schisms—For truth's sake—
What is truth?—'They were not of the seed of those men by whom
salvation was brought to Israel,' pp. 178–181.

POSTSCRIPT.

Striking analogy between the State Church of England and the State Church
of Russia—Whether we have written for the former or the latter,
pp. 182–183.

THE POPE OF ROME
AND
THE POPES OF THE ORIENTAL ORTHODOX CHURCH.

INTRODUCTION.

The events now taking place in Protestant countries, and especially in England, cannot fail to excite the deepest interest in those who have at heart the religious condition of the people.

Not unlike to a political revolution, the authors of which, after having overthrown all constituted authority, vainly endeavour to establish any settled form of government, Protestantism, after having succeeded in partially destroying Catholicism, has proved itself quite unable to take its place. From the time of Luther and the establishment of the State Church of England, many and various have been the attempts to construct some religious edifice which could stand the tests of time and of that cool reflection which time brings with it. The most skilful combinations have been tried, appeals have been made to the genius and talent of men, proposals suggested by human passions have been readily accepted, while whatever could wound our natural instincts has been curtailed or avoided. Trial after trial, attempt after attempt, has been made, but all have proved fruitless and vain, and not one of the numerous religious systems created by Protestantism has a better chance, unless supported from without, of standing the same tests, than any of those which have already failed.

And what has been the necessary consequence of this impotency of Protestantism to create any lasting religious system? That those very dogmas without which Christianity itself cannot exist, deprived as they were of a stable basis in the religious teaching of Protestants, have long since begun to lose their hold on the minds of the people. Even faith in the divinity of Jesus Christ is growing less and less, and one cannot behold without alarm the rapid progress of infidelity. We are threatened, should Protestantism be the only religion of the country, with seeing, at an early date, all faith in God, in a future life, and in everything supernatural, entirely lost.

There is, moreover, a very general desire for a change which, though it might have some good effects, might also, in Protestant countries, hasten the triumph of infidelity over the last remains of Christianity—we mean the separation of Church and State. The most effectual support for Protestant Churches, that of the civil power, is everywhere about to be withdrawn from them.

The support of the State has always proved the best means of maintaining a religious system which has no solid foundation. Leaning upon the State, that special form of Protestantism which the State supports is secured from falling as long as the State lends to it its own framework; and adhering to the State as a parasite adheres to the tree, it is secured from starvation, at least, as long as the State does not cut off those channels through which it receives vital nourishment.

But in these days many people are utterly averse to a State Church, and are ready to do all in their power to bring about a separation. It would almost seem as if, vexed beyond measure at having been so long deceived by the apparent vitality of State Churches, they were desirous of revenging themselves by getting rid of them without further delay or consideration.

This is exactly what is now taking place in England. More than once, on the occasion of the meeting of Parliament, the same authority which three centuries ago pronounced sentence of death against Catholicism, has been called upon to discuss the question whether the same sentence ought not to be passed on the Church which, for three centuries, has occupied the place of Catholicism. Not that the State Church and her adherents have any cause to fear those sanguinary edicts and bloody persecutions which were the lot of their Catholic predecessors—such things are now out of date. The State will merely withdraw its support, leaving the Church to herself, and then it will be seen how long, unsupported by the State, the Anglican Church will linger before dying.

But WHAT WILL FOLLOW? . . . This is the serious question which in our day forcibly engages the attention of every thinking man, whatever be his religious or political creed. *What will follow?* . . . It was, we believe, the gravity of this question, joined with sad forebodings and apprehensions as to the religious future of England, which, some years ago, caused English divines to make themselves acquainted with the two greatest Christian Churches abroad, the Roman Catholic and the so-called Oriental Orthodox Church, whose principal branches are the Greek and the Russian. The same forebodings and apprehensions have also caused many adherents of the State Church of England to promote any sort of friendly relations with the Oriental Orthodox Church, and to renew the ancient attempts at union with her.[1] Even lately the public

---

[1] See about these attempts: *The Orthodox Church of the East in the eighteenth century*, being the correspondence between the Eastern patriarchs

papers spoke of the arrival in London of Mgr. Licourgos, the Greek orthodox bishop of Syra, with a view of promoting the work of the union, and hopes are entertained, on both sides, that such attempts will be crowned with success.

Though Catholics, and especially desiring, as the wish nearest our heart, the return of the Oriental Orthodox Church to Catholic unity, we are far from being alarmed or dissatisfied in witnessing such feelings in England towards the Orthodox Church. The Oriental Orthodox Church is far better than Protestantism, and *Protestants* cannot but find great advantages in becoming *orthodox*. It is, even for us, a consoling thought that, on the day following the fall of the State Church of England, very many souls, whom ignorance or prejudice keeps from embracing Catholicism, would be preserved from total incredulity by having at hand the Oriental Orthodox Church. Moreover, the union of this Church with the Anglican would not only be for England one step more towards Catholicism, but would very likely remove for ever one of the chief obstacles to the reunion of the Oriental Orthodox Church herself with the Roman Catholic—we mean the contest about the procession of the Holy Ghost. Fully convinced that, with regard to this point, great misunderstanding underlies the alleged opposition between the doctrine of the Oriental Orthodox Church and that of the Roman Catholic,[1] we gladly welcome attempts at union

---

and the non-juring bishops, with an Introduction *On various projects of re-union between the Eastern Church and the Anglican Communion*, by George Williams, B.D. (London: Rivingtons, 1868).

The London *Union Review* is, in England, one of the organs of those who pursue the reunion between the Anglican and the Eastern Church. We shall designate the latter by the appellation which she gives to herself of *orthodox*, this being the title generally used for denoting her, *even by those who most vigorously attack her orthodoxy*.

[1] See about this important subject, the dissertation of F. V. De Buck, S.J., *Essai de conciliation sur le dogme de la procession du Saint-Esprit*, printed

Introduction.

which will necessarily lead to a fair and public discussion of the matter. The Anglican Church professes, as to the procession of the Holy Ghost, to hold the same doctrine which Catholics hold; hence it follows that, before the union takes place, this point ought to be discussed, and an agreement arrived at. Whatever the result may be, the discussion itself cannot but be greatly favourable to the Catholic Church.

Nevertheless, as Catholics, we cannot help offering to those who are interested in the religious future of England, some remarks concerning that Oriental Orthodox Church, which, though better than Protestantism, still

---

in vol. ii. of the *Études de théologie, de philosophie et d'histoire,* par les PP. C. Daniel et J. Gagarin, S.J. (Paris, 1857). After a diligent discussion of the matter, based upon the doctrine contained in the *Catechisms* of the Oriental Orthodox Church, F. De Buck proposes the acceptance by both sides, of the following canons, in which the Catholic doctrine is so accurately and plainly asserted as to shut out any further misunderstanding.

'Si quis dixerit Patrem solum non esse unicum fontem Trinitatis, anathema sit.

'Si quis dixerit Patrem, gignendo Filium, huic non dedisse ut simul secum produceret Spiritum Sanctum, anathema sit.

'Si quis dixerit Spiritum Sanctum non procedere ex Patre principaliter, sou tamquam ex principio primordiali, et ex Filio non tamquam principio primordiali, sed tamquam habente a Patre ut a se quoque Spiritus Sanctus existentiam, subsistentiam et essentiam acciperet, anathema sit.

'Si quis dixerit Spiritum Sanctum procedere ex Patre et ex Filio de eo in quo alii sunt ab invicem et non de eo in quo unum sunt, anathema sit.

'Si quis ergo dixerit duo esse principia, duasve productiones Spiritûs Sancti, et non unum principium unamque productionem, aut Patrem et Filium non esse principium Spiritus Sancti per unam utrique communem spirationem, anathema sit.

'Si demum quis dixerit Spiritum Sanctum ita procedere ex Patre ut simul non sit Spiritus Filii, aut ita esse Spiritum Filii, ut a Filio non simul ac a Patre existentiam, subsistentiam et essentiam accipiat, et secundum hanc notionem ex Filio non procedat, anathema sit.'—p. 346.

See also, *Persécutions et souffrances de l'Église catholique en Russie,* par un ancien Conseiller d'État de Russie (Paris: Gaume, 1842), pp. 118, 160-2, 280-2.

is not the Church possessing the fulness of religious truth. We shall speak only of *her government*. This, we are well aware, is the point on which the Anglican Church perfectly agrees with the Oriental Orthodox, and on account of which they both seem more reluctant to enter into any agreement with the Catholic. Yet, this is also the point on account of which, more than on any other, the Oriental Orthodox Church offers some features which are not possibly consistent with a Church professing to hold the constitution given to her by Jesus Christ. Such are the following:—

The Oriental Orthodox Church professes to believe that, according to the doctrine of St. Paul (Acts xx. 28),[1] the divinely-instituted visible *heads* and *rulers* of the Church are the BISHOPS. Nevertheless she has not only admitted single priests, *and even laymen*, to share in ordinary ecclesiastical jurisdiction *over bishops*, not only solemnly sanctioned and approved forms of administration entirely depriving her of any self-government, not only kept in her communion princes *and princesses* acting as real and effectual rulers of the Church, not only allowed them to profess to have been invested by God '*with the supreme authority in the Church*,' but has also tolerated that such doctrine be inserted both in her catechisms for religious instruction of the faithful, and in some of the most solemn acts issued by her, thus causing it to appear stamped with the highest approbation which might be expected from her, unless when assembled in a Council. These are the charges against the Oriental Orthodox Church, which we are going to explain, as a subject of serious consideration to English Protestant divines. How far, after this, the Oriental Orthodox Church can be

[1] 'Take heed to yourselves and to the whole flock, wherein the Holy Ghost hath placed you bishops to rule (ποιμαίνειν, ПАСТИ) the Church of God.'— Compare Matt. ii. 6. See further on, chap. i. pp. 10–13, and p. 93, note 1.

cleared from the reproach of having acted in open contradiction both to her own doctrine and to the ecclesiastical canons admitted by her, and of having sanctioned a doctrine logically leading to her destruction, if not absolutely approaching to heresy—this we shall abstain from defining, and leave to their judgment.

But further, a Papacy, viz. an *authority superior to that of the simple bishops, controlling them in the discharge of their duties, receiving the appeals of their subjects, and prescribing them laws in which the welfare of many dioceses, or that of the universal Church, is consulted rather than the convenience of a single bishop*—a Papacy, we say, is so indispensable to the Church, that the Oriental Orthodox Church, though rejecting as a heresy[1] the doctrine of *one single Pope*, entrusted by God with the government of the universal Church, in fact does not exist without *Popes*. We shall show that the chief divisions of the Oriental Orthodox Church are so constituted as to present the whole Oriental Orthodox Church divided into several separate and independent *Papacies*. Hence it is that, whatever is objected against the Catholic doctrine of a visible head of the Church, as destroying her unity by making her a double-headed one, ought, with far more reason, to be alleged against the Oriental Orthodox Church, as many Popes destroy the unity of the Church more than one single Pope does. Hence again it is that

---

[1] 'Parmi *les hérésies* qui, par des décrets que Dieu seul connaît, s'étaient étendues sur une grande partie de l'univers, dominait jadis l'Arianisme, et aujourd'hui le *Papisme*; mais ce dernier, comme l'autre qui a déjà disparu entièrement, ne tiendra pas non plus, *malgré sa vigueur apparente*; il passera et s'abîmera, et l'on entendra retentir la grande voix céleste : " *Il s'est abîmé !* " '—*Apoc.* 12, 10.

Encyclique de S. S. le Pape Pie IX aux Chrétiens d'Orient (6 janv. 1848), *et Encyclique responsive des Patriarches et des Synodes de l'Église d'Orient*, trad. du grec par le Dr. Démétrius Dallas (Paris, Klincksieck, 1850). 8vo. *Encycl. respons.* § iv. pp. 31, 32.

the Oriental Orthodox Church, in order to be consistent with herself, must either abolish every ecclesiastical dignity interfering with the *divinely-instituted* authority of the bishops, and exercising jurisdiction over them, or at least abstain from representing and condemning the Catholic doctrine of a visible head of the Church as contrary to Scripture, and altering the constitution given to the Church by her founder Jesus Christ.

But, above all, there is a practical consequence resulting from the doctrine of the Oriental Orthodox Church concerning her own government, to which we intend to call the reader's closest attention. That doctrine, we do not hesitate to affirm, contains in itself the seeds of all revolutions, logically leads to them, and does not, to say the least, insure to the government of the Church any greater stability than that which civil Governments enjoy. The proofs in support of this assertion will form the subject of an especial chapter.

After this we shall examine how it is that the same danger is not to be feared for the Catholic Church. Finally, we shall dwell on three points of the highest interest, as those to which may be reduced all objections which, from a practical point of view, can be alleged against the supremacy of the Pope; we mean, the limits of his authority, the abuse of it, and, lastly, the reason which justifies Catholics in their filial devotion and extensive obedience to the Pope.

We need hardly remind our readers that, in the whole discussion, we have exclusively in view the mere *external government* or *administration* of the Church. Our discussion is confined to that which, up to the present time, has been the chief obstacle preventing the return of the Oriental Orthodox Church to Catholic unity, that is, *the Pope's power of jurisdiction over the universal Church.*

We further call the attention of our readers to another

point. Though, when speaking of the Oriental Orthodox Church, the Greek Church of the Turkish Empire and of the Kingdom of Greece ought, on many accounts, to be foremost, nevertheless the numerical pre-eminence of the Russian Church,[1] the political importance of Russia, and, above all, the policy Russia has for many years so constantly pursued, of making herself the defender and representative of the whole Oriental Orthodox Church all over the world—these circumstances are every day raising the *Russian* Orthodox Church more and more to the first rank. Hence it is that, without ever losing sight of the rest of the Oriental Orthodox Church, we shall speak more especially of the Orthodox Church of Russia, just as, for an analogous reason, we shall mention only incidentally the Orthodox Church of Roumania, Austria, and Servia.

Throughout the whole work we have not trusted to second-hand authorities, but have deemed it our duty to consult all the documents we quote in their original languages.

[1] The Oriental Orthodox Church is to-day spread over Russia, the Turkish Empire, Greece, Austria, Servia, and Roumania. Her chief divisions are: the Russian Church, under the jurisdiction of the Holy Synod of St. Petersburg; the four Patriarchates of Constantinople, Alexandria, Antioch, and Jerusalem; and the Church of the Kingdom of Greece, under the Synod of Athens. The numerical proportion of the different branches of the Oriental Orthodox Church is, according to the *Statesman's Year Book*, 1871, approximately as follows:—

In Russia	56,000,000
In the Turkish Empire	12,400,000
In Greece	1,308,508
In Roumania	3,860,000
In Austria	3,166,000
In Servia	1,074,000
Total	77,808,508

CHAPTER I.

THE ORIENTAL ORTHODOX CHURCH IS ACTUALLY SO GOVERNED AS NOT TO ALLOW OF HER BEING CONSISTENT WITH HER OWN DOCTRINE CONCERNING THE RIGHTS OF BISHOPS IN THE GOVERNMENT OF THE CHURCH.

The chief point of difference between the Catholic and the Oriental Orthodox Church is to be found, as already said, in the doctrine concerning the government of the Church. The Oriental Orthodox Church denies that Jesus Christ has appointed any visible head to the whole Church, whereas she professes to believe that every bishop is *the real chief and head* of his particular eparchie or diocese.

If we are allowed to use, for clearness' sake, a comparison taken from what we witness in civil society, the Oriental Orthodox Church may be likened to a confederation of small States, each of them independent of the rest, and which do not recognise any authority invested with the right of enacting laws to bind them all, except a congress or council, composed of the chiefs of the different States. Let us listen to the 'Exposition of the Orthodox Faith of the Eastern Church,'[1] commonly known under the title of 'Letter of the Patriarchs of the East on the Orthodox Faith' (1672), and which, together with the 'Orthodox Confession' of Peter Moghila, is endorsed by the whole Orthodox Church as a touchstone of her faith:

' . . . The head of this Catholic (universal) Church is

---

[1] See, for the 'Expositions of the Orthodox faith,' the account given of them in the *Introduction to the Orthodox Theology* (Введеніе въ православное Богословіе) by Mgr. Makary, Bishop of Vinnitza. This account was translated by J. M. Neale, and inserted in his *Voices from the East* (London, 1859), docum. viii. p. 209.

Jesus Christ. . . . Besides, the Holy Ghost has appointed to the particular Churches, which truly are Churches and members of the universal one, the bishops as GOVERNORS *and* PASTORS, and not abusively, but *in all points and properly* CHIEFS *and* HEADS.'[1]

The best commentary on that passage is the following, which we take from the 'Dogmatical Orthodox Theology' of Mgr. Makary, Bishop of Vinnitza, and Rector to the Ecclesiastical Academy of St. Petersburg. This important work, which is highly considered by the whole Orthodox Church, was translated into French by a Russian. As we have not at hand the Russian original, we shall quote the French translation:—

'L'évêque,' it is there said, 'est enfin LE PRINCIPAL ADMINISTRATEUR DE SON ÉGLISE (Act. xx. 28, comp. Lettre des Patr., etc., art. 10). Avant tout il a autorité sur la hiérarchie, qui lui est subordonnée, et sur le clergé. Tous les prêtres, tous les diacres et serviteurs de l'Église, doivent suivre ses dispositions et ne rien faire dans l'Église sans sa décision (Reg. apost. 39; Conc. Laod. 57; Conc. Carth. 6, 42, 52; d'Antioche, 8, 25; de Chalcéd. 8; de Sardique, 14); ils sont soumis à sa juridiction (1 Tim. v. 19), en vertu de laquelle il peut leur infliger différentes punitions (Reg. apost. 15, 32, 55; Conc. Chalcéd. 18; in Trullo, 34). Outre le clergé, tout le troupeau est sous l'autorité spirituelle de l'évêque. Il doit surveiller dans son diocèse l'exécution des lois divines

---

[1] Kimmel, *Libri symbolici Ecclesiæ Orientalis* (Jenæ, 1843). *Dositheï Confessio*, cap. x. ἡγουμένους καὶ ποιμένας καὶ ὅλως οὐκ ἐν καταχρήσει ἀλλὰ κυρίως ἀρχὰς καὶ κεφαλὰς τοὺς ἐπισκόπους ἔθηκε τὸ Πνεῦμα τὸ ἅγιον—p. 436 (2nd edit., Jenæ, 1850, p. ib.). In the Russian translation of this 'Exposition of Faith,' the bishops are termed Правители, Пастыри, Начальники, Главы.

The second edition of Kimmel's work bears the title of *Monumenta fidei Ecclesiæ Orientalis*. Important corrections and additions were made to the first edition, by Herm. Weissenborn. See also, in the same work, *Confessio Orthodoxa*, quæst. 85, p. 158.

et des commandements de l'Église (Clem. Rom. Ep. 1. aux Corinth. 51, 56; Cyprian. Epist. 69). C'est lui qui, particulièrement et surtout, a le droit de lier et de délier (Lettre des Patr. art. 10), suivant les règles des Apôtres, les décrets des Conciles (Reg. Apost. 31; Conc. de Carth. 6), et le témoignage unanime des anciens docteurs de l'Église (Cyprian. Epist. 75; Tertull. de Pœnit. cap. 4, 7; Greg. M. in Evang. lib. ii.; Hom. 26, n. 5, et suivants). C'est pourquoi les hommes apostoliques pressèrent avec tant de force les fidèles d'obéir à l'évêque.'[1] And further on:—' Cependant après avoir commis L'AD-MINISTRATION VISIBLE de son Église aux Évêques, qui, par le pouvoir dont ils sont revêtus, réunissent tous les croyants en une seule société *extérieure*, le Seigneur Jésus la gouverne Lui-même *invisiblement,* comme son véritable Chef; et en la vivifiant par la seule et même grâce du Saint-Esprit, il réunit tous ses membres par un lien intérieur. (Conf. Orth. p. 1, quæst. 85; Lettre des Patr., etc., art. 10).'[2]

In the *profession of faith,* pronounced by the members of other *Christian* confessions, when being admitted into the Russian Orthodox Church, and in which are pointed out the features distinguishing the belief of the so-called *orthodoxy* from that of heretics, there is an article running as follows:—' I believe and confess that the foundation head and most supreme Pontiff and Archipastor of the holy Orthodox Catholic Church[3] is our Lord Jesus Christ, and by Him the bishops have been appointed as *pastors and teachers* FOR THE GOVERNMENT OF THE CHURCH (*k'pravlenii tserkvi*), and that the

---

[1] *Théologie dogmatique orthodoxe,* par Macaire, etc. (Paris: Cherbuliez, 1859-60). Tom. ii. § 174, pp. 266, 267.

[2] *Ibid.* § 176, p. 271.

[3] The Oriental Church calls herself, besides Orthodox and Apostolic, also *Catholic.*

governor (*pravitel*) and pilot of that Church is the Holy Ghost.'¹

Much might be said about the doctrine expressed in the preceding quotations, but we shall closely examine it in the following chapters. For the present we confine ourselves to stating that, according to the doctrine of the Oriental Orthodox Church, the *government* of the Church was entrusted by Jesus Christ to the BISHOPS, who are therefore proclaimed *governors* (ἡγουμένοι), *pastors* (ποιμένες), chiefs (ἄρχαι), heads (κεφαλαί), of the Church —all titles which necessarily imply the bishops being the *highest* authority in the Church, and positively exclude the mere supposition of any secular authority entitled to command in ecclesiastical matters over them.

We are now going to examine how far the Oriental Orthodox Church, and especially her chief branch the Russian Orthodox Church, is governed according to the doctrine laid down in her official *Expositions of Faith*, and to what extent her bishops may be considered, if not the *highest*, at least a real authority in the Church. Let us begin with the Church of the Russian Empire.

IF WE LISTEN to the Russian Orthodox divines, as well as to the official documents of the State Church of Russia, the Holy Synod of St. Petersburg is to be considered as a

¹ Вѣрую и исповѣдую яко церкви святой православно-каѳолической основаніе, глава и наивышшій Архіерей и Архіпастырь есть Господь нашъ Іисусъ Христосъ, отъ негоже Архіерее, пастыріе и учителіе къ правленію церкви уставлени суть: и яко сея церкви правитель и кормчій есть Духъ святый. (Чинопослѣдованіе соединяемымъ изъ иновѣрныхъ къ православной каѳолической восточной церкви.—Москв. 1849., 4to. p. 48. (Требникъ.—Москв. 1836, p. 257.

permanent *Council* ruling over her. 'The most holy Synod,' says Mgr. Philaret, Archbishop of Tchernigoff, 'is, as regards its composition, what a *legitimate* ecclesiastical Council is.'¹ In fact, the Russian word *sobor*, denoting generally 'Council,' and as such applied to the œcumenical and provincial Councils of the Oriental Orthodox Church, is equally applied to the Most Holy Synod of St. Petersburg; and, thanks to that homonymy, the last is commonly believed and spoken of as a Council.² There exists, moreover, a document in which the newly established Synod asked from Peter the Great a resolution as to the way in which it ought to communicate with the Senate, submitting to His Majesty's consideration the suggestion that the Synod possessed '*the honour, the power, and the authority of the former Patriarch of Moscow*, or even a greater, *because of its being a Council*.'³

Of the many remarks which are suggested by such likening of the Synod to a Council,⁴ we shall only dwell

---

¹ Святѣйшій Синодъ, по составу своему то же что законный церковный соборъ. (Исторія русской Церкви (Черниговъ 1862. Періодъ пятый, § 2, p. 3.

² In the *Statute of the Ecclesiastical Consistories* of which we shall speak further on (p. 67 *et seq.*) the bishops and their tribunals (*Consistoria*) are said to be under the jurisdiction of the Holy Synod, as *the governing Council of the Russian Church*: яко правительствующаго Россійской Церкви Собора, art. 2.

³ Духовная же Коллегія (Синодъ) имѣетъ честь, силу и власть Патріаршескую, или едва и не большую понеже соборъ. See Полное Собраніе Законовъ Россійской Имперіи, 1st series, tom. vi. (3734) 14th of February, 1721. No. 2. p. 356. See also the Пункты, at the end of the Духовный Регламентъ, before the Прибавленіе, in any edition whatever of it.

⁴ 'Cette affirmation ne supporte pas l'examen; nous nous bornerons à y opposer les paroles de M. Katkoff dans la *Gazette de Moscou*, 1866. No. 216.' '*Le Saint Synode ne peut pas tenir la place des conciles, parce que tous les évêques ne prennent pas part à ses délibérations, tandis que tous les évêques doivent absolument siéger dans les conciles provinciaux tels qu'ils*

on the one concerning its composition. According to the statutes of the Holy Synod, commonly known under the title of 'Spiritual Regulation,' the Holy Synod is to be composed of men taken from *the different ranks of the ecclesiastical hierarchy.* The creator of the Synod, and real author of its 'Spiritual Regulation,' Peter the Great, who never showed any great reliance on human virtue,[1]

ont été institués par les Apôtres et par les conciles œcuméniques.' ' Entre le concile de l'Église russe et le synode il y a la même différence qu'entre la chambre des pairs d'Angleterre et une commission composée d'une demi-douzaine de lords, choisis par la reine. Le ministre qui s'aviserait de soutenir qu'il est indifférent de soumettre une loi à la chambre des lords ou à une telle commission, commettrait une énorme hérésie constitutionnelle.'—*Le Clergé russe*, par le Père J. Gagarin, S.J. (nouvelle édit. Paris: Albanel, 1871), p. 239.

[1] The *Spiritual Regulation* is drawn up in such a style as fully to justify its having been called *Un règlement de caserne.* Theophane Prokopovich, archbishop of Pleskoff, the *alter ego* of Peter in ecclesiastical matters, wrote it down by order of the Tzar; Peter corrected it; then it was recited and corrected in a full assembly of bishops, archimandrites, and senators. After that, Peter deigned to subscribe it with his own hand. The *Appendix* (прѣбавленіе) to it he deigned likewise to correct with his own hand, and afterwards the members of the already created Synod were summoned, by an especial ukase, to subscribe to it. In quoting also the *Spiritual Regulation*, we quote, if not Peter's own words, at least Peter's own maxims, ideas, and feelings. *His* are, for instance, the following views about the virtue of his monks.

Monks, their manner of living.

23. The Principal and his brethren are not, after dinner, to carry any remains of victuals from the table into their cells, save only 'kwass.' *If this order was not given, everything would be wasted profusely*, and carried out of the monastery.

26. None but the Principal has power to give away anything out of the monastery; not even he without the concurrence of the elders of the fraternity, attesting expressly, in writing, to whom, and for what use, anything is given. *Were not this restraint to be upon all, every one would lavishly and impudently squander what belongs to the monastery amongst his relations and friends.*

27. All the revenues arising from villages belonging to the monastery, and the donations of religious persons, and ecclesiastical profits, are to be reposited in one certain place, and taken thence, to supply all the occasions of the church and monastery, and of the fraternity; *without this care there would be no end of pillaging, &c.*—*Spir. Regul.* part iii. translated into

fairly declares that, by so ordaining, he had in view to increase the obstacles to a common agreement of the members of the Synod in any iniquity whatever. The College (Synod), he says, 'consists of such members as cannot possibly all of them enter into a secret combination, that is, the persons are of a different order and vocation—bishops, archimandrites, hegoumens, protopopes. In truth, it is inconceivable how such a body should together dare to conceal a fraudulent design, much less conspire in carrying on an act of injustice.'[1]

Further on Peter the Great draws the attention of his people to another advantage resulting from such a combination of persons belonging to different degrees of the ecclesiastical hierarchy. 'Such a conciliary (*sobornoe*) government,' so he says, 'will be as a school of spiritual improvement; for each assessor, by the communication of many and different decisions, counsels, and regular reasonings (such as various cases require), will readily be instructed in spiritual policy, and, by daily exercise, be so well practised in it as to be perfectly qualified to minister in the house of God, and afterwards, by an easy step, from being of the number of the colleagues or assessors, be deservedly advanced to the episcopal dignity (*na stepen archiereistva*); and thus, by God's assistance, barbarism will speedily be banished from the spiritual order in

---

English in Consett's *The present State and Regulations of the Church of Russia*, (London, 1729), pp. 169, 170. Полн. Собр. tom. vi. (4022) p. 711.

Some time after, Peter the Great himself addressed an 'Instruction' to the Synod, *On monastic vocation* (О званiи монашеском) which Voltaire, that competent judge in matters of Christian perfection (!), qualifies as written both '*par un ministre d'État et par un Père de l'Église*' (*Histoire de Pierre le Grand et de la Russie*, chap. xiv.) See Полное Собранiе Закон. Росс. Имперiи, 1st. ser. tom. vii. (4450), January 31, 1724, p. 227.

[1] *Spir. Reg.* part i. No. 5; *Cons.* p. 18. Полн. Собр. tom. vi. (3718) p. 317.

Russia, and we have good reason to hope for a thorough reformation.'[1]

We hardly need point out the inconsistency of such considerations. The latter especially, far from conveying any evidence in support of the preference to be given to the *conciliary* form of government found out for his Church by Peter, brings forward one of the chief motives which ought to lead every Russian to condemn it. In fact, that Synod which is supposed to *govern* the *whole* Orthodox Church of Russia is there represented as a SCHOLARSHIP, a NOVITIATE, a kind of APPRENTICESHIP for *future rulers of a single diocese*, the whole Russian Church being thus compelled to bear the consequences of her *future* bishops' mistakes, and to obtain, at her own expense, the benefit derived from their daily increasing experience.

But let us return to the subject. The Holy Synod of Russia having consequently to be composed of men taken *from the different ranks of the ecclesiastical hierarchy*, in what proportion must the bishops be represented in it? 'The number of the rulers' (viz. the members of the Synod), says the 'Spiritual Regulation,' 'is *twelve* in all, and is made up of persons of different ranks, as bishops, archimandrites, hegoumens, protopopes; of which number are *three* bishops, and of the rest as many of each order as are thought requisite.'[2] Also, according to the 'Spiritual Regulation,' the care of governing the *whole* Orthodox Church of Russia, of overseeing the bishops, of receiving the appeals of their sub-

---

[1] *Spir. Reg.* ibid. No. 9, *Consett*, p. 22. Полн. Собр. tom. vi. (3718), pp. 318, 319.

We quote literally Consett's translation, and whenever we change a word, we put the corresponding Russian into a parenthesis.

[2] *Spir. Reg.*, part iii. No. 1. *Consett*, p. 104. Полн. Собр. ibid. pp. 343, 344.

jects, and of *making known*[1] laws binding every one of them, restraining, modifying, or annulling their jurisdiction, should devolve in Russia *on a body composed of* THREE *bishops and* NINE *simple priests.* What a singular *Council,* and what contempt for the divine rights of bishops!

We hasten, however, to acknowledge that Peter the Great's successors did not lay much weight on the considerations alleged by him in favour of a Synod composed of men belonging to the different ranks of the ecclesiastical hierarchy, and, braving even the danger of plots and conspiracies alluded to by Peter, they successively increased the numerical proportion of the bishops. Already, in the year 1730, Theophane Prokopovich, the very writer of the 'Spiritual Regulation,' had presented to the Synod a special memorial, in which he pointed out the necessity, according to the *ancient canons,* of the number of the bishops sitting in the Synod being greater than that of the archimandrites, '*and this was accepted as a rule.*'[2] The application, however, of that rule depending in practice on the Tsars, the number of the bishops sitting in the Synod equally depended on their will, so that the first *official* modification of the prescription laid down in the 'Spiritual Regulation' bears the date of 1763, when the Tsarina Catherine II., at the suggestion of the 'Commission on Ecclesiastical Property,' consented that the

---

[1] We shall speak in detail of the *legislative power* in the Russian Orthodox Church, and examine where it is to be found. See p. 53 *et seq.*

[2] Mgr. Filaret, Archbish. of Kharkoff and then of Tchnernigoff. Ист. русск. церкви. Черниговъ, 1862, Пер. V. § 2. p. 3. Prokopovich's memorial is unfortunately still kept in manuscript. Its existence is mentioned by Eugeny, Metrop. of Kieff, in his Словарь историческiй писателей духовнаго чина: St. Petersburg, 1827, vol. ii. p. 319. It bears the title of Разсужденiе о присутствованiи въ Синодѣ болшему числу изъ Архiереевъ.'

Synod should be composed of three bishops, two archimandrites, and one protopope.¹ Since that time the composition of the Synod has undergone other modifications, and we are glad to state that it is now almost exclusively composed of bishops. Moreover, the Holy Synod can no longer be considered as an *apprenticeship* or practical school of religious policy for future bishops, as Peter had proposed to himself to make it. The only dignitaries of the Russian Church who are now allowed to sit in the Synod, without being bishops, are His Majesty's confessor, and the chief chaplain to the army and fleet. They both belong to the *white* or secular clergy, and, being married, cannot consequently be promoted to the episcopal dignity.²

We heartily congratulate the Orthodox Church of Russia on such progress towards reinstating herself in the right of being governed only by bishops; at the same time, however, we cannot help remarking that this very progress was accomplished in such a way as to bear undeniable evidence to her being a slave of the Tsars. Peter the Great had taken care that at least some appearance of legality should not be entirely wanting in the establishment of the Synod, for in the full assembly of bishops, archimandrites, and senators which we have already mentioned, he procured the signatures of his bishops to be attached to the 'Spiritual Regulation.' Now, as any change in the composition of the *governing Synod* ought to be considered as a most important modification of Peter's reformation, one might expect that the consent of the bishops would have been required beforehand. Far from this, the Russian Tsars and Tsarinas still altered,

¹ See Полное Собраніе Законовъ, 1 ser. Tom. xliv. Книга Штатовъ Отдѣл. iii. No. 11,942. Oct. 1, 1763, pp. 21, 22.

² The monks are commonly called in Russia the *black* clergy, because of their being dressed in black. The bishops are always taken from the

changed, suppressed, or modified the prescriptions laid down in the 'Spiritual Regulation' without the slightest regard to the rights of their bishops. Moreover, if the fact proves a tendency towards having the Synod exclusively composed of bishops, still the nomination, as well as the dismissal, of its members in practice entirely depends on the will of the Tsar. Hence it is that the Russian Orthodox Church is continually exposed to the danger of seeing herself governed by an assembly the majority of which would be simple priests (if *not deacons*), an assembly, besides, in which, according to Peter's decree, *still in full force*, all the members of the Synod must BE ON A LEVEL, and consequently the bishops on a level with the simple priests. Peter ordered that the president himself must be a mere *primus inter pares*, just like the president of modern Parliaments. 'The appellation itself of President,' says Peter, 'is not an arrogant one, for it denotes nothing more than one that sits before others (*predsedatel*), for which reason he cannot think highly of himself, nor can others think so of him. . . . .'[1] So anxious was Peter for humility, equality, and fraternity among the members of the Synod!

Let us, however, suppose that the two secular priests, who, by virtue of a customary right, are still members of the Synod, be by a special decree excluded from it, let us even imagine the Tsar ordering that henceforth bishops only should be called to form the Synod, still there remain very many other laws to be abolished, in order that it may be credible that the Russian bishops are *chiefs* and *heads* in their Church.

'In the administration of the Church,' so says the Russian Code of Laws, 'the autocratical authority (the

---

monks. A secular priest cannot be bishop unless, after the death of his wife, he had embraced the religious life.

[1] *Spir. Reg.* part i. No. 7; *Consett*, p. 21. Полн. Собр. tom vi. p. 318.

'Tsar) ACTS *by means* of the Most Holy Governing Synod
'*appointed* by it.'[1] (Fund. Law, art. 43.)

Alas! this article alone evinces, more than any number of arguments, that the Russian Church is inconsistent with the doctrine laid down in her 'Expositions of Faith' concerning the government of the Church. One could hardly succeed in expressing more plainly and more distinctly the principle that the real and effectual ruler of the Russian Church is *the Tsar!* HE it is who *governs*; the Synod is but an organ, an instrument *by means of which* HE governs; finally, the instrument itself is chosen and *appointed* by the Tsar! We shall return further on to this article, and examine how it is commented on and explained by the 'Code of Laws' itself, and the Russian jurists (see p. 48 *et seq.*; p. 91, *note*). We quote it here as a fit introduction to what we are going to say on the Tsar.

The fact that the Russian Orthodox Church is really governed by the Tsar, is still advanced, and no less still contested, according to the different points of view of those who take an interest in the question. So much has been and is said every day on that subject, that it would appear impossible to do otherwise than repeat what has been already said.[2] We deemed it advisable, however, not to

---

[1] Въ управленіи церковномъ Самодержавная Власть дѣйствуетъ посредствомъ Святѣйшаго Правительствующаго Синода, Ею учрежденнаго (Сводъ Законовъ россійской Имперіи, ed. 1857, tom. i. Основ. госуд. зак. ст. 43, p. 10.

[2] A most interesting account of the Holy Synod, and the whole mechanism of the ecclesiastical administration in Russia, will be found in F. Gagarin's quoted work *Le clergé russe* (Paris, 1871). Besides, this book contains such an amount of information concerning the Russian Orthodox Church as to make the reader considerably acquainted with her. An English translation of this interesting work is announced as shortly to be published by Messrs. Burns, Oates, & Co.

See also *Persécutions et souffrances de l'Église catholique en Russie* (Paris, 1844). Theiner, *Die Staatskirche Russlands* (Schaffhausen, 1853). Schnitzler, *L'Empire des Tsars* (Paris, 1856). Silbernagl, *Verfassung*

overlook this point, as we hope that the reader will be sufficiently repaid for his perusal of our work by becoming better acquainted than is commonly the case with the official documents of the State Church of Russia..

In order to appreciate to their full extent the encroachments of the Tzars on the divine rights of the bishops, we must consider the establishment of the Synod in relation to the analogous reforms accomplished by Peter the Great in every department of the State administration of Russia. Since the year 1718 Peter the Great had abolished the ancient State-Chanceries (*prikazy*), and appointed for the various branches of the administration of the Russian Empire different Colleges, viz: 1. That of Foreign Affairs (*tchujestrannych djel*); 2. Of Revenue (*kamor*); 3. Of Justice (*yustitsia*); 4. Of Revision (*revision*); 5. Of Army (*voinskoi*); 6. Of Admiralty (*admiralteiskoi*); 7. Of Commerce (*kommerts*); 8. Of State Counting-office (*Shtats-Kontor*); 9. Of Mines and Manufactures (*berg i manufactur*). The functions of each College were fixed by an Ukase of the 12th of Dec. 1718.[1] In the year 1720 Peter completed his work by issuing a ' *Generalnyi Reglament*,' which fixed the ' mode of action,' that is the *uniform* method to which *all* the Colleges must equally conform in carrying on their affairs.[2]

In witnessing the happy success with which his efforts were crowned, Peter the Great could not help feeling that God also required from him the reformation of the Russian Church. This he himself has announced to the world. Let us hear what he says:—

'AMONGST the many cares which the empire com-

und gegenwärtiger Bestand sämmtlicher Kirchen des Orients, &c. (Landshut, 1865), etc.

[1] Полн. Собр. 1st series, tom. v. (3255) p. 601.

[2] Полн. Собр. 1st series, tom. vi. (3534) Feb. 28, 1720, p. 141.

mitted to Us by God requires for the good government of Our hereditary kingdoms and conquests, casting Our eye on the Spiritual Order, and observing in them great irregularity and a great defect in their proceedings, We should indeed *be afflicted in Our conscience, and have too just cause to fear lest We appear to be guilty of ingratitude to the Most High*, if after, by His gracious assistance, We have happily succeeded in a regulation, both military and civil, We should neglect the regulation of the Spiritual Order; and lest, when the impartial Judge shall require of Us an account for the vast trust He has reposed in Us, We should not be able to give an answer.'[1]

One immediately conceives that a man afflicted by such pangs of conscience could not long endure a similar torture, and would have soon yielded. Besides, as half-measures and compromises can never calm the conscience of strong-minded men, it must necessarily be expected that Peter the Great would have felt compelled to do for the Church *whatever* he, *in his conscience*, would have deemed the best, however radical the measures which might have been required. Let us again listen to him:—

'WE THEREFORE (because of the before-mentioned fear of conscience), after the example of former religious kings, recited in the Old and New Testaments, having taken upon Us the care of the regulation of the clergy and Spiritual Order, and not seeing any better way for it than a *conciliary* government (*sobornoe pravitelstvo*); yet, because this is too weighty a charge for any single person to whom the supreme power is not hereditary, We appoint

[1] Ukase for the establishment of the Holy Synod. *Consett*, p. 3. (Полн. Собр. tom. vi. (3718) p. 314.) In the same identical terms, Peter expresses himself in his letter to the Patriarch of Constantinople, informing him of the *already accomplished* establishment of the Synod. See. p. 36

a *Spiritual College*, i.e. a spiritual conciliary government, which is authorized to rectify, according to the " *Regulation*" here following,[1] ALL spiritual affairs throughout the Russian Church. And We require *all our faithful subjects of every rank and condition, spiritual and temporal, to* account this administration powerful and authoritative, and to have recourse to it for the direction, resolution, and determination of their most private spiritual affairs, and to acquiesce in its definitive sentence; to obey its decrees and orders in everything, under the pain of a severe punishment for disobedience and contumacy, *as in the other Colleges.* This College must also perfect hereafter their " *Regulation* " with more rules, such as the different occasions of various affairs shall require; but the Spiritual College *must not do this without Our consent*. We constitute members of this Spiritual College, as is here specified, one president, two vice-presidents, four counsellors, four assessors. And because it is mentioned in the first part of this "Regulation," in the 7th and

---

[1] The *Spiritual Regulation*, of which we have already spoken (see p. 15, note). It bears in Russian the title of Духовный Регламентъ, and is inserted in vol. vi. of the Полное Собраніе Законовъ (Complete Collection of Laws) No. 3718, Jan. 25, 1721, p. 314 *et seq.* A German translation of it appeared in the year 1724, in Dantzig, under the title of *Geistliches Reglement, auf hohen Befehl*, etc. 8vo. A French translation, but so inaccurate as not to allow the reader to rely on it, was published in the *Anecdotes du règne de Pierre le Grand*, 1745, 16mo. Another German translation (without the 'Appendix' *pribavlenie*) was inserted by Haigold (pseud. of Aug. Ludw. Schlözer) in his *Beilagen zum neuveränderten Russland* (Riga und Mittau, 1769), vol. i. Finally, a Latin and complete translation appeared in 1785, at St. Petersburg, at the expense of Prince Potemkin.

This last translation, which, on some accounts, may be considered as *official*, is extremely rare, as, according to Phil. Strahl (*Gelehrte Russland*, Leipz. 1828, p. 423), Prince Potemkin himself caused the greatest part of the copies to be destroyed. The Paris *Société bibliographique* has undertaken to reprint it, together with a French translation *made from the Russian*, and appropriate notes.

8th sections, that the president is liable to be tried by his *brethren*—to wit, in the same College—in case he does anything amiss; We therefore allow him one vote, as the rest have. All the members of this College, at their entering on their office, must take oath, and promise on the Holy Gospel, in the form of oath hereto annexed.[1]—

'Signed and subscribed with His Imperial Majesty's own hand,

PETER.

'Petersburg, the 25th day of January,
  'in the year of our Lord 1721.'[2]

Also, in force of this imperial brief, Russia must add, on the 25th of January, 1721,[3] to the College of Mines and Manufactures, a tenth *College*, called *Spiritual*, and intrusted with the government of *all* her spiritual affairs. And in order that no one might be mistaken as to the Synod being a *State College* like the others, Peter the Great ordered that, in the conduct of its affairs, the Spiritual College should entirely conform itself to the prescriptions contained in the above-mentioned '*Generalnyi Reglament*' of the 28th of February, 1720, enacted for the other Colleges.[4]

Shortly after, however, a question of some importance

---

[1] We shall presently speak of that oath (see p. 40).

[2] Полн. Собр. tom. vi. p. 314. *Consett*, p. 3.

[3] We remark here, once for all, that in quoting the official documents of the Russian Orthodox Church, we keep the date of the Russian Calendar, which is 12 days behind ours.

[4] 'Here is nothing particularly delivered of the employ or conduct of the affairs (о дѣйствахъ) of the Spiritual College, because His Imperial Majesty required them to act by the rules of the *Generalnyi Reglament* (по Генеральному Регламенту).'—*Spir. Reg.* part iii. II. *Consett*, p. 124. See, for the Russian, any separate edition of the Духовн. Регл. See also *Spir. Reg.* at the beginning of part i.

caused the *Spiritual College* to be called *Most Holy Synod*. During divine service people were accustomed to hear mentioned in the *Ektenias*, the name of the former chief authority of the Russian Church, the patriarch of Moscow. Now that the Patriarchate no longer existed, having been abolished by Peter, and the *Spiritual College* had entered on his functions, this had evidently the right of being named in the *Ektenias*, instead of the Patriarch. It seems, however, that they found the name of *College*, connected as it was with mines and manufactures, to be too profane for the purpose, as in a petition to the Tsar, the Spiritual College proposed to His Majesty the adoption of the denomination of ' *Most Holy Governing Assembly*' (*sobranie*). Peter the Great wrote with his own hand on the petition, ' *Most Holy Synod, or Most Holy Governing Synod*,' and since that time, that is since the 14th of February, 1721, the *Spiritual College* has been called MOST HOLY SYNOD or MOST HOLY GOVERNING SYNOD.[1]

In the following year appeared the 'Appendix' (*pribavlenie*) to the 'Spiritual Regulation,' drawn up also by Theophane Prokopovich. 'This *Appendix* to the " Spiritual Regulation" (so it runs near the end) His Imperial Majesty has himself been pleased to suffer to be read in His own august presence, and to give amendments to it with His own hand; and, after His approbation of it, to order it to be printed and published, in the end of April and in the beginning of May, this year 1722. And by consent of His Imperial Majesty, the underwritten members of the Most Holy Governing (*pravitelstvuiustchyi*) Synod have also subscribed to this Appendix.'[2]

[1] *Spir. Reg.* 'Points wherein His Most Serene Imperial Majesty, with his own august hand, hath vouchsafed a resolution.'—*Consett.* p. 125. Полн. Собр. tom. vi. (3734), February 14, 1721, pp. 355–356.

[2] *Spir. Reg. Consett.* p. 184. In the Полное Собраніе, the Прибавленіе къ Духовному Регламенту is printed at the end of the laws issued in the month of May 1722. Tom. vi. (4022), p. 699.

After this, Peter, by different decisions given to several propositions (*dokladnyi punkty*) of the Holy Synod, and especially by those of the 12th of April, 1722,[1] fixed the exact limits of its jurisdiction. 'Some matters' (so says Mgr. Filaret, Archbishop of Tchernigoff) '*which had hitherto been judged by the ecclesiastical authority*, were excluded BY THE WILL OF THE TSAR (*volieio Gosudaria*) from the circle of the Synod's attributions, and assigned to the civil tribunals. They were matters which, of their own nature, belong more to the State than to the Church of Jesus Christ, more to civil rights than to faith, such as successions, marriages contracted by force or against the will of the parents, blasphemy, fornication, or *such as concern impenitent sinners, and those who neglect to go to confession and to the Holy Communion.* Even in these matters, however, with the exception of the two first mentioned, the ecclesiastical penance was determined by the ecclesiastical authority.'[2]

Finally, after having so determined what matters ought to be left to the jurisdiction of the Synod, and what tried before the civil tribunals, on the 11th of May, 1722, Peter the Great issued the following decree, which we quote literally, and *in extenso*, as a model of precision, laconism, and strength:—' For the Synod, let there be chosen from among the OFFICERS a good man, who possesses *boldness,* and knows how to direct the affairs of the Synod. This *officer* shall be the Chief Procurator of the Synod; and there shall be given to him an *Instruction*, analogous to that of the *General Procurator* (of the Senate).'[3]—The

---

[1] Полн. Собр. том. vi. (3963) April 12, 1722, p. 650.

[2] Filaret, Ист. росс. церк. *Loc. cit.* pp. 4, 5.

[3] Въ Санодъ выбрать изъ Офицеровъ добраго человѣка, кто бъ имѣлъ смѣлость и могъ управленіе Синодскаго дѣла знать, и быть ему Оберъ-Прокуроромъ и дать ему

'*Instruction*' here alluded to, and of which we are presently going to speak in detail, bears the date of the 13th of June, 1722.

In less than two years Peter had thus carried out the most radical revolution which could be accomplished in the Russian Church without causing her to cease to be *orthodox*. Though deeply deploring the illegitimacy and injustice of Peter's enterprise, one cannot but admire the stupendous activity of his genius, nor can anything be more suitably compared to it than the stupendous docility of the bishops of Russia. Nay, whatever the arguments may be, by which it has been attempted to justify Peter and the Russian Church, the wonderful condescension of the Russian bishops to the will of the Tsar forcibly involves the abdication on their side, not only of their *right to be the rulers of the Church*, but even of their *personal dignity*. These two assertions are so weighty as to oblige us to allege arguments in support of both of them. We begin with the latter.

No one of our readers surely omitted to notice the peculiar style of Peter's ukases, which we purposely quoted. Never had any Pope spoken in a more authoritative manner, nor shown in his words a fuller conviction of the legitimacy of his power, than does Peter in the before-quoted ukases. HE abolishes the patriarchate; HE appoints a *Spiritual College*, to be added to that of Mines and Manufactures; HE entrusts it with the direction of *all* spiritual affairs throughout Russia; HE orders his subjects, of *whatever rank and condition, spiritual* as well as *temporal*, to recognise the *Spiritual College* as a legitimate power; HE enforces his will by the sanction of severe punishments; HE requires the *Spiritual College* to complete

инструкцію, примѣняясь къ инструкціи Генералъ-Прокурора. Полн. Собр. tom. vi. (4001) May 11, 1722, p. 676.

their 'Regulation,' *but not without his consent;* HE fixes the form of oath to be taken by the members of the Synod. All this HE does, HE alone, without even mentioning, as the Popes generally do in the most important affairs, that he has availed himself of the advice of others.[1] As to the Bishops, the divinely-instituted *governors, pastors, chiefs, heads* of the Church, they who, consequently, were immediately concerned in the establishment of the Synod, they are alluded to, it is true, yet not as advisers, but as entering into the composition of the flock of Peter's *faithful subjects, of whatever rank and condition, spiritual as well as temporal!*

The mere style of Peter is also an outrage to them, and they, the rulers of the Church, 'they bow their neck to the worst kind of tyranny'! Yet more ought to be said.

The signatures of nineteen Bishops appear at the end of the 'Spiritual Regulation.' Those English readers who know the Russian Church only by the writings of Neale, or by Mouravieff's 'History of the Church of Russia,' translated by the Rev. R. W. Blackmore, or by some other works written with the view of supporting the State Church of Russia, can hardly realise the depth of humiliation into which Russian bishops were forced to descend, in order to comply with the will of Peter, and to allow their signatures to be attached to the 'Spiritual Regulation.' They themselves subscribed, among others, articles such as the following:—'Because the above said duties (of the *bishops*) are not to be well understood, without great application to reading; *and it being uncertain whether every one of them will love reading or no, an order therefore will be issued out of the Spiritual College*

---

[1] This Peter does in his letter to the Patriarch of Constantinople, written for the purpose of obtaining from him the recognition of *the accomplished fact*. What reliance may be placed upon Peter's assertion will appear from what we shall presently say on the subject.

TO ALL BISHOPS, *that every one of them have the Canons read at his table which concern himself;* only this reading may be omitted on some great festivals, or when some honourable guests are present, or for some other just reason.'[1] And again, on the subject of the visitation of the eparchie or diocese:—'When the chanting (or service) is ended, he (*the bishop*) is to preach a sermon to the clergy and people on true repentance, and the duties of every order, especially the sacerdotal. And there, on the spot, he shall require and exhort everyone to propose to him his spiritual wants and doubts to be resolved; and also whatever is anywhere observed to want a regulation amongst the clergy. *And because every* BISHOP *is not learned enough to compose a set discourse, the Spiritual College therefore will frame such a charge as the* BISHOPS *shall read over* (prochityvat) *in the churches they visit.*'[2]

So far as to *personal dignity*. Possibly, on account of the prodigious variety of men's feelings and inclinations, there may be some one who does not see how personal dignity can be concerned with Peter's arbitrary dealings on ecclesiastical matters, and the extreme tractability of the Russian bishops. As, after all, this is matter of taste, we shall not farther dwell thereon, but hasten to speak of the abdication by the Russian bishops of *their right to be the rulers of the Church.*

Yet, before closely entering on the matter, we are glad to state that, according to a most reliable document, an appearance at least of resistance made by the Russian clergy to the encroachments of Peter was not entirely wanting, and we believe that the resisters were bishops. We were the more delighted on meeting with that docu-

---

[1] *Spir. Reg.* part ii. 'Of the Bishops.' No. 3. *Consett*, p. 35. Полн. Собр. tom. vi. p. 322.

[2] 'On the Visitation,' etc. No. 3, *Consett*, p. 55. Полн. Собр. *loc. cit.* p. 328.

ment, because the official publications of the Russian Church, as well as many works published abroad with a view to exalt her, seem to pursue, as the accomplishment of a duty, the plan of concealing any such attempts at resistance as would confer honour on the Russian bishops, thus making them appear to be like those *canes muti* spoken of in Isaias: 'They are all dumb dogs, they cannot bark' (Is. lvi. 10).

It is well known that during the reign of Catherine II. Voltaire was in great favour at the court of St. Petersburg. The orthodox Empress commissioned the French philosopher to compile a history of Peter the Great, and caused him to be supplied with every document which might be required. Peter's ecclesiastical reformation could not, of course, be passed by, and an especial memorial 'On the Russian Church and her Reformation by Peter the Great,' was consequently handed to Voltaire. A large portion of that memorial was published some years ago in Leipzig, under the title of 'Mémoire inédit sur la réforme de l'Église russe, envoyé par Catherine II à Voltaire.' Wolf. Gerhard, 1863, 8vo. The preface says: 'Ce mémoire a été trouvé dans les papiers de Jean Schouvaloff, chargé par Catherine II de fournir à Voltaire les documents pour l'histoire de Pierre I et de la Russie. Nous tenons le manuscrit original des héritiers de Jean Schouvaloff, ce favori de l'impératrice Élisabeth et Mécène russe, selon l'expression des poètes et des chroniqueurs de son époque.'

This document was by no means an unpublished one. According to Haigold (pseudonymous of Aug. Ludw. Schlözer), the very original *and complete* manuscript sent to Voltaire was in the year 1769 still preserved in the public library of Geneva, where one of Haigold's friends, having discovered it, made a copy thereof, which Haigold translated into German, and published in the first volume of his 'Beilagen zum neuveränderten Russland. Riga und Mittau, 1769,' 12mo., pp. 1–70.[1] We happened also to find an English translation of it in the work of John Glen King, who was chaplain to the British factory at St. Petersburg: 'The Rites and Ceremonies of the Greek Church in Russia': London, 1772; 4to.[2] From him we quote the following passage on the establishment of the Synod of St. Petersburg:

'On the death of the (tenth) patriarch (of Moscow, Adrian, d. A.D. 1700), Peter deferred nominating another, on account of the troubles occasioned by the war; but HE *gave the administration* of the affairs of the patriarchate to Stephen Jaworsky, metropolitan of Rezan, a man of learning and a *foreigner*,[3] and for that reason supposed to be less apt to make a bad use of the trust reposed in him. His title was *Exarch*, or Vicegerent of the Patriarchal See; but the government of the exarchy was very different from what it was under the patriarchs; small and daily occurrences were the only business which came before him; all affairs of importance *were brought before the Sovereign*, or an assembly composed of the other bishops, to deliberate upon them. These bishops resided by turns at Moscow, and sometimes were summoned on purpose. . . . In the meantime Peter constantly meditated upon introducing a better form of ecclesiastical

---

[1] Under the title of *Russische Kirchen- und Reformations-Geschichte bis auf Peter den Grossen*, in seven chapters, of which only four and a half are given in the French *Mémoire inédit*.

[2] Under the title of *History of the Russian Church and its Reformation by Peter the Great*, in seven chapters, just as the German translation of Haigold (pp. 433–468). King, however, does not mention either from whom he had this 'history,' or the author of it, or for what purpose it was drawn up. A German translation of King's work was published in Riga, under the title of *Gebräuche und Ceremonien der griechischen Kirche in Russland*. 1773. 4to.

[3] . . . 'mais puisque il était *Polonais*.' (*Mém. inéd.*, p. 17, § 15. . . . 'der dabei ein *Ausländer* war.' (Haigold, *Beilagen*, etc. i. p. 18.)

government, *though the clergy had not given over the hopes of having their patriarch restored* ; nay, some even entered into intrigues for that purpose, of which the exarch himself was suspected ; but all their endeavours proved vain. At length Peter the Great declared, in a full assembly of the most eminent and distinguished clergy, that HE *thought* a patriarch to be neither necessary for the administration of the Church, nor expedient for the State, and therefore HE *had determined* to introduce another form of ecclesiastical government, which should keep the medium between that of a single *person* and General Councils, both of which were liable to many inconveniences, on account of the great extent of the empire; and this new mode was to be a constant Council or Synod. Some of the clergy remonstrated upon this, asserting that as the patriarchate had been established in Russia not only by the consent of his predecessors, but with the concurrence of all the Oriental patriarchs, it could only be abolished by the same authority. *But such arguments had no weight. Peter understood his own rights too well.*'[1] 'Ce que je viens de rapporter' (adds the above-mentioned 'Mémoire' only), 'je ne l'ai point trouvé dans des mémoires écrits, mais *je le tiens de quelques personnes trèsdignes de foi, qui sont encore en vie, et qui peuvent en rendre témoignage.*'

In his ' Histoire de l'Empire de Russie sous Pierre le Grand,' Voltaire did not relate this attempt at opposition to the despotism of the Tsar. He was, in fact, reproached because he did not make use, as he should have done, of the

[1] *King*, pp. 440, 441; *Haigold*, pp. 17–21; *Mémoire inédit*, pp. 17–20. The last words, which we have underlined, run in French as follows :—' *On aurait pu faire de pareilles représentations avant le temps de Pierre le Grand, mais ce prince connaissait trop le pouvoir que les lois divines et humaines lui accordaient, pour se rendre à leur sentiment.*' Haigold translates them more emphatically :—' *Aber solche Schlüsse galten nur in alten Zeiten. Peter kannte die Rechte seiner Majestät.*'

precious documents forwarded to him; and the celebrated German critic Ant. Fried. Büsching goes so far as to show some regret that this history of Peter had not been written by John Schouvaloff himself, instead of Voltaire.¹ Again, how could such an attempt have any importance for a writer who equally despised every Christian Church, and for whom the *power of bishops* and *ecclesiastical jurisdiction* were merely conventional words, invented by men in order to support an edifice of hypocrisy!² Fortunately, however, the fact is stated in such a document as not to allow anybody to doubt of its authenticity. Moreover,

---

¹ See *Geschichte des russischen Reiches unter Peter dem Grossen.* Uebersetzt von Jo. Mich. Hube, herausgegeben von Dr. Ant. Fried. Büsching (Frankfurt, 1761), *Vorrede*, pp. 3, 4.

² Voltaire's History of Peter the Great offers many proofs of the inconsistency of his principles, if not rather of the mean-spiritedness of the pretended philosopher and his cowardice towards the puissant 'Semiramis of the North.' Leaving some instances to which public attention has been already drawn, we bring forward the following. No one, perhaps, of Peter's numerous orders concerning ecclesiastical matters had been urged by the Tsar with greater severity than that in force of which (English readers will wonder at it) the normal state of the monks ought to be ignorance, and science and cultivation of the mind the exception! . . . . .

'Monks are not to transcribe any writings in the cells, neither copies out of books nor out of their records, without the privity of the principal, *on pain of a severe corporal punishment;* nor to write to anyone, nor to receive a letter without his permission; and, by the rules both spiritual and civil, are not to have ink and paper more than what is *specially* allowed by the principal or abbot for their common spiritual use. And this guard against monks *is especially necessary, because nothing so much disturbs the monastic solitude as their superstitious and mischievous writings;* but if one of the brethren has some *urgent* occasion for a letter, he must write it at the table, *out of the common ink-horn, and on the common paper,* with the principal's leave, and not presume to do this of his own accord.' (*Consett.* pp. 173, 174. Полн. Собр. vi. p. 712).

That strange prescription had been among the subjects of Peter's *nominal* (именный directly emanating from the sovereign) ukase of the 31st January, 1701 (Полн. Собр. tom. iv. (1834) pp. 139, 140; it had been again enforced as a rule for the monks in the Appendix to the 'Spiritual Regulation' (*Cons.* p. 173, No. 36. Полн. Собр. tom. vi. (4022,) p. 712; and then,

we find in F. Gagarin's quoted work, 'Le Clergé russe,' pp. 291–2, that, 'Dans un article publié le 8 sept. 1862, dans la *Causerie ecclésiastique*, sous la signature du P. Athanase, il est dit à propos de ce Concile (pour l'approbation du Synode): " Sans doute, ceux qui y assistèrent ne consentirent pas tous et immédiatement à la proposition de Pierre . . . mais la volonté du Tzar, soutenue par quelques ecclésiastiques, l'emporta."' This article, as F. Gagarin remarks, appeared with the approbation of the ecclesiastical censors.

Perhaps, if it happen that some Russian bishops become acquainted with these pages, they will take into serious consideration an objection against the establishment of the Synod, alleged in 'a full assembly of the most eminent and distinguished clergy of Russia,' and to which no other answer was given by Peter than Luther's historical answer, when convicted of a wilful addition to the text of the Holy Scripture, in order to support his doctrine of justification, '*So I will, so I command; let my will stand for reason.*'[1] Perhaps they will feel disgusted with the bantering strain in which the fact is

again it had formed the only subject of Peter's *nominal* ukase, made known by the Synod, of the 19th February, 1723 (Полн. Собр. tom. vii. (4146) p. 16.

Now, the asserted philosopher, and deadly adversary of ignorance in the West of Europe, has not a single word to condemn a Tsar, forbidding, *as a rule*, to the *less ignorant* of his subjects the use of ink and paper, but rather seems to approve this measure. Let us listen to Voltaire's words:—'La Russie était inondée de moines; ils étaient riches, puissants, et quoique très-ignorants ils étaient à l'avénement de Pierre *presque les seuls qui sussent écrire*; ils en avaient abusé dans les premiers temps, où ils furent si étonnés et scandalisés des innovations que faisait Pierre en tout genre. Il avait été *obligé* en 1703 (? 1701) de défendre l'encre et la plume aux moines : il fallait une *permission expresse* de l'archimandrite, qui répondait de ceux à qui il la donnait. Pierre voulut que cette ordonnance subsistât.' (*Hist. etc.* chap. xiv.) And nothing else.

[1] Where St. Paul in his *Epistle to the Romans*, says: 'For we account a man to be justified by faith without the works of the law' (Rom. iii. 28), Luther had translated 'justified by faith *alone*:' 'So halten wir es

related in a document which almost directly emanated from an *orthodox Empress* of Russia; and a salutary feeling of shame, because of the weakness of Peter's opponents, will lead them to consider how to make amends for the sin of their predecessors, and restore to their divine and inalienable rights the bishops, successors of the Apostles, *chiefs* and *heads* of the Church.

Indeed, that document alone bears sad evidence to the fact we have undertaken to demonstrate, that the Russian bishops' condescension to the will of Peter forcibly involves the abdication on their part of the right conferred upon them by the Orthodox ' Expositions of faith,' of being rulers of the Church. Peter's crafty policy, in the way of bringing about the establishment of the Synod, as well as his real contempt for the divine authority of the bishops, are there stated in the most conspicuous and undeniable manner. The reader has just been told how Peter answered the objection that, in order to abolish the Russian patriarchate, there was required the previous consent of all the Oriental patriarchs. Once, however, that the Synod was established and proclaimed to the people throughout all Russia, Peter displayed an active zeal in order to obtain from the Oriental patriarchs its recognition. A celebrated

nun das der Mensch gerecht werde ohne des Gesetzes Werk, *allein* durch den Glauben.' This addition being made a subject of reproach to the Reformer, Luther, in a letter of the 8th September, 1530, to Wenceslaus Link, expressed himself on the subject in the following sublime terms: 'If your Papist (Emser) takes great offence at the word "sola," say to him immediately: " Dr. Martin Luther's will is, that it be so, and says: Papist and donkey are one thing—sic volo, sic jubeo, sit pro ratione voluntas."' (' *Wenn euer Papist sich viel unnütze machen will, mit dem Worte* (sola, *allein*), *so sagt ihm flugs also:* " *Doctor Martin Luther wills also haben, und spricht: Papist und Esel sey ein Ding,* sic volo, sic jubeo, sit pro ratione voluntas, etc."' . . .) *Luth r's sämmtliche Schriften,* edit. by Walch. Halle in Magdeb. tom. xxi., 1749. 4to. Letter 310, § 6, p. 314. According to Walch, the same letter is to be found in the previous editions of Luther's works, as follows: Jen. tom. v. 161; Wittemb, iv. 474; Alt., v. 268; Leipz., xii. 90.

historian of the Russian Church suggests to us a fair explanation of that apparent contradiction: ' This conciliary (*sobornoe*) form of government,' so says A. N. Mouravieff, ' was proclaimed to the people throughout all Russia; but there still needed, in order to its permanent establishment, the recognition of the other Eastern Churches, *that the unity of the Catholic Church might not be violated.*'[1] The meaning of these words is quite clear, if one only remembers that the Oriental Orthodox Church is to be likened, as to her form of government, to A CONFEDERATION OF DIFFERENT STATES, éach of them independent of the rest. The *unity of the Catholic* (Orthodox) *Church*, to which allusion is made in Mouravieff's words, was and could be only a unity of charity and friendship.[2] The new form of ecclesiastical government introduced by Peter in Russia needed the recognition of the Oriental patriarchs, just as, in political society, every new Government, be

[1] Blackmore: *A History of the Church of Russia*, by A. N. Mouravieff, (Oxford, 1842), p. 285.

Обнародовано было сіе соборное правительство по всей Россіи но еще требовалось, для вѣчной твердости онаго, признаніе прочихъ Восточнихъ церквей, дабы ненарушимо было единство католической Церкви (Исторія Россійской Церкви. Спб. 1840, p. 376.

[2] Q. How does it agree with the unity of the Church, that there are many *separate* and *independent* Churches, as those of Jerusalem, Antioch, Alexandria, Constantinople, Russia?

A. These are particular Churches, or parts of the one Catholic Church; the *separateness of their visible organisation does not hinder them from being all spiritually great members of the one body of the universal Church* —from having one Head, Christ, and one spirit of faith and grace. This unity is expressed outwardly by unity of creed and by communion in prayer and sacrament.

Q. What hierarchical authority is there which can extend its sphere of action over the whole Catholic Church?

A. An Œcumenical Council. (*The Longer Catechism of Mgr. Filaret*, translated by the Rev. R. W. Blackmore, part i., on the IX Art. of the Creed, in Blackmore's *The Doctrine of the Russian Church* (Aberdeen, 1845), pp. 77–83.

it a commune, an aristocracy, or a monarchy, needs the recognition of the other Governments, *in order to keep up friendly relations with them*. The Oriental Orthodox Church presents, in the way in which she is governed, the most striking analogies to civil and political society, as we shall fully explain in the third chapter of this book; no wonder that she should also, like the latter, present to us the phenomena of revolutions and *coups d'état*. Of this last kind was the establishment of the Synod. Peter the Great knew well how to appreciate and to bring into practice the theory of *accomplished facts*. To ask the previous consent of the Oriental patriarchs would have been, on Peter's side, an act of most awkward and mistimed simplicity, which might have greatly compromised the success of his enterprise. This explains the rudeness of his behaviour in the assembly of the clergy. But once that this danger was over, once that all his plans had been carried into execution, Peter showed himself anxious to obtain from the anciently-established Government of the Oriental Orthodox Church the recognition of the new one he had just brought about. He himself wrote, on the 30th of September, 1721, to the Patriarch of Constantinople, informing him that 'amongst the many cares which the empire committed to Him by God required for the good government of His hereditary kingdoms and conquests, casting His eye on the Spiritual Order, and observing in them great irregularity, and a great defect in their proceeding, He would indeed have been afflicted in His conscience, and have had too just cause to fear lest He appear to be guilty of ingratitude to the Most High, if after, by His gracious assistance, He had happily succeeded in a regulation both military and civil . . . ' and so on, in the very same terms used in the above-quoted ukase of the 25th of January, 1721 (p. 22). Here, however, Peter declared that he had beforehand taken the advice of counsellors, both ecclesiastical and civil! . . . . .[1] The answer of the Patriarch of Constantinople bears the date of the 23rd of September, 1723, *two years and eight months* after the establishment of the Synod, and the approbation of the other Oriental patriarchs accompanied or followed that of the Patriarch of Constantinople.

Let us now suppose that the Oriental patriarchs had refused to comply with the wishes of Peter, would he then have abolished the newly-created synod and restored the patriarchate? Just as little as it may be expected from some one who has just succeeded in transforming a republic into a monarchy, and in causing himself to be elected its king, that he would abdicate the newly-acquired dignity, and restore the republic—only because small States, from which he has nothing to fear, refuse to recognise the accomplished fact. No one, we believe, will be able to contradict our assertion; Peter's character and whole behaviour in this affair was a guarantee for the steadiness of his resolution. ' Le dessein de Pierre,' says Voltaire, ' était d'établir un conseil de religion toujours subsistant qui *dépendît du souverain*, et qui ne donnât de lois à l'Église que celles qui *seraient approuvées par le maître de l'État dont* l'Église fait partie. . . Il pensait et il disait publiquement que l'idée des deux puissances (la spirituelle et la temporelle) fondée sur l'allégorie de deux épées qui se trouvèrent chez les apôtres, *était une idée absurde*. . . . Je trouve dans des mémoires curieux composés par un officier fort aimé de Pierre le Grand, qu'un jour qu'on lisait à ce prince le chapitre du *Spectateur anglais* qui contient un parallèle entre lui et Louis XIV, il dit après l'avoir écouté : " Je ne crois pas

---

[1] Царская и патріаршія граматы о учрежденіи Святѣйшаго Синода. Спб. 1838, pp. 2, 3. Τὰ τοῦ εὐσεβεστάτου Βασιλέως καὶ τῶν ἁγιωτάτων Πατριάρχων γράμματα περὶ τῆς συστάσεως τῆς ἁγιωτάτης Συνόδου. (Athens, 1844), p. 4. See above, pp. 33–35.

mériter la préférence qu'on me donne sur ce monarque, mais j'ai été assez heureux pour lui être supérieur dans un point essentiel, j'ai forcé mon clergé à l'obéissance et à la paix, et Louis XIV s'est laissé subjuguer par le sien."' If we quote Voltaire, it is only because his history of Peter, as has been already remarked, was almost dictated by Catherine II., so that it may be considered as a faithful echo of the opinions and feelings of the Court of St. Petersburg at that time. Yet we needed not the authority of Voltaire's history, nor that of any other writer,[1] in order to be convinced that Peter aimed at making his clergy the most obedient and subservient the world had ever seen. A cursory glance at some chief features of Peter's ecclesiastical legislature, *still in force*, is, alas! more than sufficient. These we are now going to make the reader acquainted with, setting aside whatever may personally concern Peter or his intentions.

In quoting Peter's ukase of the 25th of January, 1721, for the establishment of the Holy Synod, we promised to return to the special oath taken by the members of the Spiritual College, and to which allusion is made in the just-mentioned ukase. The formula of oath is very long, and in its greatest part identical with that forced upon the members of the other colleges.[2] There is, however, an

[1] It is worthy of remark that the Protestant historians of Peter marvellously agree in considering his ecclesiastical reformation as we do, though praising him for it. As an instance, King, after having given an account of the Holy Synod and its organisation, adds, 'These are such effectual checks to the power of the clergy, that *no prince in the world can have less to fear from them.*'—*The Rites and Ceremonies, &c.*, p. 428.

[2] This document being of the greatest importance, because of the contests to which it gave rise, we prefer quoting it *in extenso*:—

'I, undernamed, promise and swear by Almighty God, on His Holy Gospel, that I am in duty bound, and according to my duty will and shall every way endeavour, in the counsels, judgments, and in all the proceedings of this Spiritual Legislative Synod, at all times to search out the very

addition which solely and exclusively concerns the members of the Spiritual College. It reads as follows:—

truth and right, and to act in all things conformably to the rules or canons prescribed in the *Spiritual Regulation*. And if any canons shall hereafter be decreed by the suffrage and concurrence of this *Spiritual Government* (сего Духовнаго Правительства) and with *the consent of His Imperial Majesty* (соизволеніемъ Царскаго Величества); these I will act by, according to my conscience, without respect of persons, free from enmity, emulation, and strife. And plainly to be influenced by no kind of fears, but that of God, always keeping in mind his unsearchable judgments, with a sincere love of God and of my neighbour; proposing the glory of God, the salvation of the souls of men, and the edification of the whole Church (всей Церкви), as the ultimate scope and end of my thoughts, words, and actions, not seeking my own, but what is Jesus, the Lord's.

'I swear also, by the living God, that, always remembering His tremendous word, "*Everyone is accursed who does the work of God negligently,*" I will apply myself to every affair of this Legislative Synod, as to a work of God, industriously, and with all diligence, to the utmost of my power, wholly disregarding my own pleasure and ease. And I will not pretend ignorance; but if I am doubtful in any case, I will labour diligently to come at the right understanding and knowledge of it, by searching into the Holy Scriptures, examining the canons and decrees of Councils, and taking into consideration the unanimous consent of the great and primitive doctors.

'*I again swear* by Almighty God, that I will, and am in duty bound to continue a faithful, good, and obedient servant, and subject to my natural and true Tsar and Sovereign, Peter the First (Первому) Autocrat (Самодержцу) of all Russia, etc., and after him to His Imperial Majesty's august lawful successors, who, by the will and uncontrollable autocratical (самодержавной) power of His Imperial Majesty are appointed, or shall hereafter be appointed, and qualified to ascend the throne; and to her Sovereign Majesty the Empress Catharine Alexievna. And every right, prerogative, or pre-eminence belonging to the supreme sovereignty, power, and dominion of His Imperial Majesty, which is legal, or shall hereafter be legally established, to guard and defend with the best of my skill, power, and ability, and, if need be, with my life and fortune. And moreover, with the greatest constancy endeavour (старатися) to promote everything that can in any way contribute to the faithful service and interest of His Imperial Majesty. As to any diminution of, or detriment and damage to His Majesty's interests, as soon as I am acquainted with it I will endeavour not only to discover it in due time, but by all means to remedy or put a stop to it. And when, for the service and interest of

'*I confess* (*acknowledge*) *upon oath, that the monarch of all Russia himself, our most gracious Sovereign,* IS THE SUPREME JUDGE OF THIS SPIRITUAL COLLEGE.'

These words speak fairly enough for themselves. So, then, the pretended authority of the Russian Church meets, in the discharge of her functions, with another authority as superior to her as a judge is superior to those upon whom he is going to pronounce a sentence!

And in order that no one might mistake as to the natural meaning of these words, or even venture to contest it, by alleging, for instance, that the quoted words—' ne se rapportent qu'aux membres du Saint Synode en leur qualité de sujets, de dignitaires de l'État, de membres d'une assemblée mixte qui a un double caractère religieux et civil,' and that ' le serment du Saint Synode se rapporte seulement à l'existence extérieure de l'Église et au souverain comme chef politique,'[1]—Peter the Great or-

---

His Majesty, or the Church, I am privy to any secret affair, or whatever kind it is which I am commanded to keep a secret, I will keep it with perfect secrecy, reveal it to no person living who is not concerned to know it, and to whom I am not required to disclose it.

'I ACKNOWLEDGE *upon oath that the monarch of all Russia himself, our most gracious Sovereign, is* THE SUPREME JUDGE *of this Spiritual College.*
(Исповѣдую же съ клатвою крайнаго Судію Духовныя сея Коллегіи, быти Самаго Всероссійскаго Монарха, Государя нашего Всемилостивѣйшаго).

'I farther swear by the all-seeing God, that all the particulars I have now sworn to I do not only explain and understand in my mind as I have uttered them with my mouth, but in the force and sense, whatever force and sense it is, which the words here written do express to those that hear and read them.

'I assert upon oath, God the Observer of hearts being Witness of my oath, that it is no lie. If it is a lie and not from my conscience, let the same righteous Judge be my avenger.

'In confirmation of this my oath, I kiss the words and cross of my Saviour.—Amen.' *Consett*, pp. 6–10. (Полн. Собр. tom. vi. (3718) pp. 314, 315.

[1] *Discussion entre Mgr. l'évêque de Nantes et M. l'archiprêtre Wassilieff au sujet de l'autorité ecclésiastique dans l'Église de Russie* (Paris, 1861). 8vo.

dained that the words: 'I acknowledge upon oath that the monarch of all Russia himself is the SUPREME JUDGE of this Spiritual College,' should, as we have already remarked, *solely and exclusively* be inserted in the formula of oath taken by the members of the *Spiritual* College, as nothing of the kind is to be found in the formula of oath previously prescribed to the members of the *other* Colleges. Moreover, still in order to shut out even the possibility of any explanation which might not agree with the natural meaning of the quoted words, Peter ordained that the members of the Holy Synod *alone* must, before concluding their oath, swear as follows: [1] 'I farther swear by the all-seeing God, that all the particulars I have now sworn to I do not only explain and understand in my mind as I have uttered them with my mouth, but in the force and sense, whatever force and sense it is, which the words here written do express to those that hear and read them.'

But let us go on, as what we are successively going to state will more and more throw light on every previous statement, and afford new proofs of them. We shall now speak of the *Chief Procurator* of the Synod, that dignitary appointed by Peter's ukase of the 11th of May, 1722, which we have quoted *in extenso* (p. 27).

We are not aware if it has been sufficiently pointed out that the *Instruction* given by Peter to the Chief Procurator (*Ober-Procurator*) of the Synod, (and which, being still in force, is to be seen in every edition of the 'Spiritual Regulation,') is identical word for word with

---

[1] The formula of oath prescribed by Peter to the members of the other Colleges begins with the words '*I (again) swear by Almighty God,*' etc. of the formula of oath for the members of the Synod, and runs word for word identically with the last, as far as the words 'I ACKNOWLEDGE *upon oath*,' *etc.*, *instead of which*, the members of the other Colleges make a general promise of obedience to their statutes and of fidelity to the Tsar. See Полн. Собр. том. vi. Генер. Регл. (3534), February 28, 1720, p. 142.

that given by him to the *General Procurator of the Senate* only with the necessary substitution of the word *Synod* for that of Senate. Whoever is acquainted with the Russian language, and desires to make such comparison for himself, will find both ' Instructions ' in vol. vi. of the ' Complete Collection of the Laws,' etc.[1] From this single, yet two-faced, Instruction we quote the following explanation of the rights equally exercised by the Tsar both over the Senate, through its General Procurator, and over the Synod through its Chief Procurator. 'The General Procurator of the Senate (*the Chief Procurator of the Synod*) being appointed through this charge as *Our(the Tsar's)* OWN EYE, and the advocate of the affairs of the State, must behave with fidelity, because it is against him that proceedings will be first taken' (Art. 11). ' The General Procurator of the Senate (*the Chief Procurator of the Synod*) is bound to assist at the sittings of the Senate (*of the Synod*), and to have a watchful eye on the Senate (*Synod*), that it fulfil its duty, and that the affairs submitted to its discussion and decision be carried on comformably to the statutes and ukases, according to truth, with zeal and good order, and without loss of time, unless some legitimate cause prevents him doing his function; and all this he is bound to register in his diary. Moreover, he ought to watch closely that affairs be not merely decided in the sessions, but that whatever has been there decided be effectually put into execution' (Art. 1).

Thus much as to the supervision and control of the Tsar over the proceedings both of the Senate and of the

---

[1] Полн. Собр. Законъ. tom. vi. (4036), June 13, 1722, p. 721, and (3979), April 27, 1722, p. 662. The Instruction of the *General Procurator* to the Senate has, however, one article more concerning the *Chief Procurator to the Senate*. It runs as follows: ' The *Chief Procurator* (to the Senate), is the General Procurator's assistant in his business, and is bound to manage it in his absence.'

Duties of Chief Procurator of the Synod.

Holy Synod. What now follows explains in what sense the members of the Holy Synod, according to their oath, ought to consider the Tsar as their SUPREME JUDGE: 'The Procurator is also bound to have a watchful and severe eye upon the Senate (*Synod*), that it proceed in its functions according to truth and without respect to persons. And if he remarks anything to the contrary, he must, on the spot, make it known to the Senate (*Synod*) pointing out, without concealment, in what the Senate (*Synod*) or any of its members do not act as they ought, in order that the matter may be set right. If they do not obey, he is obliged to immediately protest, stay the proceeding of the business, and, if urgent, refer it immediately to *Us*. If there is no urgency, the affair will be treated in the Senate (*Synod*) in *Our* presence, within the week or the month, according to that which will be ordained. The General Procurator (*Chief Procurator*) ought equally to proceed with prudence and circumspection in his public reports to *Us*, in order not to bring any discredit on anybody without reason. Hence it is that if any affair on account of which his opinion differs from that of the others, seems to him obscure and offering two different aspects, after having stayed its proceeding by the above-mentioned protest, he must not refer it immediately to *Us*, but take advice from whomsoever he deems capable of throwing light on the matter. In case he finds that the affair really is as he judged it to be, or that he is unable to clear it any more and to resolve his doubt, he shall refer it to *Us*, and never later than within a week, unless the thing be evident, and of some urgency, in which case he shall refer it to *Us* without delay; in the contrary case he shall behave as we have just stated, but no later than within a week, nor excusing himself on account of any impediment, except if *We* should be absent. In this case, however, he must supply by a report drawn up in the above-mentioned time, and this he shall send up by a special courier. If, by indulging some passion, he draws up a report which is not conformed to truth, he himself will be punished according to the importance of the case' (Art. 2).

It evidently results from these prescriptions that *the Tsar is just as much and in the same sense the judge of the Synod and its members as he is the judge of the Senate and its members.* In the Synod, as well as in the Senate, the Tsar by HIS EYE, viz., by the Procurator, stops whatever decision is going to be taken not conformably to his will; no doubt or difficulty of importance can be resolved except by Him, and not a single law can even be framed, which has not the previous, at least supposed, consent of the Tsar!—What now follows bears evidence to the degree of liberty and independence which is left to the Synod, in the mere execution even of the laws which did not meet the *veto* of the Chief Procurator, nor the dissatisfaction of the Tzar, as well as of any ecclesiastical law or canon already existing. 'He it is (the General Procurator for the Senate, and the Chief Procurator for the Synod)—he it is who must have under his direction the Chancery of the Senate (*Synod*), as well as the clerks attached to it' (Art. 5). 'The *Executor* of the Senate (*Synod*) ought to be placed under the direction of the General (Chief) Procurator' (Art. 6).

Indeed, unless we greatly mistake the meaning of the words which are made use of in the single Instruction to the General Procurator of the Senate, and the Chief Procurator of the Synod, the Russian Orthodox Church is undeniably as much enslaved as a Church can possibly be. We cannot conceive how a king may otherwise be more really king and more really govern his people than by the possession and exercise of the legislative and administrative powers (the last of the two comprising also the executive). Now the *Executor,* or officer charged to enforce the execution of whatever might be ordered by the

Synod, '*agreeably to the will of His Imperial Majesty*,'[1] is, like the *Executor* of the Senate, a *layman* and, besides, is placed under the direction of the Chief Procurator of the Synod. The Chancery, viz., the office through which the current affairs of the Synod are managed, is, together with all its clerks, under the direction of the Chief Procurator.[2] Further, the legislative power, as we are going to explain more in detail, is entirely in the hands of the Tsar. What is there left, after this, for those members of the Synod who are bishops, and for the Synod itself,— for the asserted permanent *council* GOVERNING (*pravitelstvuiustchyi*) the Russian Orthodox Church?—Finally no other guarantee is afforded to the Synod against the abuses of power and arbitrary proceedings of its chief Procurator than the recourse to the Tsar. Thus runs the ninth article of the same two-faced Instruction: 'The general Procurator of the Senate (*the Chief Procurator of the Synod*) is not subjected to the judgment of anybody but to *Ours*. And, if, during our absence, he becomes guilty of any great crime, which will not admit of any delay, as for instance of treason, the Senate (*the Synod*) is empowered to cause him to be arrested and to open an inquiry, entrusting somebody else with his functions ; the Senate (*Synod*), however, is not allowed to subject him to any torture or penalty or chastisement' (Art. 9).

Behold, then, the Holy Synod at the Chief Procurator's mercy, and at that of the Tsar or a Tsarina. How can it be believed after this that the Holy Synod is a body really *governing* the Russian Orthodox Church?

Nay, to the easy assertions of advocates or admirers of the Russian Orthodox Church, let us prefer the sober, exact, and authoritative language of the Russian Code of

[1] Words of the oath taken by the bishops. See further on, p. 66.
[2] See, for the composition of the Chancery attached to the Synod, the *Table* relative to the law of March 1, 1839 (12,069), in the Appendix to the tom. xiv. of the Полн. Собр. 2nd series.

Law and of the Russian jurists. No one has a real interest in being deceived, and truth alone can really be profitable to Orthodox Russians, as well as to Protestant Englishmen or Catholics of every country. Now, the Russian Code of Laws, as well as the Russian jurists, plainly and fairly states that both the *administrative* and *legislative* powers of the Russian Church are in the hands of the Tsar.

The Holy Synod is, it is true, termed 'governing' (*pravitelstvuiustchyi*)[1] in the Russian Code of Laws, but the Senate also is there termed *governing*, though no one may himself venture to advance that the Russian empire is not governed by the Tsar, but by its Senate. We fairly recognise that the title of *governing* may, to some extent, be suitably applied to the Synod, that is in the sense in which it is also conferred on the Senate; the Synod and the Senate being the two chief bodies by which the laws are proposed, discussed, elaborated, and drawn up *before being presented to the Tsar*. But we are enabled to assert that the Synod is no more the real chief ruler of the Russian Church than the Senate is the real chief ruler of the Russian empire. In fact, the Holy Synod is termed *governing* in the very same (43rd) article already quoted above (p. 20), to which we promised to return, and which runs as follows:—'In the administration of the Church the autocratical authority ACTS BY MEANS of the Most Holy Governing Synod appointed by him.'

When we quoted this article for the first time, we

[1] Правительствующій is *officially* translated in French by 'Dirigeant' (see *Journal de St. Petersbourg*, etc.). Yet the common English translation which we have kept, agrees with the principal signification of the verb правительствовать, which is thus explained in the *Dictionary of the Academy of St. Petersburg*: 1.) Имѣть правительственную или верховную власть (possess the supreme authority; 2.) Управлять (administer).—Слов. церковно слав. и русск. языка сост. ii отд. Имп. Акад. Наукъ. Спб. 1847. See, further on, the quotation of Speranski, p. 50, note 3.

pointed out that, according to it, the Synod is a mere *organ or instrument* by means of which the Tsar governs the Church. The expressions we made use of, however strong they may appear, are not of our invention; they are to be found in the well-known 'Course of Jurisprudence, according to the programme approved for the instruction in the military establishments of Russia,' by Mich. Mikhailoff.[1] 'Among the rights of the supreme authority (so says Mikhailoff) the chief place is taken by the legislative and supreme administrative powers' (p. 38).[2] 'As *organs* (organi) through which the supreme authority acts, as well *in the making of laws as in the administration* of the State, are the SUBORDINATE authorities and institutions (*ustanovlenia*) appointed by him' (p. 21). 'The supreme administrative authority *acts* in the State *by means* of special instruments (*orudia*) or organs (*organs*), which are called institutions (*ustanovlenia*)' (p. 38).[3]

Then (pp. 71 *et seq.*) the same author, in a special chapter termed, 'Of the Highest Institutions: the Council of State—the Governing Senate—the Most Holy Synod,' speaks in detail of each of the three: 'The supreme authority,' so he begins, 'acts in the administration of the affairs of the State through the organs appointed by itself,

[1] Курсъ Законовѣдѣнія по программѣ утвержденной для руководства въ военно-учебныхъ заведеніяхъ. Спб. 1861.

[2] Въ составѣ правъ Верховной Власти первое мѣсто занимаетъ Власть законодательная и Власть Верховнаго Управленія.

[3] Органами чрезъ которые Верховная Власть дѣйствуетъ въ Государствѣ какъ въ законодадельствѣ такъ и въ управленіи служатъ подчиненныя власти и установленія, ею учреждаемыя.

Власть Верховнаго Управленія дѣйствуетъ въ Государствѣ посредствомъ особенныхъ орудій, органовъ, которые называются установленіями.

E

and called institutions (*ustanovlenia*).'¹ . . . And speaking of the last of them: 'The Most Holy Synod is the Governing Council of the Russian Church, subject to the dominion of the Sovereign, *by means of which* the supreme autocratical authority *acts* in the administration of the ecclesiastical affairs concerning the Orthodox Confession.² And a little further on: 'For the conduct of its affairs the Holy Synod possesses a Chancery of its own, dependent on the Chief Procurator, through whom *alone* every proposition of the Holy Synod ascends to the Sovereign Emperor, and under whose chief direction is placed *the administration of the departments of the ecclesiastical property and schools attached to the Synod.*'

We confine ourselves to the quoted abstracts out of Mikhailoff's 'Course of Jurisprudence,' confidently referring our readers to any other of the Russian jurists, as they *all* perfectly agree with him in considering the Synod as he does, that is as a mere State institution, by means of which the Tsar governs the Church, just as he governs the Empire by means of the Senate and the Ministries. 'The supreme authority,' says the celebrated Speranski, '*governs* by the institutions appointed by itself; but the institutions *administer* the affairs entrusted to them according to their rules and statutes.'³

¹ Высшія Установленія.—Государственный Совѣтъ. Правительствующій Сенатъ. Святѣйшій Сунодъ.—Власть Верховная въ управленіи Государственными дѣлами дѣйствуетъ чрезъ органы Его установляемыя именуемыя Установленіями, etc. (p. 71).

² Святѣйшій Синодъ есть Правительствующій Россійской церкви Соборъ состоящій подъ Монаршею Державой, посредствомъ коего Верховная Самодержавная Власть дѣйствуетъ въ управленіи церковными дѣлами Православнаго исповѣданія (p. 88).

³ Власть верховная правитъ (*gouverne*) установленіями

Moreover, the statements of Russian jurists are but an echo of the principles fairly and plainly laid down in the Russian Code of Law. Let us take a glance at them. It is well known that the *colleges* established by Peter (one of which was the *Spiritual College,* or Most Holy Synod), were kept up till the year 1802, when Alexander I., notwithstanding the great advantages alleged by Peter in favour of his administration by means of colleges, declared, that 'For the *best* management of affairs, he had thought it proper to entrust every separate department of the administration of the State to a separate Minister chosen by him.'[1] The only *college* which was maintained was the *spiritual* one, or Holy Synod. See, now, in what terms the Ministries and the Holy Synod are defined in the 'Alphabetical Register' of the Russian Code of Laws, being at the same time a summary of the whole code of laws. We put the two definitions in juxtaposition.

| 'The Ministries are those State institutions by means of which the supreme *executive* authority acts in every department of the administration.'[2] | 'The Most Holy Synod is that State institution by means of which the supreme *autocratical* authority acts in the administration of the affairs of the Orthodox Confession.'[3] |

ею учрежденными; а установленія управляютъ (*administrent*) дѣлами имъ ввѣренными по уставамъ ихъ и учрежденіямъ. Speranski: Руководство къ познанію законовъ, Спб. 1845, art. 140, p. 90.

[1] Manifesto for the establishment of Ministries in Russia. Полн. Собр. tom. xxvii. Sept. 8, 1802 (20,406), p. 243.

[3] Министерства суть установленія государственныя, посредствомъ коихъ Вер- [3] Святѣйшій Синодъ есть установленіе государственное, посредствомъ коего

Indeed, unless it be proved that in either of the two definitions the same words do not possess the same identical meaning as in the other, these definitions alone will undeniably prove, against all sophistry, that the Tsar is as much the chief of the Synod as he is the chief of any civil or political institution appointed for the administration of the State. The definitions are identical save in one word. The power which, in reference to the Ministries, is simply called *executive*, with *regard to the Church* is called *autocratical*, in order, it seems, to remind people that, according to the explanation of this word which is alluded to in a note to the first article of the Russian Code of Laws: 'His Majesty is a monarch autocratic, who has not to give a reason for his actions to anybody on earth, but has the power and authority, as Christian Sovereign, to administer his State and country according to his own will and discretion.'[1]

Let us conclude what we have been saying concerning the supreme administrative power of the Tzar, even in

ховная исполнительная власть дѣйствуетъ на всѣ части управленія. Сводъ Закон. tom. i. Учр. Мин. ст. 189.	Верховная Самодержавная власть дѣйствуетъ въ управленіи церковными дѣлами Православной Вѣры. Сводъ. Закон. tom. i. Зак. осн. ст. 40, 42, 43.

Алфабитный Указатель къ Своду Законовъ Россійской Имперіи изданному въ 1857 году. Спб. 1860, pp. 607 and 1023.

[1] Его Величество есть Самовластный Монархъ, которой никому на свѣтѣ о своихъ дѣлахъ отвѣта дать не долженъ, но силу и власть имѣетъ Свои Государства и земли, яко Христіанскій Государь по своей волѣ и благомнѣнію управлять. (Уставъ Морск. Кн. V. гл. 1. ст. 2 толков. in the Полн. Собр. tom. vi. Jan. 13, 1720 (3485), p. 59. See also Уст. Воин. арт. 20 толк. in tom. v. March 30, 1716 (3006), p. 325.

reference to the Church, by the following article of the same Code of Laws. 'The *administrative* power belongs *in its entire extent* to the Tsar. In the supreme administration his power acts immediately; in matters of inferior administration a definite degree of authority is entrusted by him to some officers and persons acting in his name, and in pursuance of his orders.'[1]

We hasten to speak of the *legislative* power. This point is of the greatest moment for deciding, we may say, incontestably, all possible questions concerning the real and effectual ruler of the Russian Orthodox Church. 'By the *sovereign* power,' says Blackstone, 'is meant the MAKING OF LAWS; for wherever this power resides, all other

---

This explanation is given on account, and as a justification, of the prescription contained in the military and naval statutes that 'whoever has become guilty of having uttered injurious words against the person of His Majesty, despised his acts and intentions (намѣреніе), and judged them in an unbecoming (непристойнымъ) way, should be beheaded, *because* (ибо) His Majesty is a monarch autocratic, who is not to give a reason,' etc.

To the same explanation there is a reference in the 1st article of the Russian Code of Laws, which runs as follows:—

'The Emperor of all the Russias is a monarch autocratic and unlimited. God Himself commands that one should obey his supreme authority, not only from fear, but also as a matter of conscience.'

Императоръ Всероссійскій есть Монархъ Самодержавный и неограниченный.—Повиноваться верховной Его власти, не токмо за страхъ но и за совѣсть, Самъ Богъ повелѣваетъ.

[1] Власть управленія во всемъ ея пространствѣ принадлежитъ Государю. Въ управленіи верховномъ власть Его дѣйствуетъ непосредственно; въ дѣлахъ же управленія подчиненнаго опредѣленная степень власти ввѣряется отъ Него мѣстамъ и лицамъ дѣйствующимъ Его именемъ и по Его повелѣнію. (Сводъ Зак. ed. 1857, tom. i. Осп. Гос. Зак. art. 80, p. 20.

must conform to and be directed by it, whatever in appearance the outward form of government may be.'¹ 'LEGISLATURE,' says another eminent jurist, '*is the greatest act of superiority* that can be exercised by one being over another. Wherefore it is requisite to the very essence of a law that it be made by the supreme power. Sovereignty and legislature are indeed convertible terms: one cannot subsist without the other.'² It would be of no use to make analogous quotations out of the Russian jurists, as the matter is sufficiently evident of itself.³ Let us rather see what is stated in the Russian Code of Laws concerning the composition, explanation, and completion of the laws.

Tome I. 'Code of the fundamental Laws of the State.' Article 49. 'The first draught of the laws is either made through personal advertence of the Sovereign and by his immediate command, or it takes its beginning through the ordinary proceeding of business. This is the case whenever the governing Senate, *the Most Holy Synod*, or any of the Ministries, after discussion on the matter, deem it necessary either to explain and complete a law already in force, or to draw up a new prescription. In this case the above-named authorities must submit their project to the approbation of the Tsar, in the legal way prescribed for them.' —50. 'All projects of law are examined in the Council of State: after that they come up for the revision of the Sovereign; and in no other way can they attain their intended fulfilment, unless by an act of the autocratic power.' —51. 'No authority or administration whatever in the State is entitled to make of itself any new law, and no

---

¹ *The Student's Blackstone, Commentaries on the Laws of England*, abridged by Robert Malcolm Kerr. Introd. § 1.

² H. J. Stephen's *New Commentaries on the Laws of England* (London 1841). Introd. § 2, pp. 27, 28.

³ See *Speranski, Mikhailoff, Nevolin* (Энциклопедія законовѣдѣнія), *Dobrovolski* (Руководство законовѣдѣнія), etc.

law whatever can obtain its execution without its being confirmed by the autocratic power.'[1]

These articles need no comment. They concern the Holy Synod as well as the Senate, or any authority whatever of the Russian empire. Let us only recollect Mikhailoff's words: 'As organs (*organi*) through which the supreme authority acts, *as well in the making of laws as in the administration of the State,* are the SUBORDINATE authorities and institutions appointed by him,'[2] one of which, as we have already demonstrated, is the Synod itself. Finally, let us not forget what is stated in the ukase of the 25th of January, 1721, for the establishment of the Holy Synod: 'This college must perfect hereafter their "*Regulation*" with more rules, such as the different occasions of

---

[1] Art. 49. Первообразное предначертаніе законовъ составляется или по особенному Высочайшему усмотрѣнію и непосредственному повелѣнію, или же пріемлетъ начало свое отъ общаго теченія дѣлъ, когда при разсмотрѣніи оныхъ въ правительствующемъ Сенатѣ или Святѣйшемъ Синодѣ и въ Министерствахъ, признано будетъ необходимымъ или пояснить и дополнить дѣйствующій законъ, или составить новое постановленіе. Въ семъ случаѣ мѣста сіи подносятъ предположенія ихъ установленнымъ порядкомъ на Высочайшее благоусмотрѣніе.

Art. 50. Всѣ предначертанія законовъ разсматриваются въ Государственномъ Совѣтѣ, потомъ восходятъ на Высочайшее усмотрѣніе, и не иначе поступаютъ къ преназначенному имъ совершенію, какъ дѣйствіемъ Самодержавной Власти.

Art. 51. Никакое мѣсто или правительство въ Государствѣ не можетъ само собою установить новаго закона, и никакой законъ не можетъ имѣть своего совершенія безъ утвержденія Самодержавной Власти. (Сводъ Закон. Основные Государственные Законы. Разд. i. pp. 12–13.)

[2] See above, p. 49.

various affairs shall require; *but the Spiritual College must not do this without Our consent*'—nor that the members of the Holy Synod promise upon oath to conform themselves besides to the 'Spiritual Regulation;' also 'to any canons which shall hereafter be decreed by the suffrage and concurrence of the Synod, *and with the consent of His Imperial Majesty*.'[1]

We are now eager to speak of the bishops in their relations to the Synod. In order, however, that not the slightest prejudice may possess the mind of the reader, and prevent him from following without misgiving the course of our argument, we shall here say a few words respecting those limits which are said to be put by the *ecclesiastical canons* to the will of the Tsar, reserving further remarks on the subject for the second chapter of this book. First of all, let us remark that there are two kinds of canons—the *dogmatical* ones and the *disciplinary*. As to the *dogmatical* canons—that is, those which state the belief of the Church—they not only are by their own nature immutable, but they forcibly require the submission of all that do not wish to be cast out of the Church whose doctrine they express. In this respect the Tsar is on a level with the Pope, in whom we do not recognise any more power to alter the dogmatical canons of the Catholic Church than the least of the faithful has. The question is, therefore, reduced to the *disciplinary* canons, that is, to the canons concerning the *external administration* of the Church.[2]

---

[1] See above (pp. 24; 40–1, *note*). Further evidences as to the legislative power of the Russian Church being fully and exclusively concentrated in the hands of the Tsar will be found further on, especially when we shall treat of the oath taken by the bishops at their consecration.

[2] We leave aside further subdivisions of disciplinary canons, as they are of no use for the present purpose. Much might also be said as to the influence of the Tsars on the doctrine of their Church, as will appear by what we are going to say on the Russian Catechisms. See also pp. 104–106.

Сн. I.]   *The 'Kormchaia Kniga.'*   57

As respects these also, we remark that the disciplinary canons of the Russian Orthodox Church are, at any rate, very ancient laws, which existed long before Peter had made up his mind to establish the Synod. They were exhibited in the so-called 'Kormchaia Kniga' (*the pilot-book*, Gr. Πηδάλιον) a book of much importance, showing by what gross mediæval ignorance and by what curious fables the Greek schism was fixed and popularised in Russia.[1] Since 1839, the Holy Synod, to suit, perhaps, the wishes of German and other writers, that such absurdities should not be reprinted any more, publishes only that part of the 'Kormchaia Kniga' which contains the canons of the Apostles, the Councils, and the Fathers of the Church, under the title of 'Kniga pravil,' or 'Book of the Canons.' These canons, as the reader may be convinced by an inspection of them either in the Russian translation or in the original Greek,[2] are far from

---

[1] An accurate and very learned account of the Кормчая Книга was given by the celebrated Kopitar in the *Jahrbücher der Literatur* (Wien, 1823), tom. xxiii. pp. 220-274. Kopitar concludes his account by the following words: 'Möge diese *Kormchaia* endlich gar nicht mehr gedruckt, sondern über einer ganz andern, zugleich der alten, erleuchteten griechischen Kirche und des Jahrhundertes der heiligen Allianz würdigen, vergessen werden!' Instances of the curiosities of this book are to be found also in Schlosser's *Die morgenländische orthodoxe Kirche Russlands und das europäische Abendland* (Heidelberg, 1845), p. 92 et seq.
A complete essay on that book was published in 1829 by Rozenkamf. Обозрѣніе кормчей Книги. Moscow, 1829, 8vo.—The British Museum (3356, c.) possesses the edition of the *Kormchaia* of 1816, that examined by Kopitar, in the volume of the *Jahrbücher der Literatur* which has been quoted.

[2] The following are the principal canons admitted both in the Greek and in the Russian Orthodox Church. They are to be found, with others of less authority or of less importance, in the Кормчая Книга; and, since 1839, are published in the Книга правилъ Св. Апостоловъ Святыхъ Соборовъ вселенскихъ и помѣстныхъ и Св. Отцевъ. For the reader's convenience we have added references to the Greek Πηδάλιον τῆς νοητῆς νηὸς τῆς μιᾶς ἁγίας καθολικῆς καὶ ἀποστολικῆς τῶν ὀρθοδόξων Ἐκκλησίας ἤτοι ἅπαντες οἱ ἱεροὶ καὶ θεῖοι κάνονες,

favouring a Church reformation like that of Peter the Great. Yet the Russian autocrat was too powerful to refrain, on that account, from carrying out his projects.

etc. edit. of Zante, 1864, and to Beveridge's Συνόδικον, sive Pandectæ Canonum, etc. Gr. et Lat. Oxonii. 1672. Folio.

85 canons of the Apostles. Explanation of Aristenus, with various readings.—Beveridge's Συνόδικον, pp. 1–57; Πηδάλιον, pp. 1–122.

17 canons of the Apostle St. Paul.—Bev. ii. at the end of the first part, Cc. 3—Dd.

17 canons of the Apostles Peter and Paul.—Bev. ibid.

Two canons of all the Apostles together.—Bev. ibid.

20 canons of the first Œcumenical Council of Nicæa. Aristenus' text and explanation.—Bev. i. 58–84; Πηδάλιον, 123–152.

25 canons of the Council of Ancyra. Zonaras' preface (Bev. i. 375). Aristenus' text and explanation.—Bev. i. 376–401; Πηδάλ. 371–385.

15 canons of the Council of Neocæsarea. Zonaras' and Balsamon's preface (Bev. i. 402). Aristenus' text and explanation.—Bev. i. 402–414; Πηδ. 385–395.

20 canons of the Council of Gangra, out of Zonaras and Aristenus.—Bev. i. 416–428; Πηδ. (21 canons) 395–405.

25 canons of the Council of Antioch.—Bev. i. 429–453; Πηδ. 405–419.

58 canons of the Council of Laodicea.—Bev. i. 453–481; Πηδ. (60 canons) 420–442.

8 canons of the second Œcumenical Council of Constantinople. — Bev. i. 85–98; Πηδ. (7 canons) 153–165.

8 canons of the third Œcumenical Council of Ephesus. Preface (Bev. i. 99). Epistle of the Fathers to all the faithful (Harduini, Collect. Conc. i. 1622). Aristenus' text and explanation.—Bev. i. 99–110; Πηδ. 166–179.

30 canons of the fourth Œcumenical Council of Chalcedon. Preface and Aristenus' explanation.—Bev. i. 111–150; Πηδ. 180–211.

21 canons of the Council of Sardica. Preface out of Zonaras and Balsamon. Aristenus' text and explanation.—Bev. i. 482–508; Πηδ. (20 canons) 443–461.

138 canons of the Council of Carthage.—Bev. i. 509–680; Πηδ. (141 canons) 462–542.

1 canon of the Council held in Constantinople on account of Agapius and Gabadius contending for the Bishopric of Bosra.—Bev. i. 678; Πηδ. (2 canons) p. 461, 462.

An account of the fifth Œcumenical Council.—Πηδ. 211–212.

102 canons of the (quini-sext) Council of Constantinople (held in Trullo). —Bev. i. 152–283; Πηδ. 213–313.

He acted with respect to the ecclesiastical canons in the same way in which a conqueror acts with respect to the laws of the country he has just brought under his power. The Russian autocrat looked over all the ecclesiastical laws of his country; some of them—those which might

22 canons of the seventh Œcumenical Council, second of Nicæa. Aristenus' text and explanation.—Bev. i. 284-330; Πηδ. 314-342.

17 canons of the first and second Councils held in Constantinople in the Church of the Apostles. Zonaras' preface, Aristenus' text and explanation.—Bev. i. 331-359; Πηδ. 343-361.

3 canons of the Council held in St. Sophia's Church in Constantinople. Aristenus.—Bev. i. 360-364; Πηδ. 361-366.

91 canons, out of St. Basilius' epistle to Amphilochius. Aristenus' text and explanation.—Bev. ii. p. i. 47-146; Πηδ. (92 canons), 585-649.

26 canons of St. Basilius, 'De titulo et tempore peccatorum.'—Bev. ii. Append. to the first part, Dd. *verso*.

Of the same St. Basilius' 'De locis eorum qui puniuntur.'—Bev. *ibid.* Dd. 2.

St. Basilius' 'De divina gratia et sacra communione' (Bev. *ibid.* Ee. *verso* and *recto*). 'De iis qui poenas contemnunt.'—*Ibid.* Ee. *verso*.

St. Basilius' 'Epistle to Gregory the Theologian, on the monastical life.' —Bas. ep. ii. ed. Garn.

St. Dionysius' (Archbishop of Alexandria) 'De tempore quo in magno Sabbato jejunium solvere oporteat,' and 'De iis qui cum excommunicati fuerint, et pro metu mortis ad communionem admissi, postea convalescunt.— Bev. ii. Append. to part i. Bb. 2, *recto* and *verso*.

St. Peter's (of Alexandria) 14 canons, on those who had fallen during the persecution. — Bev. *ibid.* Bb. 2. *verso*; Πηδ. (15 canons far more extensive), 562-575.

St. Gregory the Thaumaturge's (Bishop of Neocæsarea) 13 canons, ' De iis qui in barbarorum incursione fuerint.'—Bev. *ibid.* Bb. 3; Πηδ. (12 canons more extensive), 551-562.

St. Athanasius' (Archbishop of Alexandria) epistle, ' De somniantibus ad Ammum monachum' (Bev. *ibid.* Bb. 3. *verso*), ' ad Rufianum' (*Ruffinianum*) Bev. *ibid.* Cc. 3, *verso*, and 'Libri veteris testamenti sunt,' etc.—Bev. *ibid.* Bb. 4 ; Πηδ. 575 *et seq.*

St. Gregory the Theologian's ' Ex versibus—de iisdem—Prima Genesia,' etc.—Bev. *ibid.*; Πηδ. 662-664.

St. Amphilochius on the same subject.—Bev. *ibid.* Bb. 4, *verso*; Πηδ. 664, 665.

St. Gregory's, of Nyssa, ' Ad Letoium Melitanes Episcopum epistola,' (8 canons).—Bev. *ibid.* Cc. ; Πηδ. 649-662.

put him to trouble—were abrogated by the mere enforcement of the 'Spiritual Regulation,'[1] as the paramount law of the Orthodox Church of Russia; those which could do him no harm whatever he left in force, and even prescribed with severity their execution. Hence it is that the collection of canons of the Russian Orthodox Church, modified by the 'Spiritual Regulation,' by the subsequent ukases of the Tsars, and by the practical interpretations of the Holy Synod,[2] may in its entirety be safely recom-

Timotheus' (Archbishop of Alexandria) 15 canons.—Bev. *ibid.* Cc. *verso*; Пηδ. (18 canons) 665-676.

Theophilus' (Archbishop of Alexandria) 14 canons.—Bev. *ibid.* Cc. 2; Пηδ. 676-686.

St. Cyrillus' (Archbishop of Alexandria) 7 canons out of his letters: 'Ad Domnum,' 'Episcopis qui sunt in Lybia et Pentapoli,' 'Ad Maximum Diaconum,' then 'Ad Gennadium Caenobii praefectum.'—Bev. *ibid.* Cc. 2. *verso*; Пηδ. (5 canons) 686-692.

St. Cyrillus', 'De fide orthodoxa contra Nestorium,' capita xii.—Bev. *ibid.* Dd. 2.

Out of the epistles of the holy Fathers, against simony. St. Basilius' 'Ad Episcopos sibi subjectos ne propter pecunias ordinent' (Bev. ii. 145). St. Gennadius' epistle on the same subject (Bev. ii. 181; Пηδ. 692-697), etc.

See also these canons in Card. J. B. Pitra's work: 'Juris ecclesiastici Graecorum historia et monumenta, jussu Pii IX. Pont. Max.' etc. Romae, 1864-1868. 2 vols. 4to.

[1] It was, we suppose, some feeling of the disagreement existing between the ecclesiastical canons and the *Spiritual Regulation*, which caused Mgr. Filaret, Arch. of Tchernigoff, to express himself as follows: 'The *Spiritual Regulation*, drawn up by Theophane Prokopovich, revised by a Council (*that mentioned in the document sent to Voltaire*), and confirmed by the Tsar, as an application of the ancient ecclesiastical canons to the condition of the Russian Church (какъ примѣненіе древнихъ церковныхъ правилъ къ состоянію русской церкви), became the law of the Church' (Ист. русс. Церк. пер. V. § 3, p. 5). A mere *application* (примѣненіе) of the ecclesiastical canons to the condition of the Russian Church needed not a Council, far less the confirmation of an Orthodox Tsar.

[2] The *Complete Collection of the Laws of the Russian Empire* contains a *nominal* ukase of the *Empress* Elizabeth to the Synod, reminding them that in matters of marriage they must not follow their own particular views, but have their decisions supported by the authority of the Holy Scripture.— Полн. Собр. tom. xiii. 20th Sept., 1752 (10,028), p. 705.

mended to kings jealous of the influence of the Church, as one which does not lay any effectual restraint upon the

As an instance, moreover, of the influence exercised by the Tsar upon the interpretation of the ecclesiastical canons, we shall quote the decision of the Holy Synod concerning the marriage of the Grand-Duke Constantine Paulovich, brother of Alexander I. The Grand-Duke had been married since the 26th of February, 1796, to the Grand-Duchess Anna Feodorovna, Princess of Saxe-Cobourg-Saalfeld. After many years he became desirous to have his marriage dissolved, which desire having been complied with, he married the young Polish Countess Jeanne Grudzinska, afterwards Princess of Lowicz.

The dissolution of the Grand-Duke's first marriage was announced to the people all over Russia in the following *Manifesto* of the Tsar, March 20, (April 2), 1820:—

'We make known to all our faithful subjects as follows: Our beloved brother, Cesarevich and Grand-Duke Constantine Paulovich addressed a petition to our most beloved mother, the Empress Maria Feodorovna, and to us, calling our attention to the domestic situation caused by the prolonged absence of his wife, the Grand-Duchess Anna Feodorovna, who having since the year 1801 gone abroad *because of her health being utterly broken* (по крайне растроенному состоянію Ея здоровья), not only did not afterwards return to him, but will never more be able to return, as she herself has personally declared; and consequently, he (the Grand-Duke) has asked that his marriage with her should be dissolved. Having received such his petition, we, with the consent of our most beloved mother, laid the affair before the examination of the Holy Synod, which, after comparing its circumstances with the prescriptions of the Church, *on the precise ground of the 35th canon of St. Basilius the Great* (по сличеніи обстоятельствъ онаго съ церковными узаконеніями, на точномъ основаніи 35 правила Василья Великаго), has declared, "The marriage of the Grand-Duke Cesarevich Constantine Paulovich with the Grand-Duchess Anna Feodorovna is dissolved, and he is allowed to contract another marriage, if he so please." Taking all these circumstances into consideration, we have decided that it would be fruitless to make any attempt to keep within the circle of our imperial family a couple united by a bond which for nineteen years has been broken, and which there is no hope of restoring in future; consequently, making known, *on the precise ground of the ecclesiastical prescriptions*, our consent that the above declaration of the Holy Synod be carried into effect, we *order* that the same declaration shall have its purport carried into execution.'—Полн. Собр. Зак. i. ser. tom. xxxvii. (28,208) March 20, 1820, p. 129.

encroachments of the civil power on ecclesiastical matters. This will, moreover, evidently appear from what we shall quote from the Russian catechisms with respect to the theory concerning the power of the Tsar in ecclesiastical matters.

We now proceed to speak of the bishops in their relations to the Synod. To the Synod also—to that authority which, according to the expressions of the Russian jurists, is a mere organ (*organ*) or instrument (*orudie*) in the hand of the Tzar—to that State institution (*gosudarstvennoe ustanovlenie*) *by means of which,* so says the Russian

> Now the canon which is alluded to in the Synod's decision runs in the Кормчая Книга (ed. 1816) as follows:—
> 'If a wife quits her husband without reason, she is liable to be punished; as to him who had to endure the dereliction, he will not be so.' Аще безъ вины оставитъ жена мужа своего, та убо повинна есть; онъ же претерпѣвъ не повиненъ есть. (Кормч. кн. p. ρξs на об.)
> Which canon is thus explained in the Кормчая Книга (by Aristenus):—
> 'The wife who quits her husband, and, without reason, absents herself from him, will be separated from the Church (excommunicated) (въ запрещеніи будетъ), and the more so if she has been with another man, for in that case she will be judged as an adulteress. As to the husband abandoned by her, he deserves *pardon*, and therefore, if he has taken another wife, he will not be excommunicated.' (мужъ же оставленный отъ нея, прощенія достоинъ есть, и сего ради аще иную жену пойметъ беззапрещенія есть.—*Ibid.*) See also Πηδάλιον, ed. Zante, 1864, pp. 612, 613. Beveridge. Σινόδικον seu Pandectæ, etc. Oxonii, 1672, ii. p. 94.)
> Certainly, no amount either of benevolent feeling towards the Holy Synod, or of Christian indulgence for an erroneous interpretation, will allow the reader to believe that the Synod did not in its decision yield to any influence whatever from the Russian autocrat. A writer, whose sympathy for Russia, together with his highly praiseworthy aversion for any exaggeration, are equally known, speaking of that dissolution of the Grand-Duke's marriage, says, 'En matière ecclésiastique, comme en toute autre, la volonté de l'autocrate ne rencontre pas d'obstacle, le Saint Synode n'y résiste pas plus que les autres grands corps de l'État.'—Schnitzler, *Histoire intime de la Russie sous les empereurs Alexandre et Nicolas.* (Paris, 1847), tom. i. p. 156.

Code of Laws, the supreme authority *acts* in the administration of the Church—to that so-called Council in which, by the mere arbitrary will of a Russian Tsar, simple priests are on a level with bishops,[1]—the members of which are appointed, maintained in power, or dismissed by the mere arbitrary will of the Tsar, and which in no way represents the Russian Orthodox Church—to that *College*, the tenth of Peter's colleges, adapted to the department of Russia's spiritual affairs, just as the others had been adapted to the departments of Russia's commerce, revenue, &c.—to the Synod of St. Petersburg are immediately subject all the bishops throughout Russia. 'Be it known,' it is said in the 'Spiritual Regulation,'—'be it known to every bishop, what degree soever he is of, whether bishop, archbishop, or metropolitan, that he is subordinate to the Spiritual College as to the *supreme power*, being obliged to obey its orders, to submit to its judgment, and acquiesce in its decrees. And, therefore, if he has a quarrel with another bishop his brother, who has injured him, he must not avenge

---

[1] 'Si dans la hiérarchie ecclésiastique, il n'y a pas d'ordre plus élevé que celui de l'evêque ; si les évêques sont tous également successeurs des Apôtres, et que, comme les Apôtres avaient tous reçu du Seigneur et possédé le même honneur et le même pouvoir, ainsi leurs successeurs ont une égale dignité, qu'ils résident à Rome, à Constantinople, à Alexandrie, ou autre part, *il s'ensuit évidemment qu'une réunion d'évêques peut seule avoir autorité* sur un évêque.

'On voit, sans qu'il soit nécessaire d'en fournir des exemples, que le droit de siéger aux Conciles, soit œcuméniques, soit *provinciaux*, et le droit d'y décider les affaires ecclésiastiques, *n'appartiennent qu'aux évêques*, comme chefs des Églises particulières, et que les prêtres, qui dépendent en tout de leurs archipasteurs locaux, ne peuvent être admis aux Conciles *qu'avec leur assentiment*, et cela seulement comme leurs conseillers, aides, ou fondés de pouvoir, *et n'y peuvent tenir que les secondes places*.'—Macaire's *Théologie dogmat. orthodoxe*, trad. par un Russe, tom. ii. § 175. *Centre de l'autorité ecclésiastique*, pp. 268, 270.

This was written in Russia, by a Russian prelate, and from the Orthodox point of view!

himself, neither by reproaches, nor by a publication of
the injury, how true soever, or by engaging great and
powerful persons, either spiritual or temporal, to chide and
reprove him, least of all shall he presume to excommunicate
the bishop his adversary, but represent the damage he has
sustained in an indictment against him to the Spiritual
College, and there sue for justice' (part ii. ' Of the
Bishops,' 'Of the Visitation,' § 13, Consett, p. 58). Before
the Synod are equally allowed the clergy and faithful, all
over Russia, to bring their complaints against their bishop.
' Consequently,' so continues the ' Spiritual Regulation,'
' every archimandrite, hegoumen, steward, parish priest,
also deacons and the inferior clergy, are free to sue their
bishop in the Spiritual College, if they have suffered any
great injustice by him. And if a man is not satisfied with
the judgment of his bishop, he is at liberty to make an
appeal, i.e. to refer the affair to the judgment of the
Spiritual College; and a bishop is obliged to allow this
privilege to all such petitioners and inquisitors against
himself, and not to restrain or threaten them, nor, when
they are gone to the Spiritual College, seal up or gut
their houses.'[1]

In this abstract of the ' Spiritual Regulation' it is
said that the Bishops are subject to the Holy Synod as to
the '*supreme power*.' Alas! the Synod is indeed the
supreme power to be appealed to whenever bishops
are striving to obtain justice and the settlement of their
disputes, the Tsar thus not taking the trouble of receiving
their appeals; but it is far from being *supreme* whenever
it is a question of submission to the will of the Tsar.
The obedience the Russian bishops are bound to show to

---

[1] *Spir. Reg.* § 14, *Cons.* p. 59. See also *Spir. Reg.* part iii. § 8, p. 107.
Полн. Собр. Зак. том. vi. Дух. Регл. (3718) pp. 329–330, §§ 13, 14,
and p. 344, § 8.

the Synod, though of prodigious extent, yet has a limit *prescribed* to it; it is when the Synod's prescriptions possibly might not agree with the will of the Tsar. However improbable such a case might be, it could not fail to be contemplated; and so it has been. The document which affords this new evidence of the slavery of the Russian Orthodox Church is the formula of the oath taken by the Russian bishops before their consecration; what we shall quote from it will at once confirm all that we have hitherto advanced. The whole rite now followed on the election and consecration of the bishops of Russia, is detailed in a special book, which first appeared in St. Petersburg in the year 1725,[1] and has since been invariably reprinted without modifications. Though unsuccessful in getting the Slavonic original of that book, we have been so fortunate as to meet with three different translations of it—one Latin, another German, and the third English. The Latin translation is to be found in Haigold's already quoted 'Beilagen zum neuveränderten Russland,' Riga, 1769-70 (tom i. p. 97), and bears the title of 'Ritus circa electionem et inaugurationem Episcoporum et Archiepiscoporum in Russia observari soliti. Secundum exemplar an. 1725 Petropoli typis expressum latine convertit Cyriacus Kondratowicz Academiæ Scientiarum Interpres.' A German translation was given very recently by Rajewski, chaplain to the Russian Embassy in Vienna, in his 'Euchologion der orthodoxen katholischen Kirche' (Wien, 1861. II. Theil). Finally, the English translation is to be found in King's work, 'The Rites and Ceremonies of the Greek Church in Russia' (p. 289 *et seq.*). From this we quote the following abstracts out of the formula of the oath taken by the Bishops:—'I do promise . . to yield true obedience all the days of my life to the Holy Legisla-

---

[1] Чинъ избранія и рукоположенія Архіерейскаго, Спб. 1725.

tive (?) Synod of all the Russias, *as instituted by the pious Emperor Peter the Great, of immortal memory, and confirmed by command of* her¹ *present Imperial Majesty*² (p. 295)...'
'To comprehend all in a few words, I do hereby bind myself, and hold myself bound by this promise, that I will faithfully observe and do all things commanded by the laws of the Most Holy Legislative (?) Synod of all the Russias, and which are written in the diploma of the Synod; which will be given me concerning the ministry committed unto me. I will also obey all other rules and statutes which shall hereafter be made by the authority of the Holy Synod, *agreeably to the will of Her Imperial Majesty*, and I will willingly exert my utmost diligence to execute whatever I am commanded with all obedience, always regarding truth and justice alone'³ (p. 298).. 'I also swear by the all-seeing God, that I do not understand these promises in my mind in any other sense than that in which I pronounce them with my mouth, and in the sense these words are written, and import to all who read them and hear them' (p. 299). Accordingly, whilst swearing obedience to the prescriptions of the Holy Synod, the Russian bishops mention the reason why they do so—in other words, the motive of their obedience. They obey the Synod as the *legitimate*⁴ *authority* appointed by Peter

---

[1] Catherine I. who was then Empress of Russia. We need hardly remark that whatever we state of the authority of the Tsar over the Russian Church, ought also to be applied to any *woman* who happens to be Empress of Russia.

[2] 'Promitto...omnibus diebus vitæ meæ obediendo morem gesturum semper Sanctæ *dirigenti* totius Russiæ Synodo, uti *legitimæ* potestati, a pie defuncto et æterna memoria digno PETRO M. constitutæ, et a feliciter imperante Imperatoria Majestate *cum bono jussu* confirmatæ.'—*Haigold*, i. p. 107.

[3] 'Obediam quoque reliquis mandatis et statutis, quæ deinceps adstipulatione illius Sanctissimæ Synodi *ad lubitum Imperatoriæ Majestatis* constituentur.'—*Haigold*, p. 114.

[4] The word *legitimate*, omitted by King, stands in the Latin, (see note 2 here above), and in the German, '*als der gesetzmässigen Gewalt*.'—*Rajewski*, ii. p. 91.

the Great, and *confirmed by the present Sovereign of Russia.*
Consequently, far from deriving the legitimacy of the Holy
Synod from its recognition by the Oriental Patriarchs,
not only is such a recognition not even alluded to, but it
is rather positively hinted that, in case the Sovereign of
Russia for the time being should refuse to give the Synod
his (or her) confirmation, they would not consider themselves bound by the oath of obedience they are just about
to pronounce. Moreover, the obedience they promise to
the Synod's prescriptions is on the condition that these
should be *agreeable to the will of his (or her) Imperial
Majesty.* Ought we, after this, to be taxed with exaggeration if we state that, by the very words of their oath, the
Russian bishops are compelled to acknowledge the Sovereign as the source of the Synod's ecclesiastical jurisdiction,
and his (or her) will as the test, both of the legitimacy of
the Synod and of the moral obligation of its prescriptions?

Let us now examine what we have deservedly termed
the prodigious extent of the Russian bishops' submission
to the Synod. Every Russian bishop has, very naturally,
his own court or tribunal for the current business and
administration of his particular *eparchie*, or diocese.
Such tribunals are known under the name of ' *Ecclesiastical Consistories*,' and their attributions are carefully
defined in the so-called ' Statute of the Ecclesiastical Consistories' (*Ustav Duchovnych Konsistorii*) of March 27th,
1841, which, together with the ' Book of the Canons,'
(*Kniga pravil.* See above, p. 57), and the ' Spiritual
Regulation,' (*Duchovnyi Reglament*) forms the ' Corpus
juris canonici' of the Russian Orthodox Church.' As

---

[1] ' Источниками для познанія нынѣ дѣйствующихъ въ
Россіи церковныхъ законовъ служатъ 1) Книга правилъ ..
2) Духовный Регламентъ ... 3) Уставъ Духовныхъ Консисторій, 1841 года ' (Mikhailoff, op. cit. p. 37.

the first three articles of the '*Ustav Duchovnych Konsistorii*' clearly exhibit the mechanism of the Russian Orthodox Church's administration, we quote them here:—
1. The Ecclesiastical Consistory is the tribunal by which are carried on, under the immediate presidency of the bishop of the eparchie (diocese), the administration and ecclesiastical jurisdiction in every special portion of the Russian Orthodox Church, called an *Eparchie*. 2. The Consistory, together with the bishop of the eparchie, are under the jurisdiction of the Holy Synod, as *the governing Council (pravitelstvuiustchii Sobor)* of the Russian Church. From the Synod alone they receive decrees; and besides the Synod and the bishop of the eparchie, there exists no other tribunal or authority entitled directly to meddle with the affairs of the eparchie, or to stop any decisions or arrangements appertaining to the sphere of action of the ecclesiastical jurisdiction. 3. Since, according to the 35th canon of the Apostles, the jurisdiction of every bishop is not extended beyond the limits of the eparchie entrusted to him, the jurisdiction of the Consistory must equally be confined within the same limits.'[1]

Now, from the same '*Ustav*' are quoted the following prescriptions concerning the Russian bishops' relations to the Synod.—The members composing the Consistory are presented by the bishop, but confirmed by the Synod, and they are equally dismissed in the same way (Art. 282). They cannot be absent for more than twenty-eight days without the permission of the Synod (Art. 285). In case of special emergency, the Synod is empowered to appoint, besides the permanent, a temporary Consistory, by the addition of three or four new members (281). The right of appeal from the tribunal of the bishop to

[1] Полн. Собр. 2nd series, tom. xvi. Царствов. Николая i. March 27, 1841 (14,409). Высочайше утвержденный Уставъ Духовныхъ Консисторій, pp. 221-222.

Сн. I.] *Russian Bishops' dependence on the Synod.* 69

that of the Synod is stated in several articles (177, 181, 185). The strictest control is constantly exercised by the Synod, through the Consistory, in what concerns the administration of ecclesiastical property (348-349).

Moreover, to the Consistory is reserved the faculty of interfering in the administration of the Episcopal house, in the way stated in Article 112, where are equally indicated the cases in which they are bound to inform the Synod. Special reports are also to be sent to the Synod, concerning the property and administration of the Churches (145, 38 *note*), and monasteries (129, 131, 132, 38 *note*). Without the permission of the Holy Synod, the bishop is not allowed to build any new church or chapel, either in the towns (46), or in the cemeteries belonging to the towns (46), or in the monasteries (48), or, finally, in private houses (49). As to the latter, if they are to be built in the two capitals of St. Petersburg and Moscow, His Majesty's permission is required (49). The Synod's permission is equally required for building oratories (47) and ordering the suppression of parish churches (61). Without the Synod's permission, no one is allowed to take the religious vows (81). Without the same permission no one, having been brought up in ecclesiastical academies or seminaries, is permitted to quit the ecclesiastical state (92). The same rule prevails with regard to any enrolled among the secular or regular clergy, who desire to enter into the secular state (91), or who are condemned to be deprived of the ecclesiastical dignity (181). No bishop is allowed to go to St. Petersburg without the Synod's consent, and a passport delivered by the Synod (88). The bishop ought to inform the Synod if any doctrine is being disseminated contrary to the teaching of the Orthodox Church (7); if any superstition is being practised or spread among the people (19); if Orthodox Russians attach themselves to any sect of the *Raskol* (21,

24).¹ In the last case, besides informing the Synod, the bishop must proceed against them according to the laws, by means of the civil authorities (21, 24). The same rule prevails in case of anybody greatly disturbing the divine service in the churches (36). Considerable abuses in the sale of wax tapers are equally to be referred to the Synod (147).

As to marriages, if any sentence is passed by the Consistory annulling a marriage, because of its being contracted by force or fraud, such sentence must be confirmed by the Holy Synod (218). This is equally the case for marriages declared illegitimate, because contracted by persons within the prohibited degrees of consanguinity and affinity, or of spiritual affinity (220–1). To the Synod must be referred the case of a marriage contracted during the life of the consort (223), and its confirmation is required for every sentence of dissolution, in consequence of the demand of the consorts (238, 259), as well as for the faculty of contracting a new marriage, in case

---

¹ By that collective name (расколъ, *schisme*) are designated the numerous sects of Dissenters in the very bosom of the Russian Orthodox Church. The origin of the Russian sects dates from the correction of the liturgical books by the great patriarch Nicon (1660). Ignorant people believed that this correction was an attempt to alter the doctrine of their Church. At the present day, in spite of two centuries of persecutions such as can hardly be found elsewhere, the Russian Raskolniks are in number about nine millions, and the Russian Government has already entered on the path of concessions to them. A collection of official documents concerning the *Raskol* was published in London by V. Kelsieff, under the title of Сборникъ правительственныхъ свѣдѣній о Раскольникахъ, составленный В. Кельсіевымъ, 1860–62. See also 'Le *Raskol*; essai historique et critique sur les sectes religieuses en Russie' by a Russian (Paris and Strasburg, 1859).— Schedo Ferroti, *Études sur l'Avenir de la Russie. La Tolérance et le Schisme religieux* (Berlin, 1858).— Eckardt, *Modern Russia* (London, 1870), &c.

On the Russian Dissenters greatly depends the future of the Russian Orthodox Church.

of the consort's disappearance, after the term of five years (237).[1]

Every bishop is bound, moreover, to send to the Synod full reports as to the state of the eparchie, under severe penalties in case he should dare to conceal any great disorder whatever (Spir. Reg. 'Of the Bishops,' Consett, p. 69). Special reports are to be made every year to the Synod, concerning the schools (14), the number of confessions and communions (16), the number of converts from the *raskol* (22 *note*) or other Christian societies (25), and from Judaism, Mahometanism, or Paganism (31); the furniture of the churches (38); the students who, having finished their course of studies in any ecclesiastical institution, are still without employment (78). An accurate description of the state of the clergy, both secular and regular is also required (96), besides a special report concerning the superiors of monasteries and the chief dignitaries of the secular clergy of the eparchie (97). The bishop is equally to inform the Synod of those, among his clergy, whom he deems worthy of any of the rewards or decorations appointed by the Government for ecclesiastical persons (98). A special account is to be sent three times every year to the Synod, concerning the donations exceeding 100 roubles which happen to be made to the churches or the clergy (142). The amount of money collected every year in the churches is equally to be made known to the Synod (146). In case the sum allowed by the Government for buildings of ecclesiastical purposes exceed what is really required, the excess ought to be returned to the Government, and not employed in

---

[1] The faculty of contracting a new marriage, even during the life of the consort, is granted, according to the Russian legislation, 1, in case of adultery on the part of the consort; 2, in case of the consort having been condemned to the privation of all civil rights (civil death); 3, in case of disappearance, if after five years no news can be obtained of him.

any use whatever without the consent of the Holy Synod (156). Every year the bishop is also to send to the Synod a report of the number of births, marriages, and deaths (109).

Finally, . . . 'As to the course of business' (so reads the 343rd article), 'the bishops ought to send to the Most Holy Synod the following reports—1. Every month: (α)—of His Majesty's orders which have not yet been executed; (β) of the decrees received from the Holy Synod;[1] (γ) of those of these last which have not yet been put into execution. 2. Every year: of the affairs not yet resolved in the Consistory, or still waiting their execution through the Chancery, with special personal remarks.'[2]

Such are the principal regulations concerning the Russian bishops' dependence on the Synod. In looking at them one cannot help thinking of the Catholic bishops' dependence on the Pope, and a comparison forcibly occurs to the mind as to the *legitimacy and extent* of the Synod's jurisdiction over its bishops and of the Pope's jurisdiction over the Catholic bishops of the whole world. Whilst a Catholic bishop, in the ordinary daily emergencies of the administration of his diocese, has scarcely occasion even to perceive the existence of that authority which yet *he believes entrusted by God with the power of full and ordinary jurisdiction over the*

[1] Two kinds of orders are here mentioned as notified to the Bishops in the course of the year. Some of them are directly issued by the Tsar, whilst others are communicated to the bishops in the form of *Synodical decrees*. The Полн. Собр. Зак. offers many instances of that double kind of orders, just as in civil matters it offers instances of ukases directly emanating from the Tsar, and others issued in the form of decrees of the Senate.

We need hardly remind our readers that no law whatever may be issued in Russia, either by the Senate or by the Synod, without the previous consent of the Tsar.—See what we have said above of the legislative power in the Russian Church, pp. 53–56.

[2] Полн. Собр. Зак. 2nd series, tom. xvi. Уст. Дух. Конс. p. 260.

whole Catholic Church, a Russian bishop, who professes to believe himself to be, not abusively but in all points and properly, CHIEF and HEAD *of his particular Church*,[1] meets at every step with the interference of the Synod, whose minute and vexatious control is exercised to such an extent that we can hardly conceive how the Russian bishops can even be termed 'CHIEFS and HEADS *in the Church*.'

Yet the just quoted prescriptions are far from representing in its real extent the enslavement of the Russian bishops. In order to appreciate it according to the truth we must pay attention to the office and attributions of a LAYMAN constantly attached to the *Consistory* or court of every Bishop, and called Secretary of the Ecclesiastical Consistory. The Secretary of the Consistory is appointed on the presentation of the Holy Synod by its *Chief Procurator* (another layman). (*Ust. Duch. Kons.* art. 287). Under the presidency of the Secretary is the Chancery for expediting the affairs of the Consistory according to the prescriptions of the Government (286). Like the bishop of the eparchie, the Secretary is placed under the *immediate* jurisdiction of the *Chief Procurator* of the Holy Synod, and is bound to execute all his orders (288). Upon the Secretary rests, beside the immediate inspection of the Chancery in every department, the responsibility as to the legality of procedure in the conduct of affairs (299). In the sittings of the Consistory, the business is brought before it either immediately through the Secretary, or through another official, under his direction (310). In case a decision be taken which he deems contrary to the laws, it is his office to remind the Consistory of the law which is transgressed (318), and if his remarks are not listened to, he is to mention the fact both in the

---

[1] *Dosithei Confessio.* Decr. x. See above, p. 11.

journal and protocol of the Consistory, and, further, to present to the Bishop a report of the matter with the exposition of the reasons urged by him in the sitting against the decision (329). The *journal* of the sittings is drawn up under his inspection, and is, like the protocols of the Consistory, countersigned by him (325, and tables xvi. xvii.). Special reports concerning the affairs treated in the Consistory are to be presented by him to the *Chief Procurator* of the Synod, besides those which are sent by the Bishops (344). He it is who overlooks the *archivist* of the Consistory in the exact discharge of his duties (357); he it is who takes care that, for expenses ordered by the Consistory, the money should be disbursed exactly and in just time (349); finally, in order, it might appear, to guarantee the Russian Church from the danger of embezzlement on the side of her bishops, and to protect these against any such temptations, he it is, again, who keeps the key of the chest out of which the expenses are to be paid (349).—' *The* HOLY GHOST *has appointed to the particular Churches, which truly are Churches and members of the universal one, the bishops as* GOVERNORS *and* PASTORS, *and not abusively, but* in all points and properly CHIEFS *and* HEADS!'[1]

The first statements we undertook to prove are now sufficiently justified. The State Church of Russia is totally deprived of any self-government; her real chief administrator and legislator is the Tsar. The Synod, as a mere organ (*organ*) or instrument (*orudie*) in the hands of the Tsar, and the Russian bishops cannot possibly be called with truth *Chiefs of the Church.*

All this, however, is not the worst. Were the slavery of the Russian Church a mere transitory fact, an abuse

---

[1] Kimmel, *Monum. fidei Eccl. orient. Dosithei Confessio.* Decr. x. p. 436. (See above, p. 11.)

of power against which the Russian Church, though enduring it, would have protested, we should not have undertaken to make it known to the world. But, alas! her slavery is not a mere transitory fact; it is grounded upon theories and principles which the Russian Orthodox Church presents us as her own; it is the immediate and necessary application of tenets accepted and sanctioned by her—a kind of dogma of her own. Nay, the Russian Orthodox Church seems to be no longer aware of the Saviour's words: 'Date ergo quæ sunt Cæsaris Cæsari et quæ sunt Dei Deo.' Nothing is more afflicting, and at the same time instructive, than the confusion and misconceptions which pervade her dogmatical teaching whenever the question is one of the government of the Church. The total distinction between the civil and ecclesiastical powers, each of them being supreme in its own sphere,[1] is almost denied by her; at any rate the independence of the ecclesiastical power seems to be confined *to the teaching of the already defined articles of faith*, as if by 'govern the Church' must be understood only 'teach the Church.' But let us allege evidence of what we have just advanced. Here also we need only interrogate the

[1] '... Civilis potestas summa quidem in suo genere est, nimirum in rebus civilibus; sed non inde efficitur, ut summa etiam esse debeat in rebus sacris quarum dissimile genus est. In eo summa est potestas ecclesiastica; et vero utraque suas habet partes, et suum certum, ac definitum genus in quo summa est. Hæc (*ecclesiastica*) nimirum curat res sacras atque divinas, illa (*civilis*) studet civium commodis, civilemque societatem administrat. Nulla hic pugna, aut absurdum, rerumque confusio, neque *status in statu* est, quod inquiunt Protestantes; sed *status uterque* diversi generis est, et habet uterque provinciam suam, cujus intra fines continere sese debet. Atque in eo quidem omnis est posita vera atque accurata distinctio Ecclesiasticæ atque Civilis potestatis, quod hæc est ordinis naturalis, illa supernaturalis, altera in res civiles, atque in temporalem hominum felicitatem incumbit, altera præest rebus sacris atque divinis et curam gerit eorum, quæ ad æternam beatitudinem pertinent.' Devoti. (Jo. Arch. Carthag.) *Jus Canonicum Universum publicum et privatum.* Nova romana editio accuratior (Romæ, 1837). Proleg. c. viii. § ix.

most authentic documents of the Russian Orthodox Church, her 'Spiritual Regulation,'[1] the ukases of her Tsars, and the principles laid down in her own 'catechisms.'

Out of the 'Spiritual Regulation' we shall quote only the chief reason alleged in its first part (together with others of no greater weight[2]) for the abolition of the patriarchate and the establishment of the Synod. 'The ignorant vulgar people do not consider how far the spiritual power is removed from (*raznstvuiet*) the regal, but, in admiration of the splendour and dignity of a high priest, consider such a ruler as a second sovereign, *equal in power to the king himself* or *above* him, and imagine the spiritual order to be another and better sovereignty.'[3] If these words need any explanation, this is afforded by that saying of Peter related by Voltaire: 'Il pensait et disait publiquement que l'idée des deux puissances fondée sur l'allégorie des deux épées qui se trouvèrent chez les Apôtres était une idée *absurde*.'[4] Again, in his nominal ukase, '*On monastic vocation*,' in which, according to Voltaire, Peter shows himself both *a minister of State*

---

[1] The *Spiritual Regulation* has been, since Peter the Great, accepted upon oath by every bishop in Russia, and its explanation is enforced in the ecclesiastical schools of the Russian Empire.

[2] It is worthy of remark, that, of all the 'weighty reasons' alleged by Peter the Great in Part I. of the *Spiritual Regulation*, in order to persuade his subjects of the convenience, utility, and necessity of the establishment of the Synod, that here quoted is, we may say, the only one which has not been disregarded and refuted by the conduct of the subsequent Tsars, successors of Peter. Those reasons which concern the advantages to be found in a *Council* of rulers, rather than in one single ruler, were refuted by the abolition of the Colleges and the establishment of the Ministries (see above, p. 51). That, concerning the *novitiate* or *apprenticeship* to be had in the Synod for future bishops of Russia was refuted by the fact of the admission at the present day into the Synod of bishops alone, with only two dignitaries of the secular clergy. (See above, pp. 17-20.)

[3] *Spir. Reg.* part i. § 7. *Consett*, pp. 18, 19. Полн. Собр. Зак. tom. vi. Дух. Регл. pp. 317, 318.

[4] *Histoire de l'Empire de Russie sous Pierre le Grand*, part ii. chap. xiv.

and a Father of the Church, the Russian autocrat gives the reason why, in the 'Spiritual Regulation,' the matter concerning the monks had not been thoroughly enough explained. The reason is because 'the greatest necessity then requiring amendment, was created by the authority of the chief prelate, which some people strove to exaggerate as being *supreme*, like that of the Pope of Rome, against the commandment of God.'[1] The reader being now more than sufficiently acquainted with Peter's opinions in ecclesiastical matters, we may proceed to deal with his successors.

About forty years after the establishment of the Synod, Catherine II., though a woman, reiterated confidently the same principles, as a blessed inheritance of her great predecessor Peter the Great. In her celebrated ukase of the 12th of August, 1762, about the possessions of the clergy, after referring to the maternal authority she possessed for the welfare of the people, Catherine complains that the Russian clergy had often made bad use of their properties, so that 'many of our predecessors (she says), *invested as they were by God, like all monarchs*, WITH THE SUPREME AUTHORITY IN THE CHURCH,[2] were obliged to prescribe them rules, etc.' Then, after having ordered that a large portion of the present possessions of the clergy should be taken from them, Catherine excuses herself for doing so by the following declaration: 'It is neither our intention nor our desire to appropriate to ourselves the possessions of

---

[1] ... тогда аще и о всемъ ко исправленію была нужда, но вящшая была о верховной Архіерейской власти, которую примѣромъ Папы Римскаго, противно повелѣнія Божія, распостранять нѣкоторые тщились. — Полн. Собр. Зак. tom. vii. (4450), Jan. 31, 1724, О званіи монашескомъ, p. 227.

[2] Имѣя порученную себѣ отъ Бога такъ какъ и всѣ Монархи, въ Церкви главную власть... (Полн. Собр. tom. xvi. (11,643), August 12, 1762, p. 51.

the Church, but we only exercise *the authority, given to us by God, to prescribe laws for the best use of them*, according to the glory of God and the welfare of the country.'[1]

Such was, in the year 1762, the language of an *Empress* of Russia. It would have been astonishing after that, if when the Russian sovereigns acted and spoke so much like *heads of the Church*, the mere expression of HEAD OF THE CHURCH in reference to the Tsar had long been wanting in the official acts of the Russian empire. What could not fail to happen we meet with a little before the end of the last century in the most solemn and most important act issued by any Tsar since Peter the Great, we mean the 'Act of Succession to the throne of Russia,' promulgated by Paul I. (1797). This document has doubtless been translated into many languages, and everyone will find in it as follows: 'If the hereditary succession should devolve to a female line, to some woman who is already governing on another throne, then she is obliged to elect which faith and throne she is willing to retain, and to renounce the other for herself and her successors; if, namely, the possession of that throne be linked to some particular faith; and this *because the sovereigns of Russia are* HEADS OF THE CHURCH.'[2]

Now it is well worthy of remark that the expression '*head of the Church*' (*glava tserkvi*) applied *in a general way* to men, occurs, if we are not wrong, only twice in *the whole Russian Orthodox literature*. Once it is applied to the Tsar, and this in Paul I.'s 'Act of Succession;' another time it is applied to a ROMAN PONTIFF, to the Pope Leo the Great, and this in the office of the saint, on

---

[1] *Ibid.* p. 52.

[2] ... Для того что Государи Россійскіе суть Главою церкви. (Полн. Собр. Зак. tom. xxiv. (17,910), April 5, 1797, p. 588.

February 18, on which day the Russian Orthodox Church thus addresses Saint Leo:—

> '*What must we call thee, O man inspired by God!*
> *Head of Christ's Orthodox Church!* or *eye of piety?*'[1]

This fact may afford a striking testimony to the ancient belief of the Oriental Orthodox Church in the supreme power of jurisdiction of Peter's successors over the Universal Church;[2] such, at any rate, will undeniably be the case if we are only allowed to understand the expression of '*head of the Church*' (*glava tserkvi*) when applied to St. Leo, *in the very sense in which the same expression was understood by Paul I.* when applied by him to himself and to any of the Tsars his successors. In fact the year following the publication of the 'Act of Succession,' Paul I. published a 'Regulation for the Churches and Monasteries of the Roman Catholic Belief in the Russian Empire.' This regulation begins as follows:—' 1. The supreme authority given by God to the Autocrat, and his paternal solicitude for the welfare of the people entrusted to him from above, is equally extended over the ecclesiastical order; hence it is that they must observe towards the Tsar, as *towards the chief chosen by God himself,* the most devoted fidelity, and show to him, in *all religious* and civil matters, the due obedience.'[3]

---

[1] Что тя именуемъ, богодохновенне? Главу ли православныя Церкве Христовой, око ли благочестья? (Мин. мѣсяч. Февр. 18. Св. Льва папы римск. На Веч.

[2] In the same office St. Leo is called '*successor* of the venerable Peter.' Петра честнаго преемникъ. (На Утр. пѣснь. 6.

[3] Верховная власть дарованная Самодержцу отъ Бога, и Отеческое попеченіе о благоденствіи ввѣренныхъ свыше ему народовъ, распространяется равно и на Духовенство; по чему оно и повинно хранить къ своему Государю, яко

2. Like the white, the black clergy also are obliged to carry out with the greatest exactness *all* legitimate injunctions and commands of the authority established over them. In case of any dissatisfaction with them, they ought to bring their complaint before the bishop of their eparchie (diocese), and in case this should not afford them the legitimate satisfaction, they are permitted to refer the case to the Roman Catholic Department of the College of Justice.'[1]

What do these words mean, we confidently ask our readers, but that every Russian Tsar is *pope* in his own states? The well-known words of the Pope St. Leo—' In the person of my humility let him (St. Peter) be recognised and honoured, with whom still abides the care *of all the pastors* and the guardianship of the flock entrusted to him, and whose dignity does not fail in the unworthy successor'[2]—do not express the doctrine of a visible head of the Church, in reference to the whole world, either so plainly or so unambiguously as Paul I.'s ukase does with regard to the Church of the Russian Empire; and the more so if we consider that they were his Catholic subjects who were concerned in it. Let us also, as we insist, only be allowed to explain the liturgical expression 'HEAD OF THE CHURCH' (*glava tserkvi*), applied to the Pope St. Leo, in the same sense in which Paul I. called himself '*head of the Church*,' and Russia's ancient belief in the supremacy

самимъ Богомъ избранному Начальнику, всеподданническую вѣрность и оказывать во всѣхъ духовныхъ и мірскихъ дѣлахъ достодолжное послушаніе.

Полн. Собр. Зак. tom. xxv. (18,734), p. 436. November 3, 1798.

[1] *Ibid.*

[2] *Sermo 2dus in anniversario assumptionis suæ.* 'In persona humilitatis meæ ille intelligatur, ille honoretur in quo *et omnium pastorum sollicitudo*, cum commendatarum sibi ovium custodia perseverat, et cujus etiam dignitas in indigno hærede non deficit.'

of Peter's successors will be undeniably proved by her liturgy itself.

The quoted abstracts of the Russian Tsars' ukases are amply sufficient, we believe, for the purpose of evincing the fact that the enslavement of the Russian Orthodox Church was considered by them as the exercise of a legitimate right. As to the Russian Church herself, her silence in presence of their pretensions, and her condescension and wonderful obedience in everything concerning her government, entitle us to consider that Church as fully conniving at her masters' will and adhering to the doctrine professed by them. Numerous and no less striking instances of the Tsars speaking of and considering themselves as real rulers of the Russian Orthodox Church are equally supplied by the ukases of Paul I.'s successors down to the present Emperor of Russia, especially by those of Nicholas, to whom the Russian Church is indebted for the ' *Ustav duchovnych Konsistorii*,' which our readers already know. For brevity's sake, however, we refer them for further instances to the ' Collection of Russian Laws,' or to Theiner's celebrated works, 'Die Staatskirche Russlands' and 'Die neuesten Zustände der katholischen Kirche beider Ritus in Poland und Russland,' or to the French work, ' Persécutions et souffrances de l'Église catholique en Russie,' &c.

Passing on now to the Russian Catechisms, we will abstain from making any choice of our own, but will be guided by the Russians themselves. Let us interrogate them and listen to them. We find in the 'Théologie dogmatique orthodoxe de Mgr. Macaire, traduite par un Russe' (Introd. p. 79), that ' Parmi les abrégés ou précis de la foi, les plus remarquables en langue russe sont: 1°. Le Catéchisme de l'éminentissime Théophane Prokopovich, *qui fut longtemps en usage dans les écoles.* 2°. Les

Catéchismes (le petit et le grand) de l'éminentissime Platon, métropolitain de Moscou, *qui eurent la même destination.* 3°. Les Catéchismes, et surtout le grand, de l'éminentissime Philarète, métropolitain de Moscou, qui se publie de nos jours, *soit pour l'enseignement scolaire, soit à l'usage de tous les chrétiens orthodoxes.*'—We are told the same by Mgr. Filaret, Archbishop of Tchernigoff, in his 'History of the Russian Church.' 'Theophane Prokopovich,' so says that prelate, 'wrote a Catechism and a Primer, with the explanation of the commandments of God, which long enough deserved *to be approved for general use.* After that *a catechism for children, the best for its epoch*, was written by the Metropolitan Plato; then another, more *profound and exact* (1st ed. 1823), was written by the Metropolitan Filaret.'¹—Accordingly we shall examine what doctrine is contained in these three catechisms, respecting the government of the Church.

The first of the three is that commonly known as the *Catechism of Peter the Great.*² In fact, the Russian Tsar was too clear-sighted not to understand that the best support for his ecclesiastical reformation would be a religious one. He therefore caused his ideas to be reduced to some practical maxims, adapted to the most vulgar intelligence, to form part of the religious teaching of the people. The man charged by him to draw up a little catechism for the purpose, was Theophane Prokopovich, the same to whom we owe the 'Spiritual Regulation.' Peter's Catechism appeared in

---

¹ Filaret: Истор. Русс. Церк. пер. v. § 14, p. 47.
Prokopovich's Catechism and Primer bear in Russian the title of Букварь, или первое ученіе отрокомъ, съ катихизисомъ (1720). See Eugeny, Metr. of Kieff. Словарь историческій о бывшихъ въ Россіи писателяхъ духовнаго чина греко-россійской церкви. Спб. 1827. ii. p. 304.

² See Kimmel's *Monum. fidei Eccl. orient.* Proleg. lix. and lxxiii.

St. Petersburg a little before the establishment of the Holy Synod, viz., in the year 1720. The German translation appeared in 1724 (very likely at Dantzig), and the English one was published before the German in London by Philipps, in the year 1723, under the title of 'The Russian Catechism.'[1]

Before quoting the passages concerning the government of the Church, we beg to call the attention of our readers to the following judgment of an Evangelico-Lutheran writer, J. W. Feuerlein. In his 'Biblioth. Symbol. Evangelico-lutherana' (Gottingæ, 1752), at the place where he is quoting the German translation of Peter's 'Catechism' and the 'Spiritual Regulation,' he says: 'It is chiefly out of these two sources that W. Fried. Lutjens, in his dissertation "De religione Ruthenorum hodierna" (Gottingæ, 1745), showed that the religion of the Great Peter *has come very near to our own*, so that the only thing to be desired is its more general reception among the Russian clergy and people.'[2]

[1] The German translation bears the following title: 'Erste Unterweisung der Jugend, enthaltend ein A B C-Büchlein, wie auch eine kurze Erklärung der zehen Gebote, des Gebets des Herrn und des Glaubens-Bekenntnisses, auf Befehl Petri M., Imperatoris von gants Russland, in den Druck gegeben.'

The English translation is mentioned by Eugeny in his Словарь, etc., ii. p. 304; yet there is given by mistake the date of 1725. An error of statement is also to be found in Philipps' preface to the English translation, as to the author of that catechism. The Rev. R. W. Blackmore, in the preface to his *Doctrine of the Russian Church* (Aberdeen, 1845), mentions Prokopovich's Catechism and its English translation, and states that this reached a second edition.

[2] 'Ex his in primis scriptis, diss. hist. theol. de religione Ruthenorum hodierna me præside a Resp. auctore Guil. Fred. Lutjens A.D. 1745, edita et publice defensa ostendit, *Religionem Magni Petri ad nostram quam proxime accessisse* ut tantum magis universalis ejus receptio apud clerum et populum Ruthenicum optanda sit.' Feuerlinius, *Bibl.* etc., App. ii. sect. iii. § 184, p. 354. See also on that subject, Kimmel, *Monum.* etc., proleg. lix. lx. F. Gagarin, S. J. *De l'enseignement de la Théologie dans l'Église russe*, in the *Études de Théologie, etc.* (Paris, 1857).

Let us now see the explanation of the fifth commandment, as it is contained in the Catechism of Peter. We quote Philipps' translation, as we were not able to get the original Russian.

'*Q.* What is required in the fifth[1] commandment?

'*A.* It is required of us to honour and respect, not only our natural parents, but those that are in dignity and place of parents, and have any degree of authority over us.

'*Q.* Who are those that can justly demand this respect

Moreover, the following prescription concerning preachers gives evidence of Peter's religious tendencies. *Spir. Reg.* part ii. No. xxiii. *Consett*, p. 86.

'That none presume to preach unless he has been educated in an Academy, and has a testimonial from the Spiritual College. But *if anyone has been educated by men* OF ANOTHER RELIGION, let him present himself first to the Spiritual College, to be there examined, what knowledge he has in the Holy Scripture, and to make a discourse on any subject which the College shall give him to discourse upon, and *if he is found to be a good scholar*, to give him a testimonial and licence to preach, if he is disposed to go into Holy Orders.' Полн. Собр. tom. vi. Дух. Регл. (3718) p. 331.

[1] The Oriental Orthodox Church follows, in the division of the Ten Commandments, the arrangement commonly adopted also by Protestants. The 'Catechism of the Council of Trent' mentions it, giving at the same time the reason why the other arrangement has been preferred.

'THOU SHALT NOT MAKE (so runs the said Catechism, quoting Exodus xx. 4),—THOU SHALT NOT MAKE TO THYSELF A GRAVEN THING, NOR THE LIKENESS OF ANYTHING THAT IS IN HEAVEN ABOVE, OR IN THE EARTH BENEATH, NOR OF THOSE THINGS THAT ARE IN THE WATERS UNDER THE EARTH: THOU SHALT NOT ADORE THEM NOR SERVE THEM. Some (continues the same Catechism), supposing these words to constitute a distinct precept, reduce the ninth and tenth commandments into one. St. Augustine (sup. Exod. *quæst.* 71, and in Ps. xxxii. Sarm. 2) holds a different opinion; considering the two last to be distinct, he refers these words to the first commandment; and this division, because well-known (*celebris*) in the Church, we willingly adopt. As a very just argument in its favour, we may, however, add the propriety of annexing to the first commandment the reward or punishment attached to its observance or violation.

'This commandment does not prohibit the arts of painting or sculpture; the Scripture informs us that God Himself commanded images of cherubim, and also the brazen serpent, to be made,' etc.—*Catechismus ex decreto Concilii Tridentini ad parochos* (*Romæ*, 1845), cap. ii. Nos. 16, 17, p. 231.

from us, and what honour and reverence is due to them *respectively?*

'*A.* I. In the *first* place kings and magistrates, who rule over us in the Lord, are to us in the place of fathers, whose duty is to defend their subjects, and *seek what is best for them, both in temporals and spirituals,* and therefore must have a watchful eye to all *ecclesiastical,* military, and civil affairs, that men do conscientiously execute their respective employments; and *this is, next God, the highest fatherly dignity.* . . . .

'II. *Next* to kings and sovereigns princes, *spiritual governors,* senators, judges, generals of armies, and other magistrates, are vested likewise with the fatherly dignity. The duty of ecclesiastical governors is to lead the people in the way of salvation. The civil magistrate should distribute justice without respect to persons. The general must promote military discipline, and inspire the soldiery with Christian courage. Inferiors must love and respect their superiors, pray for them, and cheerfully obey all their just commands.

'III. The third order of men vested with fatherly authority are our natural parents, viz., fathers and mothers; for though, according to nature, they claim the first place, yet, in a civil society, the persons above mentioned, as promoters of the public good, deserve greater honour than they . . . . .' etc. (pp. 10, 11).

'*Objection.* I am at a loss how to behave myself when one to whom I owe filial obedience commands, and another, who likewise stands in the same degree of paternal authority, forbids me the same thing.

'*Answer.* When neither of these has authority over the other, then you must have a regard to what is commanded, and not to the person that commands. For if your master, to whom you owe fidelity and service, commands you any lawful thing, and your father forbids it, obey your master and not your father. But if one is superior in dignity to the other, obey that superior person; for if thy father or thy master command thee anything that is against the order of the magistrate, obey the civil power, and not thy father or master. *But if the magistrate bids thee do anything that the Czar forbids,* BY ALL MEANS OBEY THE CZAR' (p. 14).

Before making any remarks on the doctrine contained in these abstracts, we must quote also some passages of the second Catechism—that of Platon, Metropolitan of Moscow.[1]

This Catechism appeared for the first time in 1765, and was soon received into general use for the religious instruction of the people. There exist more than eight different translations of it, two of which are in modern Greek. The first Greek translation of 1783 is dedicated to the Metropolitan of Philadelphia, Sophronius Koutoubaly;[2] the second of Korai, which appeared in 1782,[3] was reprinted in Corcyra in 1827, and, by the editor, Constantine Typaldos, dedicated to the Orthodox clergy.[4] As regards English translations, we have found two; the first made from the original Russian was published in 1814 by Pinkerton;[5] the second, made from the Greek of Korai, appeared in 1857, and is due to G. Potessaro.[6] As to the *orthodoxy* of Platon's Catechism, the following judgment

---

[1] The Russian title is Православніе ученіе, или сокращенная Христіанская Богословія. Спб. 1765 and 1780.

[2] 'Ορθόδοξος διδασκαλία, ἤτοι χριστιανικὴ Θεολογία ἐν συνόψει ... Vienna, 1783.

[3] 'Ορθόδοξος διδασκαλία εἴτουν σύνοψις τῆς χριστιανικῆς Θεολογίας. ... Leipsig, 1782.

[4] Πλάτωνος μητροπ. Μόσκας ὀρθόδοξος διδασκαλία. ... Corcyra, 1827.

[5] '*The Present State of the Greek Church in Russia, or a Summary of Christian Divinity,* by Platon, late Metropolitan of Moscow, translated from the Slavonian, etc., by Robert Pinkerton (Edinburgh, 1814), 8vo.

[6] *The Orthodox Doctrine of the Apostolic Eastern Church, or a Compendium of Christian Theology,* translated from the Greek (London: Whittaker, 1857).

was quoted by Snegireff, the Russian biographer of Platon, as having been expressed by Bacmeister: 'This work forms an epoch in the history of the Church. The doctrine expressed in it is further removed from that of the Roman Catholic than from that of the Lutheran Church, and even, in many points, agrees with the latter.'[1]

When Platon composed his Catechism, he was preceptor to the Tsarevich Paul Petrovich, afterwards Paul I., the very Tsar who introduced in the official documents of the Russian empire the designation of 'Head of the Church' (*glava tserkvi*) for himself and his successors. To his imperial pupil Platon could not teach anything at variance with the principles of his glorious ancestor Peter the Great, and the Catechism being composed for the use of the Tsarevich, no one will wonder to find in it as follows:—

Part 2. xxviii. 'Of the Government of the Church.' (Translation of Pinkerton, p. 167.) '. . . The governors of the Church consist of *pastors* and *spiritual teachers*, according to the doctrine of Paul to the Ephesians: "And he (Christ) gave some apostles, and some prophets, and some evangelists, and some pastors and teachers, for the perfecting of the saints for the work of the ministry, for the edifying of the body of Christ."—Eph. iv. 11, 12.'

'Of *pastors* some are greater, such as *bishops*; the other

---

[1] Бакмейстеръ при разсмотрѣніи Нѣмецкаго перевода сего сочиненія заключаетъ, что: 'оно составляетъ эпоху для Церковной Исторіи и будто изложенное въ немъ ученіе болѣе отдѣлено отъ Римско-Католической нежели отъ Лютеранской Церкви, и даже во многомъ согласно съ послѣднею.' (Snegireff. Жизнь московск. Митроп. Платона. (Моск. 1856, tom. ii. p. 92.

The original German, too freely translated by Snegireff, reads as follows: 'Man bemerket, dass diese (russische) Kirche weniger von der Lutherischen abweichet, und sich von der Pabstlichen mehr absondert, als man bisher, bei dem Mangel ihrer Lehrbücher, geglaubt hat.'—Bacm. *Russische Bibliotek* (1772), B. I. st. ii. No. xii. p. 120.

are lesser, such as *presbyters* or *ministers*. Christ alone is the head of this Church government and service, because, as He is the founder of His Church, so He is her only independent Governor, who ruleth her invisibly by His word and spirit. Consequently, in all matters RESPECTING THE ESSENCE OF FAITH, the Church can obey no one except Himself, and the evident testimony of the Word of God.'

P. 169.—' There have been *seven* general Councils exclusive of that of the Apostles mentioned in Acts xv. 6. 1st—of Nicæa ; 2nd—of Constantinople ; 3rd—of Ephesus ; 4th—of Chalcedon ; 5th—second of Constantinople ; 6th — third of Constantinople ; 7th — second of Nicæa. These Councils were usually called by pious Emperors, in which sometimes those great personages were present themselves ; for orthodox monarchs are the *chief* guardians and protectors of the Church.[1] A Christian monarch is bound to strive no less for the prosperity of the Church than for the general good of the State. From him the Church of Christ demands : 1st. To know the law of God. 2nd. To have the fear of God and give a pious example. 3rd. *To observe that the government of the Church be properly administered, and to encourage faithful labourers.*[2] 4th. To quench divisions, and to protect her from oppressors and revilers. 5th. To disseminate learning and liberally to support schools. 6th. To endeavour to bring the unbelieving nations to the faith. From this everyone will see what a close connection exists betwixt civil society and the Church ; because, in order that an honest citizen may rightly perform the duties of his station, it is neces-

---

[1] Государи суть главные церкве попечители и покровители. (Правосл. учен. ed. 1780, Часть. ii. § 29. p. 130.

[2] Смотрѣть чтобъ правительство церковное было порядочно, и вѣрно труждающихся одобрять. *Ibid.*

sary that he keep himself from evil and perform these conscientiously. But who can bind the conscience except God, the searcher of hearts and trier of the reins? And more particularly is it of peculiar advantage for a Sovereign to be under the influence of a holy faith; because he, *although subject to no human laws*,[1] is thereby made subject to the law of faith, and is thus preserved within the bounds of holy justice. Moreover, it enables him with firmness to perform his exalted duties; for, as a monarch *has no person on earth higher than himself*,[2] so he can be rewarded by none for his labours; hence faith alone can encourage a Sovereign in the discharge of his duty, while it promises him a real, worthy, and most exalted reward in heaven.' (Russ. ed. 1780, pp. 129–131.)

III. Part 9, p. 245. 'The fifth commandment requires that we should render to our parents, and under the same name ('first of all'—*vo pervych*—Russ. p. 196) to our Sovereign, to religious and civil governors, to instructors and benefactors, to masters and elders, all due reverence and subjection, and to every man sincere love... This commandment requires (p. 247): 1. That we should honour our parents. 2. That we obey the Sovereign, who is *the supreme magistrate and the first governor under God*.[3]

'The duty of the Sovereign is to endeavour to promote the peace and happiness of his subjects, to see that justice be dispensed and transgressors punished; that the *spiritual and civil powers* perform the duties belonging to their offices; to reward the good and punish the irregular and wicked; and in everything to show himself a father who diligently careth for the good of his children. Also to

---

[1] Яко никакому закону человѣческому неподлежащаго. *Ibid.*

[2] Государь не имѣя никого на земли вышшаго себя, ни отъ кого за труды свои награжденъ быть не можетъ, p. 131.

[3] Яко перваго по Богѣ правителя. *ib.* Часть. iii. § 9, No. 2. p. 197.

promote the prosperity of the Church, and defend her against despisers and defamers; to propagate her doctrines, and thereby civilise his subjects, and bring them to the practice of piety; for the Holy Ghost, in Isaiah xlix. 23, calleth orthodox Sovereigns, " Nursing Fathers of the Church." This commandment further requires men— 3. To be subject both to religious and civil governors; to love them unfeignedly, defend their honour, render them all due respect, and suffer patiently their reproofs. But the duty of religious powers is to *instruct men in the way of salvation* and *recommend good morality;* and that of the civil powers to administer justice, and observe that those who are subject to them perform the respective duties of their stations. 4. We are required to love our instructors,' &c.

Let us pause here. The above abstracts, we are well aware, do not *positively* and *distinctly* confer on the Tsar either the title or the functions of supreme ruler of the Church, and we should not wonder if they fall short of the expectation of the reader. A single remark, however, will enable him to realise the doctrine *virtually* contained in Peter's and Platon's Catechisms, and above all, the *practical* influence of the abstracts which we have quoted on the minds of the people.

There are cases in which no eloquence or amount of argument whatever has the force of a calculated *omission*. This system is then especially effective, when circumstances are such that people cannot supply of themselves that *omission*, but everything leads them to adopt erroneous statements conformable to the will of him by whom the omission was caused. Now the Russian people are told that—1. The highest fatherly dignity, *next God*, is that of the Tsar (Pet. Cat). 2. The Tsar is the *first* governor under God (Plat.). 3. The Tsar has nobody on the earth higher than himself (Plat). 4.

The *spiritual* governors come *next* to the Tsar (Pet. Cat.). 5. The Tsar is not subjected to any human law. Faith alone can keep him in the path of justice and reward him (Plat.). 6. The Tsar is the *chief* guardian (provider) and protector of the Church (Plat.). 7. It is in matters respecting *the essence of faith* that the Church must obey nobody but Christ Himself, and the evident testimony of the Word of God (Plat.). 8. He who rules over the people has to have a watchful eye to all *ecclesiastical*, military, and civil affairs (Pet. Cat.). 9. He has to see that the *spiritual* powers perform the duties belonging to their office (Plat.).—They were also taught, it is true, that 'the duty of *spiritual* governors is to instruct men in the way of salvation;' but at the same time they learned that—10. A king has *to seek* what is the best for his subjects both in temporals and spirituals (Pet. Cat.).

How could simple people infer from these premisses alone the conclusion that the spiritual power is separate and independent in its own sphere from the civil? And the more so as people heard their Tsars and Tsarinas, without any opposition from the clergy, openly declare that—11. The Tsar has been invested by God with the *supreme authority* in the Church (Cath. II.). 12. The Tsar is the *head* of the Church[1] (Paul I.). 13. The supreme autho-

[1] In order to prevent people from considering the Tsar as '*head of the Church*' in the same sense in which Jesus Christ is so, the following article, with the annexed note, was inserted in the Russian Code of Laws :—

Article 42. 'The Emperor, as Christian Sovereign, is the *supreme* defender and protector of the dogmas of the orthodox faith, the guardian of orthodoxy and of all good order in the Holy Church.

Note.—It is in that sense that the Emperor is called Head of the Church in the Act of succession to the throne. Law of April 5, 1797 (17,910). Св. Зак. ed. 1857, pp. 10, 11.

Then *immediately* follows the 43rd article, which our readers already know, and which runs as follows :—

rity given by God to the Tsar, being equally extended over the ecclesiastical order, the clergy ought to obey him as the *chief* (*nachalnik*) chosen by God Himself in all civil as well as *religious* matters (Paul I.);—and knew that the 'Spiritual Regulation,' the very manual of canon laws explained to the clergy in the seminaries and ecclesiastical schools, stigmatised as '*a prejudice of ignorant people*' the doctrine that 'the spiritual order constitutes a sovereignty superior, or even equal, to that of the Tsar!' (Spir. Reg. See above, p. 76.)

No one, we believe, will accuse us of exaggeration if, out of this series of aphorisms, we draw the only conclusion that the mere idea of the ecclesiastical power's independence of the civil power has long since disappeared in Russia, and that the *government of the Church*, with which the bishops are entrusted, is in Russia understood only in the sense of their being entrusted with the administration of the sacraments, the teaching of the Word of God, and the *execution* of orders enacted either directly by the Tsar or by a *State institution* representing the Tsar. As to the right the Church holds from Jesus Christ of governing herself—this right of *self-government*, which every English Dissenter immediately feels to be a condition of his Church's very existence as a Church—this right, which everyone feels to be a thing quite distinct and separate from the mere right of performing religious services or teaching particular doctrines—this is not even claimed as a right by the Russian Orthodox Church!!

'In the *administration* of the Church, the autocratical authority *acts by means* of the Holy Governing Synod appointed by him' (Art. 43). See above, pp. 20 and 48–56.

No more is required in order that the Pope be just as much the *administrator* of the whole Catholic Church as the Tsar is so for his own. We remind our readers that there is no question here of the *doctrinal* authority of the Pope, but only of his *administrative* power, viz., his *supreme power of jurisdiction over the universal Church*.

The Catechism of Mgr. Filaret.

Nay, it is with sorrow that, from the last of the three mentioned Catechisms—that of Mgr. Filaret, the late illustrious metropolitan of Moscow—we exemplify this *omission* in his speaking of the episcopal power: 'Q. What is it to *feed* the Church?'[1] (S. Paul, Acts xx. 28).—*A.* To instruct the people in faith, piety, and good works.—*Q.* How many necessary degrees are there of orders ?—*A.* Three: those of *bishop, priest,* and *deacon.*—*Q.* What difference is there between them?—*A.* The deacon serves at the sacraments; the priest hallows the sacraments in dependence on the bishop; the bishop not only hallows the sacraments himself, but has power also to impart to others, by the laying on of his hands, the gift and grace to hallow them.'[2]

The Catechism of Mgr. Filaret, we are very glad to be able to say, is far more orthodox than the two we have been dealing with; moreover, in speaking of the Holy Synod, and of its holding in the hierarchy the same rank with the Eastern Orthodox patriarchs, he supports his assertion by referring the reader to the Letters of the Most Holy

---

[1] The passage of the *Acts of the Apostles* (xx. 28), here alluded to, is translated in the Latin Vulgate:—'Attendite vobis et universo gregi in quo vos Spiritus Sanctus posuit Episcopos *regere* Ecclesiam Dei.' The Greek word translated by *regere* is ποιμαίνειν, which in the New Testament alone is four times rendered by *rule* in the English translation 'appointed to be read in the Churches':—

'Shall (J. C.) *rule* my people Israel.'—Matt. ii. 6.
'He shall *rule* them with a rod of iron.'—Rev. ii. 27.
'Who was to *rule* all nations with a rod of iron.'—*Ibid.* xii. 5.
'He shall *rule* them with a rod of iron.'—*Ibid.* xix. 15.

See Bruder (Car. Herm.), Ταμεῖον τῶν τῆς καινῆς διαθήκης λέξεων, sive Concordantia omnium vocum *Testamenti Græci* (Lipsiæ, 1842); und *The Englishman's Greek Concordance of the New Testament* (London: Central Tract Depot, 1839).

See, for the Old Testament, Abr. Trommii *Concordantia Græcæ Versionis vulgo dictæ LXX Interpretum.* Amstelodami et Trajecti ad Renum, 1718.

[2] Filaret: *The Longer Catechism of the Orthodox Catholic Eastern Church,* translated by the Rev. R. W. Blackmore, in 'The Doctrine of the Russian Church,' part i. On Faith, x. art. On Orders, pp. 95, 96.

Patriarchs on the institution of the Most Holy Synod, and not to any ukase of the Tsars.[1] Finally, in speaking of those who stand to us in the place of parents he puts well in the first place the *Sovereign* (adding, however, '*and our country*'); but he does not at all confer on the Tsar any right of high inspection over the bishops, far less of enacting laws for the welfare of the Church, and totally abstains from mentioning the independence of the Tsar on anybody upon the earth.[2]

All this we readily acknowledge and make known; yet still we deplore the *omission* we have already alluded to, and that *the episcopal office is reduced to the bare administration of the sacraments and the teaching of the Word of God*. Nay, the prescriptions we have quoted from the 'Spiritual Regulation' and the 'Statute of the Ecclesiastical Consistories,' the statements of the Russian jurists, the enactments of the Tsars and the language of their ukases, the principles laid down in the two Russian Catechisms, which up to the year 1820 were generally made use of for the religious teaching of the people, the important omissions in the Catechism of Mgr. Filaret — all this evidently proves that the very theory of the government of the Church is profoundly altered and curtailed in the Russian Empire.

It has cost us much trouble to get together all the evidence we have hitherto brought forward; and it was one thought only, viz. that of contributing, by the publicity given to the fact of the enslavement of the Russian Church, towards hastening the day of her delivery, that made us persevere in the toilsome task. The same thought induces us not to overlook what we are going to state—we mean the tokens of servility to-

---

[1] *The Longer Catechism*, part i. 'On Faith,' Article ix. p. 83.
[2] *Ibid.* part iii. 'On Charity,' Fifth Commandment, pp. 132, 133.

wards the Tsar which overspread the very performance of the religious services of the Russian Orthodox Church, and which are exhibited in her liturgical books.

Whoever casts a glance on any liturgical books whatever cannot help remarking a peculiarity which they possess in common with dedicatory epistles or other writings of that kind. The monotonous uniformity of characters is broken by some words in large type, and always in capital letters. These are the names of the Tsar and other members of the imperial family, or even the mere title by which they are designated. A special ukase of the Senate prescribed that the Emperor's title should always and everywhere (in official papers) be written in capital letters.[1] The same privilege is also extended to the relative pronoun *ego* (his), *eya* (her), when designating the same personages. We need not comment on the adoption of the same rule in the liturgical books, as the comparison of the imperial family's names to the name of God, of the Blessed Virgin, and of the Saints, which are left without any token of distinction, forcibly occurs to the mind. Moreover, the exact and *complete* enumeration of the imperial family's members is to be found in the so-called *ektenias*,[2] as well as in the *formula of approbation*, prefixed to the printed volume of the Holy Scriptures, and to all the liturgical books of the Russian Church. The terms in which this approbation is couched, and which are invariably the same, deserve consideration.

---

[1] Полн. Собр. tom. x. 7 Nov. 1739 (7934) p. 934. Императорскій Титулъ печатать и писать вездѣ и всегда крупными литерами. *Ib.* tom. xlii. Указ. Алфаб. part i. Императорскій и Царскій Титулъ. p. 768.

[2] The *ektenia* (ἐκτενὴς, *extended*) is an *enlarged* prayer. It consists of short petitions or biddings, with a response from the singers and people to each, such as 'Lord, have mercy,' ' Господи помилуй ' (Κύριε ἐλέησον), or 'Lord, hear us,' or 'Grant us, O Lord.'

As an instance, we translate the formula of approbation of the Rite for admitting Dissenters into the bosom of the Oriental Orthodox Church' (ed. 1849):—

'To the glory of the most holy, consubstantial, lifegiving, and indivisible Trinity, Father, Son, and Holy Ghost, by order (*poveleniem*) of our most pious and most autocratic Great *Hossoudar*, NICOLAS PAULOVICH, EMPEROR of all Russia; with HIS consort, the *most pious* Hossoudarina, the EMPRESS ALEXANDRA FEODOROVNA; HIS heir the orthodox Hossoudar the Cesarevich and Grand-*prince* ALEXANDER NICOLAEVICH; and HIS consort, the orthodox *Hossoudarina* Cesarevna and Grand-*princess* MARIA ALEXANDROVNA; with the orthodox Hossoudars the Grand-princes, NICOLAS, ALEXANDER, and VLADIMIR ALEXANDROVICHI; the orthodox Hossoudar the Grand-prince CONSTANTINE NICOLAEVICH, and HIS consort the orthodox *Hossoudarina* the Grand-*princess* ALEXANDRA JOSEPHOVNA; the orthodox *Hossoudars* the Grand-*princes* NICOLAS and MICHAEL NICOLAEVICHI; the orthodox Hossoudarinas the Grand-*princess* HELENE PAULOVNA, the Grand-princess MARIA NICOLAEVNA, and HER consort; the Grand-princess OLGA NICOLAEVNA, and HER consort; the Grand-princess CATHERINE MICHAELOVNA; the Grand-princess MARIA PAULOVNA, and HER consort; and the Queen of the Netherlands, ANNA PAULOVNA, and with the blessing (*blagosloveniem*) of the Most Holy Governing SYNOD,[1] this book—"The rite for admitting into the Orthodox Catholic Oriental Church the members of other confessions'—has been printed in the

[1] The word *Synod* is printed sometimes in capital letters, sometimes, as in the Ektenias, in common letters.

imperial great city of Moscow, in the printing-office of the Synod, in the year from the creation of the world 7358, and from the nativity in the flesh of the Word of God 1849, in the 8th of the indiction, in the month of October.'

No doubt, church books might be printed by 'order' (*poveleniem*) of the Tsar, and with the 'blessing' (*blagosloveniem*) of the Primate, and the Tsar's name might be put first too without sin; and if the names of the Tsarina and of all the Tsar's children and their consorts were added, this might be done to associate them in a pious work, and to include them under the same blessing.[1] But since, unquestionably, the *less is blessed of the greater*, and no 'College' or 'Synod' created by the Tsar can be greater than the power which created it, the enumeration of all those names in the formula of approbation prefixed to ecclesiastical books and in the offices themselves, and the printing of them since Peter the Great,[2] and especially since 1739, in huge letters, and the frequent repetition of them all aloud in the church, produces now an impression suiting only too well the State supremacy established by Peter I., and *unbalanced* by the existence of any *canonical primate whose blessing might be denied*, and whose ban might be feared by the Tsar as well as by the peasant.

These reflections lead us to speak of the 'Rite for the election and consecration of a Bishop,' as they are equally applicable to some expressions made use of in that rite.

---

[1] The names of the children of the Tsar are to be seen, in small type however, previously to Peter the Great, in a book containing the office, life, and an account of the miracles of St. Nicholas printed at Moscow in 1672, and possessed by the British Museum (1018. g. ¹⁴⁄₇) pp. ρξζ'-ρξη' verso.

[2] In a Prayer-book (МОЛИТВОСЛОВЪ) possessed by the British Museum (3355 a), and published at Kieff in 1729, the name of Peter II., then the only living member of his family, is already printed in large capital type.

From the formula of oath taken by the Russian bishops before being consecrated, we have already quoted the words by which they engage themselves to yield true obedience to the Holy Synod, '*as the legitimate authority instituted by the pious Emperor Peter the Great, of immortal memory, and confirmed by command of his* (or her) *present Imperial Majesty*,' and to obey, besides the existing, 'all other rules and statutes which shall be hereafter made by the authority of the Synod *agreeably to the will of his* (or her) *Imperial Majesty*.'[1] To these we must now add the following words taken from the same formula of oath. 'Furthermore, I do testify by this my writing that I have not received this province in consideration of gold or silver promised or given by me, forasmuch as I have neither given nor promised anything to any person whatever in order to obtain this dignity; but I have received it *by the free will* of our most serene and most puissant (sovereign by name) and by the *election* of the Holy Legislative Synod.'[2] Moreover, at the beginning of the ceremony the Bishop-consecrator thus addresses the newly elected bishop: 'Reverend Father N.—The most serene and most puissant Tsar N.N. hath *commanded, by his own singular and proper edict*, and the Holy Legislative Synod of all the Russias gives its benediction thereto, that you, holy sir, be bishop of the city of N.; whom God preserve.' The future bishop is made to answer: 'Since the most serene and most puissant Tsar N.N. has *commanded*, and the Holy Legislative Synod of all the Russias has judged me worthy to undertake this province, *I give thanks* therefore, and do undertake it and in no wise gainsay.'[3]

---

[1] See above, pp. 65, 66.
[2] King: *The Rites, etc.*, p. 295. For the Latin, Haigold, *Beilagen*, etc., i. p. 108; and for the German, Rajewski, *Euchologion der orthodoxen, etc.* ii. p. 91.
[3] King, *ib.* p. 291; Haigold, i. p. 101-2; Rajewski, ii. p. 86.

Here, again, we should indeed be happy to state that the '*free-will,*' '*command,*' and '*singular and proper edict*' of the Tsar enforce a free election made by a *canonical* Primate and Synod. Even the '*thanksgiving*' forced upon the newly elected bishop might then be explained in the sense that, being really unwilling to undertake the episcopal office, yet forced by his brethren and *commanded* by the Ruler of the State, he thanks them for their good opinion. But, unfortunately, we possess documents which prevent us from explaining, in such a Christian and charitable way, the expressions made use of in the rite for the election and consecration of bishops.

Among the 'points wherein His Most Serene Imperial Majesty, with his own august hand, hath vouchsafed a resolution' (see above, p. 26), and which are printed at the end of the 'Spiritual Regulation,' there is one in which the 'Spiritual College,' as it was still termed, though shortly afterwards to be re-named the 'Most Holy Governing Synod,' asks His Majesty to decide whether, *for the vacant eparchies*, the Spiritual Assembly (Synod) must propose any person to His Majesty's approbation. Peter the Great deigned to write on the petition: 'Let there be elected two persons, and let that one of the two whom we shall select be consecrated and selected.'[1] Undoubtedly Peter the Great might just as well have written on the petition: 'I take the care of this entirely on myself,' or, 'The Senate will appoint them,' or anything else according to his own *will and pleasure.* The mere fact of having asked the decision of the Tsar evinces that the newly created Synod did not consider the election of bishops to belong to itself as of right, so that, the presentation of two persons being usual,

[1] Полн. Собр. Зак. tom vi. (3734) Feb. 14, 1721, p. 356. *Consett*, p. 127.

as it is, in consequence of a free decision of the Tsar, *must* be considered like all other presentations for civil employments made by the Senate or any of the Ministers. He who asks for a decision makes himself *less* than he from whom the decision is sought, and subjects himself to all the uncertainties of his *will and pleasure*. We must bear in mind, moreover, that the members of the Synod are appointed, maintained, and dismissed solely by the free will of the Tsar, and that apparent election by the Holy Synod will then appear, as it is in truth—let us say it again—nothing more than any similar presentation which might be made in any other department of the civil government. Finally, with regard to the 'thanksgiving' forced upon the newly elected bishop, we refer the reader to the way in which the episcopal office is spoken of in the 'Spiritual Regulation,' as the existence of any supernatural feeling in him who becomes a bishop is there no more supposed or alluded to [1] than it is in the same document with regard to monks.[2]

Fancy, now, Athanasius, Chrysostom, Basilius, Gregorius, those great bishops of the ancient Greek Oriental Church, being summoned to utter, before their consecration, some analogous words in reference to the Emperor of Constantinople; fancy those men, so full of the spirit of St. Paul, who so eloquently pointed out the heavy burden of the episcopal office, being compelled to say: 'Since the Emperor has *so commanded*, . . I give *thanks* therefore ! !' Indeed from a Church whose bishops are compelled so profoundly to bow their neck to the Tsar, what more can be needed in order that the whole world be convinced that she is the slave of her Tsars? But still more can be said.

---

[1] See *Spir. Reg.* part ii. 'Of the Bishops,' Nos. 14, 15 *Cons.* and pp. 41–3 Полн. Собр. Зак. tom. vi. Дух. Регл. (3718), pp. 324, 325.

[2] See above, pp. 15, 16, *note*.

We have already alluded to Neale's (Rev. John Mason's) writings on the Oriental Orthodox Church. Besides his great work, 'A History of the holy Eastern Church,' (London, 1850), dedicated to the Tsar Nicholas I., he published, among others, a pamphlet with the tempting title of 'Voices from the East: documents on the present state and working of the Oriental Church, translated from the original Russ, Slavonic, and French, with notes' (London, 1859). The last of these documents, and that to which our attention has been specially drawn, is headed, 'Expositions of Faith employed by the Holy Eastern Church, translated from the Russ of *Macarius*, Bishop of Vinnitza, &c.' (doc. viii. p. 209). After having spoken of the 'Orthodox Confession of the Catholic and Apostolic Church of the East,' and of the 'Letter of the Patriarchs of the East,' both of which have been mentioned at the beginning of this work,[1] Mgr. Makary, whom we have already quoted several times, goes on in the following terms:—
'Besides these two general confessions, there are particular confessions for particular cases as: 1. *The oath of bishops*. Important as any oath must be as a matter of faith, this is so additionally, because he who pronounces it is a man destined to be *pastor and guardian* of one particular Church, because he takes it solemnly in the Church, in presence of a vast number of the faithful, and before an assembly of prelates from whom he expects to receive Divine grace for the purpose *of preaching the word of truth, and of feeding well the spiritual flock entrusted to him...*' The reader is sufficiently acquainted with this *oath*, and with the doctrine therein asserted relating to the government of the Russian Church. Other remarks might well be made, but as they are not strictly connected with our subject, we pass them over in silence. Mgr. Makary then quotes:

---

[1] See above, p. 10. In Kimmel's *Monumenta Fidei*, etc., the 'Letter o the Patriarchs of the East' has the title of *Dositheï Confessio*.

'2. Dogmatical questions to Jews and Saracens . . ; 3. The profession of faith pronounced by the members of other Christian confessions . . ; 4. *The Formula of excommunication, composed of twelve articles, and pronounced in Orthodoxy Week*' (*Neale,* pp. 213–14).

Let us pause here. This formula of excommunication forms part of the so-called *Office of Orthodoxy*,[1] which is performed on the Sunday of the first week of Lent. The original Greek is due, according to the 'Historical Account of the Liturgical Books of the Russian Greek Church,'[2] to the Patriarch of Constantinople, Methodius (A.D. 846), and is to be found in the *Triodion*.[3] Catherine II. seems to have found it too long, and by a special *ukase* charged the archimandrite Gabriel, afterwards metropolitan of Novgorod and St. Petersburg, to shorten and recast it, which order having been complied with, the Russian *Office of Orthodoxy* was first printed in its actual form in the year 1761.[4]

The formula of excommunication was also reduced to twelve articles, in which the *greatest* heresies which afflicted the Church are pointed out, and their chiefs and followers pronounced three times over to be excluded from the Church. One of these articles runs as follows:—
'To those who think that Orthodox Sovereigns are not raised to their throne by a special good pleasure of God concerning them, and that at *the unction* (pri pomazanii) *the gifts of the Holy Ghost are not poured out* (izlivaiotsa) *upon them in order to the fulfilment of this great vocation,*

---

[1] Чинъ православія. It is printed in a separate book, under the title of ' Послѣдованіе въ недѣлю православія.' The edition we have made use of is that of Moscow, 1850.

[2] Историческое обозрѣніе богослужебныхъ книгъ греко-россійской церкви. Kieff, 1836.

[3] Τριώδιον. Κυριακὴ τῆς αʹ ἑβδομάδος τῇ κυριακῇ τῆς ὀρθοδοξίας.

[4] This account is taken from Eugeny's Словарь историческій, etc. Спб. 1827, i. p. 83; and the Историч. обозр. p. 191.

and who, in consequence, dare to rebel against them and to betray them, as Grishka, Otrepieff, Ivan Mazeppa, and others like them, anathema! anathema! anathema!'[1]

We altogether abstain from commenting on this anathema, and hasten to make a last quotation from official documents, in order to complete our work. Nothing has been more pernicious to the Orthodox Church of Russia than the praises and approbation which the acts and policy of her Tsars have met with, and that saying of Tacitus, '*Pessimum inimicorum genus laudantes*' (Agr. xli.), has in no case, perhaps, been more strikingly justified. Leaving therefore other writers to extol as they please Peter's ecclesiastical reform, and to cry out, with Theophane Prokopovich : 'Behold, O Church of Russia, thy David and thy Constantine!'[2] we will go on with our own observations.

---

[1] Помышляющимъ яко православные Государи возводятся на престолы не по особливому о нихъ Божественную благоволенію и при помазаніи дарованія Святаго Духа къ прохожденію великаго сего званія въ нихъ не изливаются; и такоⷣ держащимъ противъ ихъ на бунтъ и измѣну, яко Гришкѣ, Отрепьеву, Ивану Мазепѣ, и прочимъ подобнымъ: анаѳема. (Трижды)   Чинъ прав. ed. Mosc. 1850, p. 8.

See Rajewski, *Euchologion*, etc., Theil III. p. 136; King, *The Rites*, etc. p. 404.

[2] See *Lacrymæ Roxolanæ, seu de obitu Petri Magni totius Rossiæ Imperatoris brevis narratio, duæque de laudibus ejusdem* divi *principis orationes*, auct. Theophane Archiep. Novo-Grodensi (Revaliæ, 1726), p. 22. These orations have been translated into English by Consett, *The Present State*, &c., tom. ii. See p. 283.

Haigold's admiration for Peter's ecclesiastical reform soars almost to the height of lyric poetry, though of a comical kind : 'Wie weislich *schuf* er (Peter) seinen *Pabst* (the Patriarch) in eine Synode *um*; wie künstlich flocht er das Band des Staats, der Kirche und der Klöster wieder, das der Aberglaube zerrissen hatte!'—*Beilagen zum neuveränderten Russland*, Band I. Vorrede, p. 62, *verso*.

The Russian code of laws has some articles concerning the secret of confession. They are the following:—

(Criminal Code, book ii. divisions iii. and vii.)

Art. 245. 'Priests are forbidden to reveal, in giving evidence, what their penitents may have said to them in confession, except in the (following) cases':—

Art. 598. 'If a man, in confession, discloses to his confessor the existence of a plot against the honour and health of the Sovereign, or of intention to excite rebellion and treason, and whilst he makes this disclosure does not show repentance nor the intention of desisting from it, but mentions it in confession solely in order that, by the consent or silence of his confessor, he may be the more confirmed in his criminal design, then the confessor is to give information of this immediately, seeing that *such is not a legitimate confession, because the penitent does not repent of* ALL *his iniquities.*'[1]

We leave to the reader to judge for himself what must become of the secret of confession if it be once admitted

---

[1] 245. Священникамъ запрещается объявлять во свидѣтельство то, что духовныя ихъ дѣти скажутъ имъ на исповѣди, исключая случаевъ (сейчасъ) означенныхъ.

598. Если кто при исповѣди объявитъ духовному отцу своему объ умыслѣ на честь и здравіе Государя, или о намѣреніи произвести бунтъ и измѣну, и объявляя о томъ, не покажетъ расканія и намѣренія оное отложить, но единственно исповѣдуетъ о семъ, дабы согласіемъ или молчаніемъ духовника въ преступномъ намѣреніи своемъ болѣе утвердиться; то духовному отцу доносить о томъ немедленно, такъ какъ таковая исповѣдь не есть правильная, ибо исповѣдывающійся не о всѣхъ беззаконіяхъ своихъ кается. (Сводъ Закон. ed. 1857, tom. xv. Зак. Суд. Уголовн. Кн. ii. Разд. iii. p. 46, and Разд. vii. p. 113.

that the want of repentance for any sin not only prevents the confession from being legitimate and true (which is also the Catholic doctrine if the sin is a mortal one), but moreover justifies the confessor in giving information of such sin to others, at the command of the civil government. But, to proceed.

'Nevertheless' (so runs the following article, 599), 'it is the duty of the confessor, in giving such information, not to reveal in detail what has been disclosed to him in confession, but *only* to say that such an one, naming him, and mentioning his condition, has an evil design against the Sovereign or the State, and persists in it without repenting. In *consequence of this information* the suspected person must be immediately apprehended and put under arrest. *After he has been arrested*, and the criminal process against him has begun, the confessor is bound to reveal *all* that he has heard concerning that criminal design, without any sort of reticence, in all details.'[1]

A note appended to these articles in the Russian code of laws, refers the reader to the ukase of May 17, 1722 (4012), and to the Nos. xi. and xii. of the 'Appendix' to the 'Spiritual Regulation.' In No. xi. the reader will find the arguments alleged in order to tranquillize the conscience of the priest. Besides the one already quoted, and which was incorporated in Article 598, the 'Appendix' to the

[1] Однакожъ надлежитъ духовнику, въ томъ объявленіи, не открывать именно показанное на исповѣди, но токмо въ ономъ сказать, что такой-то, показавъ его имя и званіе, имѣетъ злой умыселъ противъ Государя или Государства и перасказанное къ тому намѣреніе; въ слѣдствіе сего извѣщенія, подозрѣваемый немедленно долженъ быть взятъ подъ стражу. По взятіи же его и начатіи уголовнаго слѣдствія, духовникъ обязанъ все о томъ зломъ намѣреніи слышанное объявить безъ всякой утайки во всей подробности, ib., art. 599.

'Spiritual Regulation' points out another taken *from the Holy Scripture*.

'The priest' (it is there said in No. xi.) 'shall declare all that he has heard of that villanous design, explicitly and plainly, without any disguise or hesitation— for by this declaration the spiritual person (the confessor) does not discover a perfect (*soverchennoi*) confession, nor offend against the canons (*pravil*), but rather *fulfils Our Lord's doctrine*, which teaches that, '*If thy brother trespass against thee, go and tell him his fault between thee and him alone; if he shall hear thee thou hast gained thy brother; but if he will not hear thee, then take with thee one or two more, that in the mouth of two or three witnesses every word may be established. And if he shall neglect to hear them,* TELL IT TO THE CHURCH.' (Matt. xviii. 15, 16, 17.[1])

This is certainly an interpretation of Holy Scripture which needs no comment!

Those histories of Peter's life and acts which have been written out of Russia, when speaking of the establishment of the Synod, commonly relate that, in an ecclesiastical assembly, when some allusions had been made to the Patriarchate as unsuppressed—'*I am*,' said Peter, '*your Patriarch*.'—Some Russians have denied the authenticity

---

[1] . . . Ибо симъ объявленіемъ духовникъ не объявяетъ совершенной исповѣди, и не преступаетъ правилъ, но еще исполняетъ ученіе Господне, тако реченное: 'аще согрѣшитъ къ тебѣ братъ твой, иди и обличи его между тобою и тѣмъ единымъ; аще тебе послушаетъ, пріобрѣлъ еси брата твоего,' и прочая. 'Аще же не послушаетъ, повѣждь Церкви.' (Матѳ. гл. xviii. 15, 16, 17). *Spir. Reg.* Append. No. 11 *Cons.* pp. 137, 138, and Полн. Собр. Зак. tom. vi. (4022) p. 701.

of these words, and we are, indeed, indisposed to make it a subject of discussion. Still it is instructive to notice the way in which the same fact is related by a Russian writer, as having happened in the very first meeting of the 'Spiritual College' (Synod).

'The idea,' so says Nic. Polevoy, 'that spiritual matters do not appertain to the authority of the Sovereign was still so deeply rooted in men's minds that, in the very first session of the Spiritual College, some members *dared* (*osmelilis*) to ask the Emperor: "*Is then the patriarchal dignity suppressed, although nothing has been said about it?*" —'*I am your Patriarch* (*ya vash Patriarkh*)' exclaimed angrily (*gnevno*) Peter, striking his breast. The questioners were dumb (*umolki*). The long habit of seeing the Church governed without a patriarch *had this effect, that the people accepted with submission the establishment of the Spiritual College.*'[1]

This account of Peter's *coup d'état* (see above, p. 38) was printed at St. Petersburg in the year 1843, and, be it observed, not without the approbation of the censors.

No more is required, we think, to show that with the Tsar who in 1843 ruled over Russia—'*still abode the care* OF ALL THE PASTORS, *and the guardianship of the flock, and that Peter I. and Paul I.'s dignity had in* 1843 *not failed in their successors.*' (See above, p. 80).

Now, before English Protestant divines we lay these questions: *Whether that Russian Church of which we have spoken, bears sufficient marks of her being governed according to the will of Jesus Christ?* And if not, *whether she may confidently be relied upon as possessing the fulness of revealed truth?* That Russian Church, we mean, which has been ruled by Peter the Great

[1] Ист. Петра Великаго, сочин. Николая Полеваго. Спб. 1843, т. iv. p. 212.

and the Voltairian Catherine II., that Church which adopted for *general* use in the schools the Catechisms of Prokopovich and of Platon, both which were judged by the Protestants themselves to be rather Protestant than Orthodox; that Russian Church, which is spoken of in the classical works of the Russian jurists;—the Russian Church, in a word, as she is represented in imperial ukases *still in force*, in the ʻSpiritual Regulation,' in the ʻStatute of the Ecclesiastical Consistories,' and the Russian Code of Laws.

Can Anglican divines safely and confidently, in the spirit of union, hasten to greet and embrace this Church?

AS TO THE REST of the Oriental Orthodox Church, we lay again before them the question: Whether the solemn approbation given by her Patriarchs to the establishment of the Synod; her forbearance in presence of the Tsar's encroachments upon their Church; her silence concerning the Catechisms of Peter the Great and of Platon being generally adopted in the Russian schools; the way in which her writers[1] speak of Peter's ecclesiastical reform, and his successor's acts, completing his work—in a word, whether the Orthodox Church's connivance at the pretensions and dealings of the Tsars in the Russian Empire does not constitute a serious charge against her? And the more so if one considers that, standing beyond the limits of the Russian empire, her bishops had not to

---

[1] See, for instance, Meletius, Metrop. of Athens. Ἐκκλησιαστικὴ Ἱστορία (Vienna, 1783–95), tom. iv. c. iv. § 10, pp. 32, 33.

For the bibliography of the Greek Oriental Orthodox Church see the Νεοελληνικὴ Φιλολογία of Papadopulos Vretos, and especially Const. Satha's most useful work: Νεοελληνικὴ Φιλολογία.—Βιογραφίαι τῶν ἐν τοῖς γράμμασι διαλαμψάντων Ἑλλήνων ἀπὸ τῆς καταλύσεως τῆς Βυζαντίνης αὐτοκρατορίας μέχρι τῆς Ἑλληνικῆς ἐθνεγερσίας (1453–1821). Ἐν Ἀθήναις, 1868.

fear, like the Russian, the ill-treatment and tortures by means of which the Russian autocrat, more than once, stifled not only attempts at, but even mere aspirations after liberty?[1] We search in vain for a single protest, or any other act of the kind! But, moreover, she herself offers such features as should lead English divines to ask again if she is governed according to the will of Jesus Christ, and consequently if they can safely and confidently embrace her? We confine ourselves to some few statements concerning, first, the Orthodox Church of the Kingdom of Greece, and then that of the Turkish Empire.

'On the 15th (27th) July, 1833,' says J. M. Neale, 'a national Synod met at Nauplia, then the seat of government, to devise some plan for the regeneration of the Greek Church. It must be confessed that this body was *uncanonically* assembled, owning no higher convocants than Tricoupi, Minister of Worship, and Schinas, of Education. The two following propositions[2] were presented to

---

[1] The striking contradiction between the conduct of the Patriarch of Constantinople in 1722, when he solemnly recognised the Holy Synod of St. Petersburg, and the conduct of his successor, who in 1833, *alleging the violation of the holy canons*, so strongly opposed the establishment of the Synod of Athens, created *after the model of the Russian Church*, could not fail to be made a subject of reproach to the Church of Constantinople, and so it has been. See further on, chap. ii. pp. 134, 135, note, and chap iii. p. 152.

[2] These propositions form the two first articles of the "Declaration of the Independence of the Greek Church" officially published by King Otho on July 23 (Aug. 4) 1833. They read as follows:

1. Ἡ ὀρθόδοξος Ἀνατολικὴ Ἀποστολικὴ Ἐκκλησία τοῦ Βασιλείου τῆς Ἑλλάδος, ἐν Πνεύματι μὴ ἀναγνωρίζουσα ἄλλην κεφαλὴν παρὰ τὸν Θεμελιωτὴν τῆς Χριστιανικῆς πίστεως τὸν Κύριον καὶ Σωτῆρα ἡμῶν Ἰησοῦν Χριστὸν, κατὰ δὲ τὸ διοικητικὸν μέρος ἔχουσα ἀρχηγὸν τὸν βασιλέα τῆς Ἑλλάδος, εἶναι αὐτοκέφαλος καὶ ἀνεξάρτητος ἀπὸ πάσης ἄλλης ἐξουσίας, φυλαττομένης ἀπαραχαράκτου τῆς δογματικῆς ἑνότητος, κατὰ τὰ παρὰ πασῶν τῶν ὀρθοδόξων Ἀνατολικῶν ἐκκλησιῶν ἀνέκαθεν πρεσβευόμενα.

2. Ἡ ὑπερτάτη Ἐκκλησιαστικὴ ἐξουσία ἐναπόκειται, ὑπὸ τὴν τοῦ βασιλέως κυριαρχίαν, εἰς χεῖρας Συνόδου διαρκοῦς, φερούσης τὸ ὄνομα· "Ἱερὰ

it, and in a free and private deliberation (members of the Government having withdrawn), approved by thirty-six prelates:—" 1. The Eastern Orthodox and Apostolic Church of Greece, which SPIRITUALLY *owns no Head but the Head of the Christian Faith, Jesus Christ our Lord*, is dependent on no external authority, while she preserves unshaken dogmatic unity with all the Eastern Orthodox Churches. With respect *to the administration of the Church*, which pertains to the crown, she acknowledges THE KING OF GREECE AS HER SUPREME HEAD, as in nothing contrary to the holy canons. 2. A permanent Synod shall be established, consisting entirely of archbishops and bishops, appointed by the King: to be the highest ecclesiastical authority, after the model of the Russian Church." [1] Accordingly, what, as regards the Russian Tsars, we have been proving, with much trouble and long research, as regards the kings of Greece was fairly and plainly asserted by the national Synod of Nauplia, composed of *all the bishops of Greece!* Besides, the Statute-law (νόμος καταστατικὸς) of the Holy Synod of Greece contains the following article: 'To the Holy Synod there will be appointed by the King a royal delegate, who, before entering on his functions, will take, in presence of the King, the oath prescribed by law. And since to the supreme royal authority, in which the governing power is lodged, belongs also the inspection of whatever happens within the kingdom, the royal delegate has a mission to assist, without a vote, at every sitting of the Holy Synod, and to countersign the original of whatever is decided or put in force by the Holy Synod, whether as concerns its internal or external affairs. Moreover,

---

Σύνοδος τοῦ βασιλείου τῆς 'Ελλάδος," *Nicolopoulos and Kakoulidi*, Συλλογὴ ἁπάντων τῶν νόμων, etc., Athens, 1859, tom. i. (49), p. 118.

[1] Neale (J. M.), *A History of the Holy Eastern Church*, Gen. Introd. i. p. 60.

every decision and act of the Holy Synod, taken in the absence of the royal delegate, or not bearing his countersign, will be null.[1]

We are well aware, and are extremely glad to state it on most reliable information, that in practice the King's interference in the administration of the Hellenic Orthodox Church is by no means so extended and vexatious as to be compared to that of the Tsar in the administration of the Russian Orthodox Church. Let us, however, take here notice of the fact that all the bishops of Greece, assembled in a national council, have solemnly professed to hold, as in nothing contrary to the holy canons,[2] that, with respect to her *administration* (or *government*— διοικητικὸν) the Supreme *Head* (ἀρχηγὸς) of the Hellenic Church is the King of Greece.

FINALLY, as to the Greek Orthodox Church of the Turkish Empire, the Church of the Patriarchates of Constantinople, Alexandria, Antioch, and Jerusalem, the following judgment was passed upon her by an eminent dignitary of the State Church of England: "In Con-

---

[1] Νόμος καταστατικὸς τῆς Ἱερᾶς Συνόδου τῆς Ἐκκλησίας τῆς Ἑλλάδος τῆς 9 Ἰουλίου, 1852, art. 6.

. . . Παρὰ τῇ Ἱερᾷ Συνόδῳ διορίζεται ὑπὸ τοῦ Βασιλέως βασιλικὸς ἐπίτροπος, ὅστις, πρὶν ἢ ἀναλάβῃ τὰ καθήκοντα διὰ τοῦ, δίδει ἐνώπιον τοῦ Βασιλέως τὸν νενομισμένον ὅρκον τοῦ δημοσίου ὑπαλλήλου. Ἐπειδὴ δὲ εἰς τὴν ὑπερτάτην βασιλικὴν ἐξουσίαν, εἰς ἣν ἐναπόκειται ἡ κυριαρχία τοῦ Κράτους ἀνήκει καὶ ἡ ἐποπτεία ἐφ᾽ ὅλων τῶν ἐντὸς τοῦ Βασιλείου γινομένων, ὁ βασιλικὸς ἐπίτροπος ἔχει τὸ καθῆκον νὰ παρευρίσκηται, ἄνευ ψήφου, εἰς ὅλας ἐν γένει τὰς συνεδριάσεις τῆς Ἱερᾶς Συνόδου, καὶ νὰ προσυπογράφηται εἰς ὅλα τὰ πρωτότυπα τῶν παρὰ τῆς Ἱερᾶς Συνόδου ἐκδιδομένων ἀποφάσεων καὶ πράξεων, ἀναγομένων εἴτε εἰς τὰ ἐσωτερικὰ εἴτε εἰς τὰ ἐξωτερικὰ αὐτῆς καθήκοντα. Πᾶσα δὲ ἀπόφασις ἢ πρᾶξις τῆς Ἱερᾶς Συνόδου, γινομένη ἐν ἀπουσίᾳ τοῦ Βασιλικοῦ ἐπιτρόπου, ἢ μὴ φέρουσα τὴν προσυπογραφὴν αὐτοῦ εἶναι ἄκυρος. Rhalles, Οἱ Ἑλληνικοὶ κώδικες. (Athens, 1856), tom. ii. p. 634 *et seq.*—Συλλογὴ etc. tom. ii. (810) p. 732 *et seq.*

[2] See Pitra, (Card.), *Des Canons et des Collections canoniques de l'Église grecque* (Paris, Durand, 1858), pp. 35–37.

stantinople the Sultan still exercises the right which he inherited from the last of the Cæsars; and the virtual appointment and deposition of the patriarchs *still places in his hands the government* of the Byzantine Church—a power, no doubt, more scandalous and more pernicious in the hands of the Mussulman than it was in the hands of the Christian despot, but not more decided and absolute. And how high a place is occupied by the Emperor of Russia will be seen,' &c.[1]

Besides, in a Letter '*to all the Orthodox faithful of the world*' (May 6, 1848), in answer to that of Pius IX. 'to the Christians of the East' (January 6, 1848), the four Patriarchs of Constantinople, Alexandria, Antioch, and Jerusalem solemnly profess to hold as follows:—
' Les patriarches d'Alexandrie, d'Antioche, de Jérusalem, dans les cas extraordinaires et difficiles, écrivent au patriarche de Constantinople, parce que cette ville est le siége de l'Empire, et à cause de la préséance de ce siége dans les Synodes; et si le concours fraternel remédie à la perplexité, la chose en reste là; *sinon on s'en refère au pouvoir temporel suivant les lois*. Mais ce concours fraternel, dans les affaires de la foi chrétienne, ne s'exerce pas au prix de l'asservissement des Églises de Dieu.'[2]

The temporal power or government (διοίκησις) here alluded to is that of the *Sultan*. On the Sultan then

---

[1] Stanley (A.P., Dean of Westminster), *Lectures on the History of the Eastern Church*, 4th. ed. (London, 1869.) Lect. I. p. 41.

[2] Οἱ Πατριάρχαι τῆς 'Αλεξανδρείας, τῆς 'Αντιοχείας, τῶν 'Ιεροσολύμων εἰς τὰ παραδόξως συμπεσόντα καὶ δυσδιευθέτητα γράφουσιν εἰς τὸν Κωνσταντινουπόλεως, διὰ τὸ εἶναι ἕδραν Αὐτοκρατορικὴν, ἔτι δὲ καὶ διὰ τὸ Συνοδικὸν Πρεσβεῖον· καὶ εἰ μὲν ἡ ἀδελφικὴ σύμπραξις διορθώσει τὸ διορθωτέον, εὖ ἔχει· εἰ δὲ μὴ, ἀναγγέλλεται τὸ πρᾶγμα καὶ εἰς τὴν Διοίκησιν κατὰ τὰ καθεστῶτα. *Encycl.*, p. 60. Pitzipios' *L'Église orientale*, part i. p. 140.

The above-quoted French translation is taken from the *Lettre encyclique de S.S. le Pape Pie IX aux Chrétiens d'Orient, et Encyclique responsive des Patriarches et des Synodes de l'Église d'Orient*, traduites du grec par le Dr. Démétrius Dallas (Paris, 1850). *Enc. resp.* p. 51.

devolves the final settlement of the questions which cannot be ended by the sentence of the Œcumenical Patriarch of Constantinople. One is entitled to ask after this, if, when recently the Sultan himself undertook to settle the question concerning the independence of the Bulgarian Church, he did anything but exercise a right solemnly conferred upon him by the representatives of the whole Greek Orthodox Church of the Turkish Empire?

But, moreover, this policy, the recourse to the final decision of the Sultan, is quoted by the Oriental Patriarchs and their Synods in opposition to that followed in the Catholic Church, and pointed out as the one which does not trench upon *the freedom and independence of the Churches of God!*

What a strange idea of ecclesiastical freedom and independence! It agrees only too well with the exaggerations of the following address, presented to the Sultan on the occasion of the concessions granted by him in 1853 to the different religious communities of the empire. We have translated it from the original Greek, as it may be seen in the Greek newspaper, the 'Ἀθηνᾶ,' together with the address of the Jews.

Address of thanksgiving of the Œcumenical Patriarch, and of that of Jerusalem, to the Ottoman Government.

'The Greek patriarchs of Constantinople and Jerusalem, the metropolitans and bishops of the supreme order, the principals of the nation, and the chiefs of the corporations (τῶν συντεχνιῶν), subjects of the Sublime Porte, submit the present address of thanksgiving at the feet (εἰς τοὺς πόδας) of the most high and most just throne, and of the most merciful autocratic threshold (βάθρου), may it be preserved (εἴη διατηρούμενον) to the end of the world! Our humble nation, which glories (τὸ σεμνυννόμενον) in its faithful subjection and submission to the autocratic Government, be it blessed for ever! (ἣν εὔχεται αἰώνιον) of His

I

Majesty the Sultan, our master and benefactor, having called together, in our patriarchate, an assembly of our nation (γενικὴν), in order to have there read, in presence of your servants, now in Constantinople, the metropolitans, the principals of the nation, and the chiefs of the different corporations, the Hatti Sheriff of His Highness, by which are confirmed the special conditions, concessions, and spiritual privileges granted by the great Autocrats and illustrious Sultans of everlasting memory, &c. . . . the undersigned were overwhelmed with infinite joy and everlasting gratitude.

'It is beyond the range of our possibility, by act or word, to make due acknowledgment for one only (καὶ μόνον) of the kindnesses, privileges, or concessions which have been granted to our humble nation, in such a manner as to attract the jealousy of the other nations (*of the empire*), and make the glory of our own, according to the usual compasssion (ἐκ τῆς συνήθους εὐσπλαγχνίας) of His Imperial Majesty the most august and most powerful Sultan, compassionate toward all, who is glorified by his own deeds, benefactor of the world (τοῦ ἐνεργέτου τοῦ κόσμου), our peculiar benefactor, who is the ornament of the crown of the Sultans, and who gains the admiration of the whole earth by his bounties and by all his other perfections (καὶ τὰς ἄλλας αὐτοῦ ἐντελείας).

'All the world knows (πασίγνωστον) that the security (ἀσφάλεια) and the tranquillity (ἡσυχία) of all his subjects are *perfect* (τέλειαι), thanks to the protection, full of justice, of the Imperial Government, to which is confided, as a divine pledge (ὡς θεῖον ἐνέχυρον), the wellbeing and contentment (ἄνεσις) of all the inhabitants of the empire. Thus our nation considers, as the very first of its religious and legal (νομίμων) duties, to remain, with all its heart and soul, for ever constant in its submission and subjection to the Imperial Government, and to shed its last drop of blood for the august person of His Majesty; and night and day it prays God the Almighty, with its women and children, with uncovered head and shedding tears ("Εύχεται δὲ διαπύρως εἰς τὸν παντοδύναμον Θεὸν ἡμέραν τε καὶ νύκτα σὺν γυναιξὶ καὶ τέκνοις, δακρυρροοῦν καὶ ἀσκεπῆ τὴν κεφαλὴν ἔχον), that He may preserve the august person of His Majesty, our most magnanimous sovereign, on the throne of the Sultanate of eternal duration, in good health (ὑγιὴς) and through long years, and preserve the ministers of the Imperial Government, who are the intermediates of so great imperial kindness, in honour and glory under the gracious benevolence of His Imperial Majesty.

'We pray Your Highness to deign to take cognizance of the present address, and to submit at the feet of the most august Sultan (καὶ ὑποβάλῃ εἰς τοὺς πόδας τοῦ τρισεβάστου Σνλτάνου), that shadow of God (τῆς θείας ταύτης σκιᾶς), our perfect gratitude, and joy, and sincere thanks.'[1]

We hasten to conclude this chapter. Neither in Russia, nor in the Kingdom of Greece, nor in the Turkish Empire are the bishops of the Oriental Orthodox Church what, according to the doctrine of that Church, they ought to be. In none of her three chief branches do they really constitute the *chief supreme* authority; in the Kingdom of Greece their authority is considerably lessened and curtailed, and in the Russian Empire they scarcely constitute any authority whatever.

[1] Ἀθηνᾶ, No. 1986, June 27, 1853, pp. 3, 4: Εὐχαριστήριος τοῦ Οἰκουμενικοῦ Πατριάρχου καὶ τοῦ τῶν Ἱεροσολύμων πρὸς τὴν Ὀθωμανικὴν Κυβέρνησιν.

CHAPTER II.

THE ORIENTAL ORTHODOX CHURCH IS REALLY DIVIDED INTO SEVERAL SEPARATE AND INDEPENDENT CHURCHES AND EVEN PAPACIES, WHILST CATHOLICS ADMIT ONLY ONE CHURCH AND ONE POPE.

ONE of the most striking instances of the misunderstandings by which mainly religious discussions are perpetuated and increased, is afforded by the way in which the Catholic doctrine of a *visible head of the Church* is spoken of in the works of 'Orthodox' divines, and generally whenever Orthodox Russians or Greeks are treating of the Pope. As many Protestants, even in our day, hate Catholicism because, *so they are told*, Catholics pay divine worship to the blessed Virgin; assume that, provided one goes to confession, one can freely sin, obtain by money the remission of sins, &c. &c.; so also many Orthodox Russians and Greeks have no better reason for repudiating Catholicism than its 'monstrous' doctrine of a visible head of the Church, the Pope thus being an usurper of the authority of Jesus Christ, a simple man thus becoming invested with the attributes of God Himself, and the Church thus being made to be double-headed. Now as, in the first case, the Protestants we allude to do not hate a Catholicism really existing, but an imaginary Catholicism of their own; so, likewise, the Orthodox Russians and Greeks whom we have in view do not repudiate the true Catholic doctrine concerning the Pope, but a fancied Catholic doctrine, created, let us say, not by passion but by want of acquaintance with the fact, or by prejudice. Indeed, one cannot help smiling when listening to them, especially when they represent the doctrine of a *visible head of the Church* as *destroying her unity.* Of the innumerable instances which one might bring forward of such misconception of the true Catholic doctrine concerning the Pope, we confine ourselves to quoting the following:—' Jesus Christ' (so says the Archimandrite Makary, in his 'Orthodox Doctrine of the Oriental Orthodox Church ')[1] ' has promised that the Church shall last for ever (Matt. xvi. 18); moreover He has declared that He alone is the sole head of the Church (Eph. i. 22): but the Church is a body (Coloss. i. 18); consequently the Church will never fail, and will for ever have Jesus Christ as her head, inasmuch as she is united with Him, receives from Him spiritual life and being, and is by Him governed and justified. Can the Pope do this—the Pope, I say—that monarch of the Church, *violator* of the holy equality against the precept of Jesus Christ (Luke xii. 24), and *usurper* of the authority of Jesus Christ (2 Coloss. ii. 4)? Among us there are to be found in the Church only *brothers,* and not fathers.'[2]

How far the Pope deserves such epithets and qualifica-

---

[1] Церкви восточныя православное Ученіе. Спб. 1783. Ch. x. § 97, p. 114.

'De tous les Essais de Théologie dogmatique que nous avons mentionnés jusqu'ici' (says the *other* Makary, Bishop of Vinnitza), 'ceux que l'on reconnaît à juste titre comme les meilleurs comparativement, au point de vue de la solidité et de la plénitude, ce sont ceux de *l'Archimandrite Macaire* (édit. 1783, 1790), de L. E. Irénée (Falkovsky) et Théophylacte (Gorsky).' *Théol. dogm. orth.,* trad. par un Russe (Paris, 1859), Introd. p. 76.

[2] Можетъ ли сіе Папа учинить, Папа, говорю, монархъ онъ церковный, святаго равнодушія нарушитель, противу заповѣди Христовой. (Лук. 12, 24.) и похититель Христовой власти. (2 Col. 2, 4.) У насъ ничего въ Церкви кромѣ братій и отцевъ нѣтъ. (Церк. вост. прав. Учен. p. 114.

The passages of the Holy Scripture are only indicated by Makary, not quoted.

tions will appear from what is stated by the same author concerning the *visibility* of the Church. 'Jesus Christ alone' (so he says further on) 'is the Monarch of the Church, and she is His *spiritual* (*duchovnoe*) kingdom. Of the faithful, many of them have already attained their happiness in heaven, the others are preparing for it. Hence the Church is divided into Church triumphant and Church militant. Some of the *militant* Church walk in sanctity, but others show only the exterior appearance of Christianity. *These form a visible Church, but the former form at the same time the* VISIBLE *and the* INVISIBLE *Church.*'[1]—Accordingly, a portion of Jesus Christ's *spiritual kingdom* is formed by a *visible* Church. Now, to cause this Church to be governed by a single man rather than by a large number of men, each of them independent of the others—can this be deservedly termed *a usurpation of the authority of* JESUS CHRIST?[2] One might indeed speak of usurpation of the fellow-bishops' authority, but to represent the Pope as an usurper of *Jesus Christ's* authority in the Church, cannot be explained but by that extreme misconception of the Catholic doctrine concerning the Pope which we are just complaining of.

What is the Pope? The Pope is the *visible head of the visible portion of the Church* alluded to by the Archimandrite Makary. That the portion of the Church here on earth constitutes a *visible* society is clearly asserted in the Catechism of Mgr. Filaret, whose words on this

[1] Сія видимую, а тѣ вмѣстѣ и невидимую составляютъ Церковь. *Ibid.* at the end : Догматы Богословскіе, Nos. 76, 77, p. 139.

[2] It is well known that up to the definition of the Vatican Council on the 18th of July, 1870, the infallibility of the Pope was not obligatory on belief as an article of the Catholic faith, and its non-acceptance did not even prevent Catholics from becoming bishops. This divine prerogative of the successor of Peter could not consequently be seriously alluded to in 1783 by the Archimandrite Makary.

subject perfectly agree with those of the 'Catechism of the Council of Trent.' 'The Church,' says Mgr. Filaret, 'though *visible so far as she is upon earth, and contains all orthodox Christians living upon earth*, still is at the same time invisible, so far as she is also partially in heaven, and contains all those that have departed hence in true faith and holiness.'¹ On the other hand, the Catechism of the Council of Trent, after mentioning the two parts of the Church, called the one 'the Church triumphant,' and the other 'the Church militant,' adds: 'We are not, however, hence to infer that there are two Churches, but there are two constituent parts of the same Church; one of which has gone before and is now in the possession of its heavenly country; the other following every day, until at length, united with our Saviour, it repose in endless felicity.'²

Now, since the Church on earth constitutes a *visible society*, she needs an external government and *visible governors*. Whatever the form of that government might be, the appellation itself of *chief* or *head* of the Church, applied to one single man, or to many men, cannot possibly be spared, as a special word must necessarily be made use of for designating the *man* or the *men* entrusted with the external government of the Church. But neither the Catholic nor the Oriental Orthodox Church has deemed it necessary to avoid as heretical the word *chief* or *head* of the Church when speaking of such men, and both agree in applying to them the denomination of *head* (or *chief*) of the Church. The Oriental Orthodox Church, professing to believe that the bishops are the *common*

---

¹ *The Longer Catechism*, part i. 'On the Ninth Article' in Blackmore's *The Doctrine of the Russian Church*, etc. p. 76.

² *Catechismus Romanus ex decreto Concilii Tridentini*, ed. Romæ, 1845, pars i. cap. x. 'De Nono Articulo' quæst. 6: 'Ecclesia militans et triumphans una est,' pp. 59–60.

rulers of the Church, applies the forementioned denomination to them;[1] the Catholic Church, on the contrary, professing to believe that above the bishops there exists another divinely instituted authority commanding over them, and causing the Church to be constituted into a monarchy, *specially* applies the said denomination to that supreme authority, and calls the Pope *the head of the Church*. Yet to the Pope by the Catholic Church, just as little as to the bishops by the Oriental Orthodox Church, is such denomination applied in the same sense in which Jesus Christ is called *head of the Church*. The catechisms of the two Churches again marvellously agree in stating the different meaning which that denomination bears when applied to men and when applied to Jesus Christ.

'We are taught,' so reads the 'Orthodox Confession of the Catholic and Apostolic Eastern Church,' 'that Christ is the only head of His Church, according as we are taught by the Apostle (Ephes. v. 23): " *For the husband is the head of the wife, and Christ is the head of the Church; and He is the Saviour of the body.*" And again (Colos. i. 18): " *He is the head of the body of the Church, who is the beginning, and the first-born from the dead; that in all things He might have the pre-eminence.*" However the rulers of the Church are called *Heads* (κεφαλαί) in their several Churches over which they are placed: *but this is only as stewards and vicars* (τοποτερηταί) *of Christ in His several provinces over which they are said to be heads* (κεφαλαί—главы).'[2]

On the other hand, the 'Catechism of the Council of

---

[1] See chap. i. p. 11 and note, 'Episcopi qui nequaquam abusive sed verissime *capitum* instar suis præsunt Ecclesiis' (οὐκ ἐν καταχρήσει ἀλλὰ κυρίως ἀρχὰς καὶ κεφαλὰς). *Kimmel. Monum. fid.—Dositheii Confess.* Decr. x. p. 437. In the Russian translation: ГЛАВЫ, НАЧАЛЬНИКИ.

[2] *The Orthodox Confession*, &c., in English (London, 1762), quest. 85, p. 82, 83. *Kimmel, Monum. fidei*, etc., *Confessio Orthod.* p. 158.

Trent,' after having said that 'The ruler and governor of the Church is *one*, the invisible one indeed, Christ, *whom the Eternal Father hath made* HEAD *over all the Church, which is His body* (Eph. i. 22, 23); but the visible one he who, as the legitimate successor of Peter, the Prince of the Apostles, occupies the See of Rome,'[1] thus proceeds to state in what sense the Pope is called the *head* (*caput*) of the Church: ' Quest. XIII. (part i. chap. x.): How, besides Christ, does the Church require one visible head? *Ans.* Should anyone object that the Church, content with one head and spouse, Jesus Christ, requires no other besides, the answer is at hand; for, as we have Christ the Lord, not only the author of every sacrament, but also their inward giver (*præbitorem*) (for He it is that baptizes and absolves, and yet He instituted men the external ministers of the sacraments), so has He placed over His Church, *which He rules by His inward spirit*, a man to be the VICAR (*vicarium*) and minister of His power; for, as a visible Church requires a visible head, so our Saviour appointed Peter head and pastor of the faithful of every sort, when, in the most ample terms, He committed to him His sheep to be fed, so that He wished His successor to have the very same power of ruling and governing the whole Church.'[2]

Consequently, since the 'Catechism of the Council of Trent,' in speaking of the *single supreme visible head* of the Catholic Church, designates him by the very same expression of *Vicar* of Jesus Christ used in the 'Orthodox Confession' for designating the *many visible heads* of the Oriental Orthodox Church—since the Pope, in the same 'Catechism of the Council of Trent,' is asserted to

---

[1] *Catechismus Rom. ex decr. Conc. Trident.* ib. quæst. xi.: 'De notis veræ Ecclesiæ, et primo cur una dicatur,' p. 61.
[2] *Ibid.* quæst. xiii.: 'Quomodo præter Christum Ecclesia uno capite visibili indigeat,' p. 62.

be only the *visible* MINISTER of the government of the Church, exactly as priests are the external ministers of the sacraments, Jesus Christ still being the inward giver of the sacraments and the inward *ruler* of the Church—in a word, since the Pope is called *head of the Church* in the ' Catechism of the Council of Trent ' IN THE VERY SENSE in which the bishops are called *heads of the Church* in the ' Orthodox Confession,' we are entitled not to pay any further attention to the unqualified imputations that the Catholic doctrine respecting the Pope ' destroys the *unity* (!) of the Church,' that ' the Pope is a usurper of the authority of JESUS CHRIST,' and others of the same kind.

The Catholic doctrine being thus cleared from misconceptions and mistakes, the question is solely of the *number* of those *visible heads,* who cannot possibly be spared in the visible portion of the Church ; in other words, the question is one of the Church's *form of government.* Now, whilst the *unity* of her external and visible organisation forms one of the chief features of the Catholic Church, in looking, on the contrary, at the Oriental Orthodox Church, we cannot help being struck by the *separateness* of her visible organisation and the want of unity in her external government. ' Why is the Church one?' it is asked in the Catechism of Mgr. Filaret, and the answer is, ' Because she is one *spiritual* body, has one head, Christ, and is animated by one Spirit of God. *There is one body and one Spirit, even as ye are called in one hope of your calling ; one Lord, one faith, one baptism, one God and Father of all.*' (Eph. iv. 4, 6.) [1]

---

[1] Blackmore, *loc. cit.* ' On the Ninth Article,' p. 77.

' The Orthodox Confession ' (quest. 83) says :—' The Church is *one*, holy, catholic, and apostolic, according to the doctrine of the Apostle (2 Cor. xi. 2): " I have espoused you to one husband, that I may present you as a chaste virgin unto Christ." For like as Christ is only one, so his spouse also can

Thus far, the character of unity is equally claimed by every one of the innumerable sects brought forth by Protestantism. Each of them pretends to be a *spiritual body*, to have one head, Christ, and, above all, to be animated by one Spirit of God. We cannot possibly believe that the Fathers of the Council of Constantinople, when they pointed out the UNITY of the true Church as one of her four external characters or marks distinguishing her from every pretended Church whatever, did not attach to the word UNITY any more meaning than Mgr. Filaret does.

In spite of this the Orthodox Church positively rejects the doctrine that unity in the visible organisation of the Church is required in order to cause her to be *one*, and positively states that her UNITY is expressed outwardly by '*unity of creed, and by communion in prayer and sacraments.*'[1]

A doctrine so analogous to that of Protestantism must necessarily lead to consequences very analogous to those of Protestantism. As Protestants—after having rejected the visible head divinely appointed to the Church by Jesus Christ—in order to exist, could not help calling

---

be but one; as is manifest from the Epistle to the Ephesians (iv. 5), "One Lord, one faith, one baptism, one God and Father of all."'

In other words: the Church is *one* because she is *one*. An inquirer after the one Church of Jesus Christ is no further advanced by such explanations than before.

[1] *Q.* How does it agree with the unity of the Church that there are many separate and *independent* Churches, as those of Jerusalem, Antioch, Alexandria, Constantinople, and Russia?

A. These are particular Churches, or parts of the one Catholic Church; the *separateness of their visible organisation does not hinder them from being all spiritually* great members of the one body of the universal Church, from having one head, Christ, and one spirit of faith and grace. This unity is expressed outwardly by unity of creed, and by communion in prayers and sacraments.

Blackmore, *ibid.*

others to be *visible heads* over them instead of the Pope, and either submitted to kings and queens, or, getting rid of their authority and passing through manifold revolutions, experienced the greatest variety of governors and governments, the Oriental Orthodox Church also, whilst rejecting, as contrary to the precepts of Jesus Christ, the authority of the Pope of Rome, has, in fact, never existed without some other *Popes*;—moreover, in the stead of bishops, kings and queens have ruled over her like Popes—and revolutions and a variety of governors and governments have equally formed, and still constantly form, the history of the Oriental Orthodox Church. Let us look attentively into such a *fact*, as, putting aside the arguments taken from Holy Scripture and tradition, we propose to confine ourselves to it, in order to deduce from it alone a special evidence of the *divinely instituted* authority of the Pope. In this chapter we shall treat of the Popes of the Orthodox Church, as we shall speak in the next of her revolutions and variety of governments.

The Oriental Orthodox Church, we have said, had never existed without some *Popes*. By *Pope*, we mean here the *visible, supreme, and independent head of some special branch of the Oriental Orthodox Church, commanding not only the faithful (lambs) but also their pastors the bishops (sheep)*,[1] *and exercising jurisdiction over all of them, without being commanded by them*. The Pope of Rome, with regard to the *government* of the Church, is all this, and nothing else than this. We say: 'with regard to the *government* of the Church'—as it is only the *government* of the Church we are concerned with—and in order to prevent misunderstandings, we add here some few words concerning the different powers of the Pope.

[1] 'Feed my lambs,' said Jesus to Peter; 'feed my sheep.'—John xxi. 15–17.

In the Pope (of Rome) must be distinguished three powers, the *doctrinal* power, the power of *order*, and, finally, the power of *jurisdiction*. The *doctrinal power* is that by which the Pope is constituted, according to the expression of the Council of Florence, 'TEACHER OF ALL CHRISTIANS.' '*Infallibility*' is attached to the Pope whenever (and only when) he exercises this power under conditions constituting a definition *ex cathedrâ*.— The *power of order* is that which the Pope holds by virtue of the EPISCOPAL CONSECRATION. This power entitles him to consecrate priests and bishops, and to be the ordinary minister of the sacrament of confirmation.— Finally, the *power of jurisdiction* is that by virtue of which the Pope is entrusted with the GOVERNMENT properly so called of the Church, that is, with the supreme *legislative* and *administrative* power over her. Other bishops may indeed have been called *by God* to share in the government of the Church, the Pope being just as much unable to administer by himself the whole Church as a king is unable to administer, alone and without aid from other men, his particular kingdom. Yet this participation of the bishops in the *government* of the Church no more prevents the Pope from being their chief, than the *unavoidable* assistance of local governors in the separate provinces of a State prevents a king from being really their king.

Now, of these three powers, the only one which is here in question is the last, that is, the Pope's *power of jurisdiction over the universal Church*. The doctrine we have in view is only that which has hitherto been the chief obstacle in the way of the reunion of the two Churches, and we shall indeed be happy if, supposing the recent decree of 'infallibility' to constitute a new one, we may by this book help toward reducing all causes of division to the infallibility of the Pope. Let us, therefore, be faithful to our programme, and not engage in any controversy which does not concern the Pope's *power of jurisdiction* over the universal Church.

We must, however, dwell a little on the Pope's *power of order*, as a great confusion of ideas generally prevails on this subject. The *power of order* we have already defined as that which the Pope holds in virtue of the episcopal consecration, and which enables him to consecrate priests and bishops, and to be the ordinary minister of the sacrament of confirmation. With regard to this power, the Pope is on a level with the last bishop *in partibus*, and the last bishop *in partibus*, if elected Pope, has not in the least increased his power of order. Moreover, the *power of order* is essentially distinct and separate from the *power of jurisdiction*. The above bishops *in partibus* whom we have just named have the first, without possessing the second. Many apostolic vicars in mission countries are invested with the second without possessing the first, as, without being bishops, they exercise in their mission a real *jurisdiction* like that of bishops. Again, the *power of order* is so separate even from the *power of jurisdiction over the universal Church*, that one might, for a while, be invested with the latter without being necessarily a bishop. Let us only suppose the case that, on the death of a Pope, the cardinals present at Rome, and invested, *ad interim*, with the power of governing the Catholic Church, be all either deacons or priests and none of them bishops. In that case the *jurisdiction* over the universal Church, during the vacancy of the Holy See, would be exercised by men who do not even possess the power of episcopal order, and who, besides, do not exercise the said jurisdiction (which is extended also over bishops of whatever rank) because they are *priests* or *deacons*, but because they are *cardinals*. Finally, even a layman, if elected Pope, is immediately, on his acceptance of the dignity, invested with the power of full jurisdiction over the whole Catholic Church, and enters at once upon the exercise of it, without needing for it the episcopal consecration, which is only subsequently conferred.

One could hardly find, we believe, a better instance of the practical difference and *separateness* of the two powers of *order* and *jurisdiction*. What makes the Pope to be *the visible head of the Church* is not his power of *order* (on account of which, let it be remarked again, he is on a level with the last bishop *in partibus*), but his power of *jurisdiction*. The 'Tradition of the Syriac Church of Antioch,' which we here beg to point out to our readers as well worthy public attention, affords us, on that point, passages in which the said difference between the two powers and the special prerogative of Peter are so clearly asserted and explained, that we cannot help quoting two of them. 'In the imposition of hands,' so runs the first, 'in the invocation of the Holy Ghost, and in other episcopal offices, patriarchs, metropolitans, and bishops are all equal, as Peter and the Apostles, his associates, did all equally partake of the gifts of the Holy Ghost and of the priestly order. For *government*, however, Peter (alone) was appointed head of his colleagues. (John Bar-Wahbun, in "Expos. Sacram." cap. 29, art. 15.)' 'The disciples,' so reads the second passage, ' were all Apostles; each of them had received the imposition of hands from our Redeemer, all of them were made bishops; but, for the sake of the *government*, Simon was appointed chief.'[1]

---

[1] *The Tradition of the Syriac Church of Antioch, concerning the primacy and the prerogatives of St. Peter, and of his successors the Roman Pontiffs*, by the most Rev. Cyril Behnam Benni, Syriac Archbishop of Mossul (Nineveh), translated, under the direction of the author, by the Rev. Jos. Gagliardi (London: Burns, Oates & Co., 1871), Nos. lxxiv. lv. p. 57.

From this work, which, because of the new and striking evidence it contains in favour of the Popes' primacy and prerogatives, is so well adapted to strengthen the faith of Catholics, we will add here the following passage:—

We ask the reader not to lose sight of the distinction between the Pope's two powers of *order* and *jurisdiction*, as it is only by getting a clear conception of this distincttion that he will be enabled to understand and discuss the matter which we are dealing with in this chapter. We proceed now to speak of the several *Popes* dividing among themselves the government of the Oriental Orthodox Church.

FIRST OF ALL, what, we ask our readers, are the Tsar of Russia and the King of Greece, if we listen to the documents discussed above and to the declaration of the Greek bishops assembled at Nauplia on the 15th (27th) of July, 1833? Does the Catholic Church acknowledge in the Pope of Rome a more extended *power of jurisdiction* than that conferred upon the said Sovereigns by the Russian and Hellenic Churches? However paradoxical such a question might appear, some reflections will lead the reader to conclude that the answer is by no means so obvious as at first sight he may have believed.

'The Tsar,' so we are told in Platon's Catechism, 'has nobody on earth higher than himself, and is not subject to any human law.' Where, then, are to be found the limits to the extent of his jurisdiction over the Church? Is it in the ecclesiastical canons? We have already examined this question (pp. 56–62). Let it be so with regard to the *dogmatical* canons of the Russian Church (the Pope also

---

' Christ Himself (so runs this testimony) did not confer the high priesthood upon the virgin John, full of zeal though he was besides, but on the married Simon, who had also experienced weakness by denying him (xlvii. p. 45).' Accordingly, on Peter was conferred a *high priesthood not conferred upon John*, though this latter was not only an Apostle like Peter, but of all the Apostles was the happiest—the happiest one, '*whom Jesus loved*' (John xiii. 23, xx. 2, xxi. 20, xix. 27); who during the last supper '*was leaning on Jesus' bosom*' (John xiii. 23, xxi. 20); and who, still *lying on Jesus' breast*, had then dared to say unto him, 'Who is it?' (John xiii. 25.)

being bound by the *dogmatical* canons of the Catholic Church), but as to the *disciplinary* ones, the documents which we have discussed in the first chapter of this book, and the most cursory inspection of the Laws of the Russian Empire, must convince everyone that the Russian Tsars never considered themselves bound by the disciplinary canons of their Church. And in doing so, not only were they consistent with the doctrine virtually contained in the Russian Catechisms (see above, pp. 90–2), but they were also fulfilling a *duty* logically resting upon them. In fact, the disciplinary canons of the Church are, by their own nature, liable to be suppressed or modified according to circumstances of time and place, and whenever such changes and suppressions are required for the welfare of the Church, the supreme authority is not only entitled but even *bound* to effect them. Now, since the Tsars must '*seek what is the best for their people both in spiritual and temporal things,*' and since they depend on no one on earth, but are rather charged by God to '*overlook the pastors of the Church in the discharge of their duties,*' whenever conscience suggests to a Tsar that some canonical prescriptions have become no longer good either for the Church or for the State, or that the episcopal jurisdiction ought to be restrained, or that modifications are to be brought into the legislature concerning the impediments to marriage, how could he refuse to obey his conscience? and where on earth is to be found the authority by which he should be prevented from bringing about whatever he may deem to be best for the Church? Accordingly, the power of the Tsar over the disciplinary canons of his Church follows as a natural and necessary conclusion from the mission with which the Russian Catechisms assert that he has been entrusted by God.

But, if not by the disciplinary canons of his Church,

by what else can a Tsar's jurisdiction over her ever be limited and restrained? The answer is at hand in Platon's Catechism, and we have already quoted it: 'Who can bind the conscience EXCEPT GOD, the searcher of hearts and trier of the reins? And more particularly is it of peculiar advantage for a Sovereign to be under the influence of a holy faith; because he, although subject to no human laws, is *thereby* made subject to the law of faith, and is *thus preserved within the bounds of holy justice.*'[1] After this how could we be deservedly taxed with exaggeration in stating that the Tsar had no more limits to his power of *jurisdiction* over his Church than the Pope has? Let us listen again to an author already quoted by us, as one having a great aversion to exaggeration: ' Pour ce qui est des *fonctions extérieures du gouvernement de l'Église,*'[2] says Schnitzler, ' l'empereur les exerce *avec un pouvoir beaucoup plus étendu que celui du pape.* Il nomme à toutes les places, et ne s'est imposé qu'une restriction *toute volontaire* en *permettant* au Saint Synode et aux évêques de lui présenter des candidats; il a également le droit (indirectement exercé) de déplacer ou même de destituer tel prêtre qu'il juge indigne de ses fonctions. Cependant il ne s'est jamais arrogé celui de *décider en matière de foi. Son influence est grande, prépondérante même, en toutes choses,* mais il est moins le chef de l'Église que son organe supérieur, son protecteur né, son tuteur si l'on veut; *dans tous les cas il n'en est que le chef séculier.* S'il s'agissait d'être juge dans un débat sur des matières de doctrine, l'empereur renverrait l'affaire au Saint Synode ou réunirait un Synode spécial, et dans un cas majeur il enverrait prendre l'avis des quatre patriarches d'Orient. Il ne se réserverait à lui-même,

[1] *Platon's Catechism*, translated by Pinkerton, 'The Present State of the Greek Church,' p. 171. See above, p. 89.

[2] The *power of jurisdiction* could hardly be better defined than by Schnitzler's words: ' *external functions of the government of the Church.*'

directement que l'exécution de la décision rendue, de la sentence prononcée.'[1] We have preferred to quote this passage *in extenso*, as what Schnitzler says in order to attenuate the effect made on the reader by his having previously likened the power of the Tsar to that of the Pope,

[1] *Les Institutions de la Russie, depuis les réformes d'Alex. II.* (Paris, 1866), t. ii. p. 66. Schnitzler, on this point, refers the reader to Tourgeneff's (Nic.) work, *La Russie et les Russes* (Paris, 1847), tom. ii. p. 280. The illustrious Russian writer who had so glorious a part in causing the emancipation of the Russian serfs to become finally a fact, did not bring to the discussion of this point the same amount of doctrine and thorough acquaintance with the matter as distinguishes other parts of his work. He states that: 'Aucun autre titre (que celui de *protecteurs* ou *défenseurs* de l'Église) n'a été jamais donné officiellement aux Tsars, et moins que tout autre celui de chef de l'Église, qu'on ne voit pas d'ailleurs qu'ils aient jamais pris.' (p. 286). The reader knows that the Tsar is officially termed 'Head of the Church,' in Paul I.'s *Act of Succession*, and in explaining this title, we merely quoted Paul I.'s ukase of November 3, 1798, and the Russian Code of Laws. (See above, pp. 78–81, and note p. 91.) But what we were more painfully struck by, is Tourgeneff's misconception of the Catholic doctrine concerning the Pope. After having said, 'L'Empereur de Russie est un souverain *complètement absolu* ; sa puissance embrasse *tout*, la vie civile du peuple comme sa vie *religieuse*; il commande à *tout*, il régle *tout*; il permet, il défend, il ordonne,' he adds, 'Mais le fait ne prouve pas le principe ; or, en principe, le peuple russe, le clergé russe, ne reconnaissent et n'ont jamais reconnu d'autre *chef* de l'Église que Jésus-Christ. . . .' And further on, 'En effet, d'où pourrait-elle naître cette doctrine de tant de gravité, *qui investirait un homme des attributs de Dieu même!*' (pp. 281–3). What doctrine does the illustrious writer mean? The above-quoted abstracts of the *Catechism of the Council of Trent* compared with those of the *Orthodox Confession* and Filaret's *Catechism*, would certainly have prevented him if he had only made the same comparison, from expressing himself on the matter as he did. Nay, the Russian Church did always declare and profess in her Catechisms, and on every occasion, that the only *head* of the Church is Jesus Christ ; but at the same time she did *always* declare and profess that *the* VISIBLE *portion of the Church, the* MILITANT *Church on earth, wants an external government.*—Now this external government must be necessarily entrusted to some human being, *vicar of the invisible Jesus Christ*, and minister of His power (see above, p. 191). In the Catholic Church this 'human being' is the Pope with the bishops *under him*; in the 'Expositions of the Orthodox Faith' the bishops ; in the Russian Empire, with the consent of the Russian Church, the Tsar and the bishops UNDER HIM.

cannot but confirm the correctness of his statement, and the thesis we have undertaken to prove. In fact, the *doctrinal power* of the Pope, viz., his 'droit de décider en matière de foi,' is not in question here; as even the recent definition of the Pope's infallibility did not add anything to his previous 'full power of JURISDICTION over the universal Church.' What Schnitzler remarks —that, at any rate, the Tsar is only the *secular* head of his Church—shows that this writer, too, did not pay sufficient attention to the distinction between the *power of order* and the *power of jurisdiction*. The Pope is called, and is, 'Pope,' *because of the latter*, and not because of the former, in respect of which, let it be repeated again, he is on a level with the last bishop *in partibus*. Finally, as to the Tsar's deference to the Oriental patriarchs, to which Schnitzler alludes, see what we have said in Chapter I. pp. 33–38. Accordingly the Tsar's *jurisdiction* over his Church has the same limits as the *jurisdiction* of the Pope, of which last we shall speak again further on. Depending only on God, having nobody on earth higher than himself, being subject to no human law, the Tsar is preserved only by *faith* within the bounds of holy justice. Yet, whilst the man acknowledged by Catholics as entrusted with the power of ruling the Church independently of everyone but God, is enabled to discharge the formidable duties of 'head of the Church,' by the *special* graces attached to the episcopal consecration, the same power is conferred in the Russian Orthodox Church on whomsoever happens to obtain the throne of Russia—even on women, even on such as publicly protect, honour, and encourage the leaders of impiety and incredulity. It was, perhaps, the feeling of the terrible responsibility resting on the Tsars, which led the Russian Orthodox Church to create a kind of eighth sacrament in favour of the Tsar, by pronouncing '*ana-*

thema' against those who '*think* that Orthodox Sovereigns are not raised to their throne by a special good pleasure of God concerning them, and that *at the unction the gifts of the Holy Ghost are not poured out upon them, in order to the fulfilment of this great vocation,* and who, in consequence, dare to rebel,' etc. (See Chap I. pp. 102–103).

What the Tsar is in Russia, the King of Greece was unanimously proclaimed by all his bishops to be in his kingdom. 'The Eastern Orthodox Apostolic Church of the Kingdom of Greece (it is said in the proclamation of the independence of the Hellenic Church), which *spiritually* (ἐν Πνεύματι) does not recognise any other head but the founder (θεμελιωτὴν) of the Christian faith — our Lord and Saviour Jesus Christ—*as regards the government of the Church has for her chief* (ἀρχηγόν) *the King of Greece.*'[1]—Indeed, one is tempted to believe that the Greek bishops assembled at Nauplia on the 15th (27th) July, 1833, when being about to write down their declaration, afterwards inserted in the 'Royal Proclamation' of July 23rd, 1833, had beforehand caused to be read in their presence the above-quoted (p. 121) lines of the 'Catechism of the Council of Trent': 'Jesus Christ has placed over His Church, *which He rules by His inward Spirit,* a man to be the vicar and minister of His power, for (as) a visible Church requires a visible head, &c. . . .' Let it only, instead of 'Eastern .. Church of the Kingdom of Greece,' be said, '*Catholic* or *Universal* Church,' and instead of '*The King of Greece,*' be said, '*The Successor of Peter,*' and the first article of the said 'Proclamation'

---

[1] Ἐν Πνεύματι μὴ ἀναγνωρίζουσα ἄλλην κεφαλὴν παρὰ τὸν Θεμελιωτὴν τῆς χριστιανικῆς πίστεως τὸν Κύριον καὶ Σωτῆρα ἡμῶν Ἰησοῦν Χριστόν, κατὰ δὲ τὸ διοικητικὸν μέρος ἔχουσα ἀρχηγὸν τὸν βασιλέα τῆς Ἑλλάδος... (Διακήρυξις περὶ τῆς ἀνεξαρτησίας τῆς Ἑλληνικῆς Ἐκκλησίας. See above, pp. 109–111.

would express THE PURE CATHOLIC DOCTRINE CONCERNING THE GOVERNMENT OF THE CHURCH. Accordingly, the King of Greece is, with respect to the government of the Hellenic Church, her *visible head*.

Where, then, are to be found the limits to the exercise of his *jurisdiction?* He also is bound by the *dogmatical* canons of his Church (just in the same way, let us repeat, as the Pope is by the dogmatical canons of the Catholic Church); but with regard to the *disciplinary* canons, we may apply to the King of Greece whatever we have just advanced in reference to the Tsar. To be *chief* of the Church is to depend on no being on earth, but on God, and to be entrusted by God with the care of ordaining what one deems to be best for the Church. Therefore, whenever the Hellenic King's conscience causes him to judge some canons to be of no use, and their abrogation or derogation to be required for the welfare of the Church, nobody on earth can prevent him from acting according to his conscience. The King's personal character may indeed make him accessible to advice; but only let a man like Peter the Great ascend the throne of Greece, and none can foresee to what extent he would consent to have himself bound by ancient laws enacted in the first centuries of the Church, when society presented an aspect so different from its modern one. Men like Peter the Great are not conservative, and the respect for antiquity and the practical wisdom of our ancestors in faith, is not likely to form a characteristic feature of anyone who would strive to imitate that Russian Tsar.[1]

[1] Some Greeks may object that the Acts of July 1833 were corrected by the Συνόδικος Τόμος of the Church of Constantinople (see further on p. 150 *et seq.*), and the Νόμος καταστατικὸς τῆς 'Ιερᾶς Συνόδου τῆς 'Εκκλησίας τῆς 'Ελλάδος (see above, pp. 110-111) of 1852. But as that Concordat with the Church of Constantinople has never been honestly carried into execution, we need not here discuss its value. The Συνόδικος Τόμος recognised the independence (αὐτοκεφαλεία) of the Hellenic Church, but on the condition

Convocation of an Œcumenical Council.

Here we are met by an objection. Above the Tsar and the King of Greece, we are told, there exists an authority admitted by both of them as being superior to them, and as having the power of enacting even disciplinary canons binding them: there exists still above them an *Œcumenical Council*, whilst the Pope is asserted to be higher than that Council itself. A few words will show the real weight of such an objection. First of all, who in the Oriental Orthodox Church has the power of assembling an Œcumenical Council? The way in which Orthodox divines speak of the convocation of the seven General Councils admitted by their Church, clearly and plainly shows that this power is not acknowledged as appertaining to any particular bishop, of whatever rank. Still in consequence of having lost the *dogma* that the ecclesiastical power is quite independent of the civil, the Oriental Orthodox Church shows herself quite unable to answer, in a satisfactory way, this elementary question. We have already, after the very words of Filaret's Catechism, likened the Oriental Orthodox Church to a confederation of separate *independent* States, which all agree in not acknowledging any authority entitled to enact laws to bind them all, except a Congress or Diet of the representatives of the different States. Yet the Oriental Orthodox Church finds herself in a still worse condition than such a confederation. In fact, in the statutes of any such political confederation of independent States, the question is constantly foreseen

---

that the Synod of Athens ' is to govern her *according to the divine and sacred canons, freely and without hindrance from any secular interference*' . . . . γνωρίζουσα Σύνοδον . . . . διοικοῦσαν τὰ τῆς ἐκκλησίας κατὰ τοὺς θείους καὶ ἱεροὺς κανόνας ἐλευθέρως καὶ ἀκωλύτως ἀπὸ πάσης κοσμικῆς ἐπεμβάσεως. Οὕτω δὴ καὶ ἐπὶ τούτοις καθισταμένην διὰ τοῦ παρόντος Συνοδικοῦ Τόμου τὴν ἱερὰν ἐν 'Ελλάδι Σύνοδον, ἐπιγινώσκομεν αὐτὴν, etc. ('Ο Συνοδικὸς Τόμος, in the Greek newspaper the ''Ἀθηρᾶ,' No. 1707, August 14, 1850, p. 2. These words, in the mouth of a Patriarch of Constantinople, are well worthy of consideration.

and resolved, to whom it appertains *authoritatively* to assemble the said Congress or Diet; whilst in the 'Catechisms' and 'Expositions of Faith' of the Oriental Orthodox Church the question is still pending, and will, very likely, remain pending for ever. A recent most striking instance of the correctness of our statement is afforded by the convocation, on the part of the Œcumenical Patriarch of Constantinople, of an Œcumenical Council of the Oriental Orthodox Church for settling the question concerning the independence of the Bulgarian Church. The Holy Synod of St. Petersburg (*instead of the Russian bishops*) answered that, though it regretted the Sultan's interference in this affair, *it deemed* the assembling of an Œcumenical Council to be *unnecessary*. A good encouraging example, which any one of the separate independent Churches composing the Oriental Orthodox Church will not, at the proper opportunity, fail to imitate!

Moreover, if we listen to some expressions of the Greek-Russian liturgy, of the Orthodox Divines, and, above all, of the Encyclical Letter of the Oriental Patriarchs (May 6, 1848) in answer to that of Pius IX. (Jan. 6, 1848), and addressed to *all the Orthodox*, the number of the Œcumenical Councils is fixed for ever. The seven Œcumenical Councils, admitted by the Oriental Orthodox Church, are likened to the seven pillars supporting the House of Wisdom (Prov. ix. 1), and to the seven seals of the Holy Ghost (Apoc. v. 1).[1] Now, as neither the number of the said pillars, nor that of the seven seals

---

[1] 'Cette piété filiale envers notre mère commune (l'Église) est la source de notre obéissance à la vérité et à la doctrine marquée des *sept sceaux de l'Esprit* (*Apoc.* v. 1), c'est-à-dire, les sept Conciles œcuméniques. . . . Les vénérables Conciles œcuméniques, *ces sept colonnes de la maison de la Sagesse*, ont pris naissance dans notre foi et dans nos pays.'—*Lettre encycl. de S.S. Pie IX, et Encyclique responsive des Patriarches et des Synodes de l'Église d'Orient* (Paris, 1850), *Enc. resp.* § 16, p. 56, and § 21, p. 63.

See also Macaire, *Théol. dogm. orthod.*, Introd. pp. 17, 18, *note*.

sealing the mystical book spoken of in the Revelation of St. John, is likely to be increased, it would appear that no other Œcumenical Council of the Oriental Orthodox Church is ever to be held in future.—Yet what, above all, shows plainly how little the Tsar of Russia and the King of Greece have to fear from any Œcumenical Council, is the circumstance that no Council whatever can be held without their consent. Let us suppose that not only the Œcumenical Patriarch of Constantinople, but also those of Antioch, Alexandria, and Jerusalem urge with great earnestness the convocation of an Œcumenical Council; let us even suppose that the bishops of the Kingdom of Greece and of the Russian Empire are willing to attend it, the *veto* of the Sovereign who, listening to his conscience, deems it to be of no use, but rather pernicious to the Church, will still be sufficient to prevent their pious desire from being carried out. The Oriental Patriarchs have no jurisdiction whatever either in Russia or in Greece, and their wishes or will *in disciplinary matters* have no claim whatever to be listened to when in collision with the will of the Sovereigns of the two countries.

Finally, let us remark again that the disciplinary canons are by their own nature liable to be suppressed or modified according to circumstances of time and place, and whenever such changes or suppressions are required for the welfare of the Church, the supreme authority is not only entitled, but even *bound*, to effect them. The application which Orthodox Sovereigns have in time past made and which they still make of this principle in dealing with the existing canons of THE SEVEN ŒCUMENICAL COUNCILS admitted by them,[1] is the surest pledge of the

---

[1] With how great earnestness, for example, do the canons of the Œcumenical Councils, confirming the prescription of the thirty-seventh canon of the Apostles, urge the convocation of Provincial Councils twice, or, at least,

similar line of conduct they would follow with regard to any future *disciplinary* canons of future Œcumenical Councils of the Oriental Orthodox Church.

We must now pass to the Oriental Orthodox Church of the Turkish Empire. Here, at least, we are happy to say that the heads of the Church of whom we are going to speak, are not kings or queens; they are *bishops*. Though, being aware of the influence exercised by the Sultan in the affairs of the Greek Orthodox Church of his empire, and of the right conferred by *her* upon him of settling disputes which the authority of the Patriarch of Constantinople is not able to end,[1] we prefer not to lay much stress upon this point, and will rather suppose that the Sultan does not even exist.

The four Patriarchates of Constantinople, Alexandria, Antioch, and Jerusalem constitute four separate and *independent* Churches, each of them under the authority of his own patriarch.[2] We dare not say that to the four Oriental Patriarchs may be fairly applied whatever we have just stated concerning the *extent* of the jurisdiction of the Tsar and of the King of Greece in ecclesiastical matters. First of all, the Patriarch of Constantinople being

once a year! Are those canons listened to? See the first Œcum. Council (of Nicæa) can. 5; second (of Constant.) can. 2; fourth (of Chalcedon) can. 19; sixth (of Constant. *in Trullo*) can. 8.

[1] See Chap. I. pp. 112, 113.

[2] *Q.* What hierarchical authority is there which can extend its sphere of action over the whole Catholic Church?

A. An Œcumenical Council.

Q. Under what hierarchical authority are the chief divisions of the Catholic Church?

A. Under the most holy Patriarchs, and the most holy Synod.

Catech. of Mgr. Filaret, part i. 'On the Ninth Article.' Blackmore, p. 83.

See also the question quoted above, p. 123, *note*.—*Q.* How does it agree with the unity of the Church that there are many separate and *independent* Churches, as those of Jerusalem, etc.?

at the same time the civil chief of all the Greek subjects of the Sultan, his influence must necessarily be felt, in ecclesiastical matters also, by the three Patriarchs of Alexandria, Antioch, and Jerusalem. It would be little advisable for them to do anything in open contradiction to the ecclesiastical canons, as this would assuredly give the Patriarch of Constantinople a pretext for urging on the Government to depose them, as perturbators of the *national* religion.[1] Moreover, even as to the Patriarch of Constantinople himself, there are many restraints laid upon him also by the very circumstance of his being at once the *Patriarch of the new Rome*, and the representative to the Government of a special nationality distinguished only by the religious belief of those who belong to it.[2] Finally, considering the concurrence of the patriarchal Synods (composed of bishops) in the administration of the general affairs of the patriarchate, and, to some extent, even the rights conferred, in certain cases, upon simple bishops, we freely grant that we are not entitled to call them Popes, or supreme independent heads, each in his own patriarchate.

[1] See M*** d'Ohsson, *Tableau général de l'empire ottoman* (Paris, 1824). '*Berat, ou Diplome d'investiture d'un patriarche grec de Constantinople*,' tom. v. p. 120.

[2] It is well known that when the Turks took possession of Constantinople in 1453, the conquered nation was offered the alternative of conversion to Islamism with the rights of citizenship and all the privileges of '*true believers*,' or of retaining *their own religion and civil rights* upon condition of becoming tributary, and therefore inferior to their conquerors in political and social position. The various populations then composing the Byzantine Empire formed in consequence different separate communities; and the same diversities of language, of manners, and of religion still continue to distinguish them from the people with whom they are incorporated. The *Greeks*, the *Armenians* (divided into *United Armenians* and independent *Armenians*), and the *Jews*, compose four communities, designated by the name of *Milleti erbaa*, and represented to the Government by their religious chiefs.

See Ubicini, *Letters on Turkey*, transl. by Lady Easthope (London, 1856); Madden, *The Turkish Empire* (London, 1862); etc.

Yet, treating them as constituting together a sort of Oligarchy, and even admitting that they may naturally be repelled by what seems to them the prodigious development of the Roman papacy, we must still remark that they cannot avoid the necessity of choosing between one development and another; if they will not have the Pope of Rome, they must have, or be liable at any time to have, the lay-popes of Russia and of Greece, and even among themselves they have, in their own way, gone even further than Rome has ever gone *in setting the patriarchate above the episcopate.* The Popes have never been reconsecrated when bishops before their election to the papacy, but when a fifth patriarchal chair was erected at Moscow, Jeremiah, Patriarch of Constantinople (1589), and after him also Theophane, Patriarch of Jerusalem (1619), themselves, with their own hands, in spite of the 68th Canon of the Apostles, reconsecrated a second time those who were raised to it.[1] *'There needed a double grace to be Patriarch,'* remark, on that point, after the documents of the time, A. N. Mouravieff and Mgr. Filaret, Archbishop of Tchernigoff,[2] both forgetting whilst

---

[1] See Mouravieff, Ист. Росс. Церк. Спб. 1840, pp. 175, 235, 409, and its English translation, by the Rev. R. W. Blackmore (Oxford, 1842), pp. 129, 176, 308.—Mouravieff, Сношенія Россіи съ Востокомъ по дѣламъ церковнымъ. Спб. 1858, tom. i. pp. 210, 342.—Zampelios (Spiridion), Καθίδρυσις Πατριαρχείου ἐν 'Ρωσσία (Athens, 1859), p. 19.— Кормчая Книга (ed. 1816), p. 18 *verso et seq. etc.*
Of the ten Patriarchs of Moscow (1589–1700), four were *twice* consecrated bishops; the first Patriarch, Job, even *three times.* The fact is stated by the Patriarch Nikon himself (1653–1667), in his *Replies of the humble Nikon, by the mercy of God Patriarch, against the Questions of the Boyar Simeon Streshneff, and the Answers of the Metropolitan of Gaza, Paisius Ligaridis,* pp. 14, 15. This precious manuscript was translated from the Russian, and lately published (London: Trübner & Co.) by W. Palmer, M.A., of Magdalen College (Oxford), author of *Dissertations on Subjects relating to the 'Orthodox' or 'Eastern' Catholic Communion* (London, 1853).

[2] Сугубая благодать нужна была высшему пастырю

writing, that, according to the doctrine of their own Church, the sacrament of order, like the sacrament of baptism, cannot be conferred a second time.[1]

Let us also add that their Oligarchy, taken as a whole, constitutes a true separate and supreme government, far less dependent, if possible, on the Churches of Russia and Greece than these have shown themselves to be with regard to the four patriarchates. Again, we need hardly remark, when we think of what has actually occurred, that the Greek Church of the Turkish Empire is by no means secured at any moment from seeing one or other of her Patriarchs transgress the limits of his power, and either by getting rid of that limited authority over him, which in certain cases is allowed to his fellow-patriarchs, or by dealing with them as their chief, become a real Pope. The language of the Patriarch of Constantinople (and naturally, as he is the first) often resembles that of the Pope of Rome. For instance, he professes to have

Церкви. Mouravieff, p. 175 (Blackmore p. 129).—Filaret, Ист. русс. церкви, пер. iv. p. 9

[1] Ἐντίθησι δὲ τὸ βάπτισμα καὶ χαρακτῆρα ἀνεξάλειπτον, ὥσπερ καὶ ἡ ἱερωσύνη. Καθὼς γὰρ ἀδύνατον, τὸν αὐτὸν δὶς ἱερωσύνης τυχεῖν τῆς αὐτῆς· οὕτως ἀδύνατον ἀναβαπτισθῆναι, etc.—Kimmel, *Monum. fid. Eccl. Orient.— Dositheï Confessio* (or *Letter of the Patriarchs of the East on the Orthodox Faith*) decr. xvi. p. 456. See also Macaire, *Théologie dogmatique orthodoxe*, tom. ii. part v. § 240: 'Côté visible du sacrement de l'ordre, ses effets invisibles et sa *non-répétition*,' p. 590.

It is worthy of remark that both Russian and Greek writers take care to prevent us from even supposing that the reconsecration to which we allude was not a real consecration. 'The whole order for the consecration of a bishop,' they say, ' was repeated over the elected Patriarch' (Mouravieff, *ll. cit.*)—' without any change' (ἄνευ οὐδεμιᾶς καινοτομίας), adds Zampelios (Spiridion) *loc. cit.*

After this, one might perhaps say, in order to excuse the Oriental Orthodox Church, that the reconsecrations of the Patriarchs of Moscow have all preceded the Synod of Jerusalem of 1672, in which the 'Letter of the Patriarchs of the East on the Orthodox faith' was drawn up. But has not, then, the Oriental Orthodox Church *created a new dogma* in 1672?

been entrusted by God with 'the care of all the Churches.'[1] The extent of this care, and the way of practically showing solicitude for the welfare of all the Churches, is a matter only of personal appreciation and of circumstance.

We go on now to the conclusion which follows from what we have been saying.

In Chapter I. we have stated that nowhere in the Oriental Orthodox Church of Russia, Greece, and the Turkish Empire do the bishops constitute the supreme authority in the Church. Here we state, after what we have hitherto proved, that the Oriental Orthodox Church is really divided into several separate and independent Churches, and even Papacies. But if so, the real difference between the Oriental Orthodox and the Catholic Churches as to the *government*, properly so called, of the Church, is practically reduced, as we have undertaken to prove, to a difference in the number of her *independent visible heads, vicars of Christ*—in other words, of her *Popes*. Whilst the Catholic Church admits only *one* of them, the Oriental Orthodox Church assumes that they may be *several*; whilst the Catholic Church is still constant in acknowledging the supreme power of JURISDICTION to be in the Bishop of Rome, the Oriental Orthodox Church confers it *according to circumstances*—at one time on single bishops—at another time on patriarchs —at a third on kings and queens; finally, whilst the Catholic Church is constituted into a *single Papacy*, the Oriental Orthodox Church is constituted into *a number of separate and independent Papacies.*

[1] . . . 'Ἡμεῖς οἱ ἐλέῳ Θεοῦ τὴν ἀποστολικὴν μέριμναν ΠΑΣΩΝ τῶν ἐκκλησιῶν ἀναδεδεγμένοι, καὶ τῆς περὶ αὐτὰς οἰκονομίας ἄνωθεν ἐμπεπιστευμένοι τὴν δ.αχείρησιν . . . . Letter of the Patriarch of Constantinople, Anthimos, concerning the independence of the Hellenic Church, see 'Ο Συνοδικὸς Τόμος ἢ περὶ ἀληθείας (Athens, 1852), p. 606. Of this book we shall have more to say further on.

Which, now, of the two Churches, we are entitled to ask our readers, more truly answers to the images by which Jesus Christ represented His Church—to a house governed by a single father of a family, to a flock ruled by a single pastor, to a kingdom ruled by a single king? And can it be assumed that the doctrine asserted in the Orthodox Catechisms concerning the external unity of the Church comes from Jesus Christ? Rather is it not from the time in which this doctrine began to prevail, i.e. from Photius' patriarchate, that the dogma of *the Church's independence of the State, each being supreme in its own proper sphere*,[1] begins to disappear in the teaching of the Oriental Orthodox Church? And at the present day, with the exception of what *directly* concerns faith, has not the power of jurisdiction over the Church even been asserted to appertain to kings? What dreadful progress towards complete abdication of all the rights which Jesus Christ has conferred upon His Church! To that progress, and to the remarkable coincidence of the great Oriental schism with the *enslavement* of the Oriental Orthodox Church, we call the attention of our readers, as to a *first fruit* borne by the denial of the Church's external unity of government as a *mark* of the true Church of Jesus Christ. We purposely say '*a fruit*,' since if it be once admitted that the Church, though externally broken up into many particular Churches dependent only on an Œcumenical Council, still remains the *one* Church of Jesus Christ, there is no more any reason why every Christian king or queen should not transform the Church of his or her State into a national one, and give it such laws as, *the*

---

[1] See above, p. 75, *note*, and Papp-Szilágyi (Jos.) Enchiridion juris Ecclesiæ Orientalis Catholicæ.—M. Varadin, 1862. 8vo. pars 1, § 180. '*Limites utriusque sacræ et civilis potestatis*,' p. 288.

ABSTRACT *articles of faith still being preserved*, may better suit the exigencies of their political system. Can, now, a doctrine which, in its logical and necessary deductions, as well as by an experience of a thousand years, has proved so highly pernicious to the Church, be safely ascribed to its founder, Jesus Christ?

But there is also another *fruit* of the same doctrine which, just as little as the enslavement of the Church, can be produced by a doctrine coming from Jesus Christ! This is '*revolution.*' Let us examine it.

CHAPTER III.

THE ORIENTAL ORTHODOX CHURCH IS LIABLE TO ANY REVOLUTION, JUST AS CIVIL SOCIETIES ARE.

IN ORDER to prevent misunderstandings and misconceptions, we must state beforehand in what sense we use here the word *revolution*. By *revolution* we mean every violent change in the form of government of a society, whatever its causes and consequences may be—whether arising from within or from without. Just as, when speaking of the civil and political history of peoples, one generally designates as *revolutions* the violent changes of government encountered by them during their existence, so we also designate as revolutions any analogous transformations in the government of the Oriental Orthodox Church. Often, in civil and political history, *revolutions* are followed by *enslavement*; this is equally the case with the Oriental Orthodox Church. Yet in this chapter we take into consideration the fact alone of *revolution*, as our purpose here is to show that '*there is no stability whatever in the government of the Oriental Orthodox Church.*'

In order now to appreciate to its full extent the danger of revolutions, to which the want of external unity of government constantly exposes the Oriental Orthodox Church, we need only look at what is passing every day in political society, and examine to what political revolutions are owing. When does a revolution occur? When people are, or fancy they are, ill governed, and when they see, or fancy they see, their ruler overstepping the limits of *his* rights and encroaching upon *theirs*. Revolutions are always and solely the result either of real or of fancied incapacity and abuses of power in rulers; and insurgents never fail to justify themselves by alleging the bad administration of the Sovereign, and by thus representing their act as a legitimate, *though violent*, attempt to rectify his abuses and to regain their rights.

How far, now, may it be expected that religion should interfere and prevent a revolution? As far as religion makes both people and kings more attentive to the fulfilment of their duties than jealous of the preservation of their rights, thus causing *virtue* to interfere on both sides in the determination of their reciprocal rights and duties. Without *virtue* the most clever and elaborate political constitutions will constantly prove insufficient to prevent a single revolution, as no political constitution whatever is able to prevent rights and duties from coming into occasional conflict. Yet religion itself is not likely to obviate all revolutions. A heavy and terrible responsibility rests upon those who create a revolution, and the more so as, even admitting the legitimacy of their grievances, they are bound to weigh before God the relative value of their forfeited rights and the consequences, though but the probable ones, of the revolution they are meditating. Besides, many virtues may strictly forbid what justice alone might perhaps seem to consent to; in a word, no grave theologian would presume to give a rash and perfunctory decision even as to the theoretical legitimacy of a revolution. All this is true, but still there are circumstances which lead people to be deceived as to the lawfulness of a revolution. Moreover, since the appreciation of such circumstances depends on men (and these have long ago chosen to rid themselves of the arbitration of that supreme authority which, in former times, was regarded as invested with the power of settling disputes between peoples and their Sovereigns), men, even without taking into account their passions, are still liable to mistake the extent of the violation of their rights, and to form a wrong judgment, resulting in a revolution.

Now, what happens in politics cannot fail to happen also in religion, *on the assumption that Jesus Christ himself did not determine who ought to be entrusted with the supreme authority in the Church.* In religion also, as in politics, rights and duties may come into conflict; justice too may seem to consent to a violent recovery of one's rights; here also, in a word, revolutions may threaten; and the more so as religious prejudices and passions have always proved to be the worst and most indomitable. Yet, if this may be generally asserted of every religious society the chief of which is not acknowledged as having been appointed by God Himself—this is especially true with regard to the Oriental Orthodox Church. The reason lies in the fact that those very conflicts between rights and duties which may result in revolutions are *constantly* impending over the Oriental Orthodox Church on *two sides* at the same time. Not only has she to fear *the rebellion of her sons*, but she must also constantly be on her guard lest her government be *overthrown or absorbed by the secular power.* Her condition, on that account, is like that of a State threatened at the same time by dissensions from within and by a conquest from without; yet, being constantly exposed to both those dangers, she is hardly more secured against them than civil societies are. Instances of the twofold *revolutions* to which we allude, and of the impotency of the Oriental Church to prevent them, are plentifully afforded by her own history. Let us notice two—the first taken from Russia, the second from Greece.

The so-called reformation of Peter the Great was, in fact, nothing else than a *revolution originating in con-*

tinual *conflicts between the civil and ecclesiastical powers.*
Peter the Great himself took care to make this known
to the world: let us quote his words: ' This is an argument of great weight and moment (*in favour of the establishment of the Synod*), that a nation has no suspicion
or apprehension of tumults and sedition from a conciliary
(*sobornoe*) government, which yet it has too just cause
to fear from a single spiritual ruler (*the Patriarch of
Moscow*). For the ignorant vulgar people do not consider
how far the spiritual power is removed from (*raznstvuiet*)
the regal, but, in admiration of the splendour and dignity
of a high-priest, consider such a ruler as a second
sovereign, equal in power to the king himself, or above
him, and imagine the spiritual order to be another and
better sovereignty: and thus the vulgar do usually think
with themselves; and if seditious disputes of some aspiring
ecclesiastics are set on foot, they take fire like dry stubble;
their silly minds are so biass'd with these conceits, that
in every affair they regard not so much the prince as the
high-priest; and on the report of a quarrel between
them, they blindly and distractedly adhere to, and take
part with the spiritual rather than with their civil ruler;
and impudently gather together, and raise a tumult in his
defence, and—poor, miserable men—flatter themselves
that they come together for God's service, and do not
pollute their hands, but sanctify them, when they proceed
even to the shedding of blood.

' They are no simple, but a crafty part of a kingdom,
that greatly rejoice in this disposition of the people; and
being disaffected to their sovereign, and observing a misunderstanding between him and the priests, embrace this
opportunity as most favourable to the execution of their
malice, and, under a pretence of zeal for the Church,
make no scruple to lift up their hands against the Lord's
anointed (*the Tsar, not the Patriarch*). The commonalty

are excited to this impiety as to a work of God, especially when the chief pastor is puff'd up with a great opinion of himself and will not rest quiet; 'tis miserable to reflect what calamities will hence ensue. And we are not only capable of making this conjecture in our thoughts, which God inspires us with, but it has very often been demonstrated in fact in many countries, and is particularly manifested in the history of Constantinople down from the reign of Justinian to this time. And the Pope effected so great things by this means, he did not only overthrow the Roman Empire, and grasp a great part of it himself, but more than once has almost shaken the power of other dominions, and threatened them with the last destruction; to say nothing of the like contentions that have been amongst us. In a conciliary spiritual administration there is no place for such a mischief; to wit, on the president himself, the great and extravagant applauses of the people are not therein bestowed; nothing more than the titles of eminence and respect: there are no high opinions of him, nor can flatterers exalt him with immoderate commendations, for what is well done in such an administration cannot be ascribed to the president alone. The appellation itself of president is not an arrogant one, for it denotes nothing more than one that presides (*predsedatel*, one that sits before, or in presence of others); for which reason he cannot think highly of himself, nor others think so of him. And when the nation is farther convinced that this synodical power is established by a law of the monarch, with the advice of his Senate, they will entirely acquiesce under it, and lay aside all hopes of having their seditions supported by the assistance of the spiritual order.'[1]

With the '*great things effected by the Popes,*' to which

---

[1] *Spir. Reg.* part i. § 7; Полн. Собр. Зак. tom. vi.; Дух. Регл. p. 317; *Consett*, pp. 18-21.

Peter refers, as well as with the calm procured to the Russian Church by the establishment of the Synod, and *which might perhaps be likened to the calm succeeding agony, and preceding death,* we are not at present concerned. So we now only point out the fact that the overthrow of the Patriarchate of Moscow and the consequent revolution effected by Peter in the Russian Orthodox Church were due to conflicts between the civil and ecclesiastical powers. And with such conflicts the Oriental Orthodox Church is constantly threatened. In Russia and Greece, it is true, thanks to the complete absorption of the ecclesiastical into the civil power, she may enjoy, for some years, the calm spoken of by Peter; but wherever she has preserved a shadow of independence, she is permanently in danger of revolutions, like that accomplished by the Russian autocrat. And what can she oppose to them? Is she able to say, like the Catholic Church, *non possumus?* Can she allege, without condemning herself, the precept ' *Date Cæsari quæ sunt Cæsaris et quæ sunt Dei Deo*'—' Render to Cæsar the things that are Cæsar's, and to God the things that are God's ' (Matt. xxii. 21)? or is she entitled to make an appeal to the conscience of the faithful for the maintenance of rights she has so willingly, in other countries, conferred upon kings?

The second *revolution* to which we alluded, as an instance of such originated in the Oriental Orthodox Church *by the rebellion of her sons,* is afforded by what took place in Greece. At the time of the Hellenic war of independence, the Church of Greece was subject to the Patriarch of Constantinople. As soon as the Greeks had succeeded in delivering themselves from the dominion of the Sultan, they became equally desirous of getting rid of the spiritual jurisdiction of the Patriarch of Constantinople. They did not wait for his consent. In spite of his strong opposition, the independence of the Hellenic Church was unanimously proclaimed by the bishops assembled at Nauplia on the 15th (27th) July, 1833, *no less than seventeen years before the Patriarch of Constantinople had given his consent thereto* (29th June [11th July] 1850). In the meantime, the Hellenic Church behaved just as if the Patriarch of Constantinople did not exist. Moreover, when the celebrated Συνοδικὸς τόμος, or the solemn act by which the Patriarch Anthimos, at the request of the Greek Government helped by the good offices of Russia, finally consented to recognise the independence of the Hellenic Church, was made known, instead of calling forth praises and thanksgivings, it encountered from some the most bitter criticism. Though granting his confirmation to the independence of the Hellenic Church, the Patriarch pointed out the uncanonical nature of their existing organisation and what changes were necessary to justify his recognition (see above, p. 134, *note*). In all this, moreover, he spoke with full conviction of the *past* rights of the Patriarchs of Constantinople over the Hellenic Church, and used the language of a father towards children, granting them some concessions, but not all they required. No more was needed in order to arouse a storm of contumely against the ἱερὸς Συνοδικὸς τόμος (Holy Synodical Volume). A complete refutation of every word contained in the Τόμος was shortly after undertaken, and appeared in 1852, in Athens, under the title of ' The Synodical Volume, that is, On Truth.'[1] The very first words show what the refutation is. They read as follows:—'We have written against the Volume of the Synod of Constantinople. Yet, the Synodical Volume is termed *holy, most holy, admirable!* Oh, impiety!' etc.[2]

[1] 'Ο Συνοδικὸς τόμος, ἢ περὶ ἀληθείας—'Εν 'Αθήναις τύποις Νικολάου 'Αγγελίδου. 1852. 8vo.

[2] 'Εγράψαμεν κατὰ τοῦ τόμου τῆς συνόδου τῆς ἐν Κωνσταντινουπόλει

But what, in this refutation, deserves more attention are the *principles* laid down in it. We refer our readers to the chapters 'On the Unity of the Church' (Περὶ ἑνότητος ἐκκλησιαστικῆς, p. 161) and 'On the Jurisdiction of the Archbishop of Constantinople over the Hellenic Church' (Περὶ δικαιοδοσίας τοῦ Κωνσταντινουπόλεως ἀρχιεπισκόπου ἐπὶ τῆς Ἑλληνικῆς ἐκκλησίας, p. 219). The following is the *general* conclusion of the last quoted chapter: 'According to the dogma of faith and the order of the Catholic Orthodox Church, as it has been handed down from the beginning, *the Church of every State* is entitled to be governed by an ecclesiastical authority of her own, without being subject to the Archbishop and Œcumenical Patriarch of Constantinople, or to any other of the existing patriarchs.'[1] A little before the same author had spoken in the following terms of the jurisdiction of the Patriarchs of Constantinople over the Hellenic Church. We preserve the same difference of type of the original Greek: 'From all the particulars, in fine, which we have compendiously stated, what is the proper conclusion? That the Church of Greece was NEVER subject CANONICALLY to the Archbishop of Constantinople, NEVER was dependent upon him CANONICALLY; NEVER was the Archbishop of Constantinople the PROPER CANONICAL Archbishop of that country.'[2]

ἐκκλησίας. 'Αλλ' ὁ Συνοδικὸς τόμος λέγεται ἱερὸς, ἱερώτατος, προσκυνητός! *Ω ἀσέβεια! etc.

J. T. Pitzipios, in his 'L'Église orientale' (Rome, 1855), speaks of this same book, but giving it the title of 'Ἀντίτομος ἢ περὶ ἀληθείας, iv. p. 57, note. The author of it is the Archimandrite Pharmakides.

[1] Κατὰ τὸ δόγμα τῆς πίστεως καὶ τὴν ἀνέκαθεν παραδεδεγμένην τάξιν τῆς καθολικῆς ἐκκλησίας τῶν ὀρθοδόξον δύναται παντὸς Κράτους ἡ Ἐκκλησία νὰ κυβερνᾶται ὑπὸ ἰδίας ἐκκλησιαστικῆς ἀρχῆς χωρὶς νὰ ὑπόκειται εἰς τὸν τῆς Κωνσταντινουπόλεως ἀρχιεπίσκοπον καὶ οἰκουμενικὸν πατριάρχην, ἢ εἰς ἄλλον τινὰ τῶν ὑπαρχόντων πατριαρχῶν, p. 272.

[2] Ἐξ ὅσων λοιπὸν ἐν συντόμῳ εἴπομεν, τί συμπεραίνεται; Ὅτι ἡ Ἐκκλησία τῆς Ἑλλάδος ΟΥΔΕΠΟΤΕ ὑπετάχθη ΚΑΝΟΝΙΚΩΣ τῷ ἀρχιεπισκόπῳ τῆς

Finally, as a last illustration of its contents, we quote the following passage concerning Peter's revolution in the Russian Orthodox Church. It will at once, should any of our readers have called in question the exactness of our statements when speaking of the establishment of the Synod, bear evidence to whatever we may have affirmed on that subject.

'But the clearest demonstration of deceit, fraud, and artifice is seen in what follows. The autocrat of Russia, the glorious Peter the Great, when he had suppressed BY HIS OWN AUTHORITY the patriarchate (of Moscow) which had been constituted by the common sentence and agreement of the four Patriarchs of the Eastern Church, set up in its place the Most Holy Governing Synod. Having appointed it on the 25th of February [? January], 1721, by letter of the 30th of September he informed the Church of Constantinople of his proceedings. The autocrat's letter to this Church is nearly identical with that of the Hellenic Council of Ministers. Whence is it, then, that, the conduct of Russia and that of Greece being almost identical, the Church of Constantinople being still the same, the Holy Ghost the same, the declaratory letter the same, yet the conduct of the Church of Constantinople is in all respects different, and her reply quite another!!! Why? Because,' &c.¹

Κωνσταντινουπόλεως, ΟΤΔΕΠΟΤΕ ἐξήρτητο ἐξ αὐτοῦ ΚΑΝΟΝΙΚΩΣ, ΟΤΔΕΠΟΤΕ ἦτον οὗτος αὐτῆς ΟΙΚΕΙΟΣ ΚΑΝΟΝΙΚΩΣ ἀρχιεπίσκοπος, Ibid. p. 271.

¹ 'Ἀλλὰ τῆς ἀπάτης, τοῦ δόλου καὶ τῆς ἐπιβουλῆς τρανωτάτη ἀπόδειξις καὶ τοῦτο. Ὁ αὐτοκράτωρ τῆς 'Ρωσσίας, ὁ ἀοίδιμος Πέτρος ὁ Μέγας, καταργήσας ΑΥΤΕΞΟΥΣΙΩΣ τὴν κυνῇ γνώμῃ καὶ συγκαταθέσει τῶν τεσσάρων πατριαρχῶν τῆς 'Ανατολικῆς ἐκκλησίας καταστᾰθεῖσαν πατριαρχίαν, ἀνήγειρεν εἰς τὸν τόπον αὐτῆς τὴν ἁγιωτάτην διοικοῦσαν Σύνοδον. Καταστήσας δὲ αὐτὴν τὴν κε' Φεβρουαρίου τοῦ ψκα' ἔτους, τὴν λ' τοῦ Σεπτεμβρίου τοῦ αὐτοῦ ἔτους ἀνήγγειλε τὴν αὐτοῦ πρᾶξιν πρὸς τὴν ἐν Κωνσταντινουπόλει ἐκκλησίαν. Ἡ πρὸς αὐτὴν ἐπιστολὴ τοῦ αὐτοκράτορος εἶναι ἡ αὐτὴ σχεδὸν τῇ ἐπιστολῇ τοῦ ἑλληνικοῦ ὑπουργικοῦ συμβουλίου. Ὅθεν ἡ ῥωσσικὴ καὶ ἡ ἑλληνικὴ πρᾶξις σχεδὸν ἡ αὐτή, ἡ ἐν Κωνσταντινουπόλει ἐκκλησία ἡ αὐτή, τὸ ἅγιον Πνεῦμα τὸ

Such quotations need no comment. The seed of all revolutions, and the previous apology for them, are both to be found in this book. The jurisdiction of the Patriarch of Constantinople is there discussed in such a way as to incite other provinces, still under the same jurisdiction, to call it in question, and, after the example of Greece, to refuse to obey it. Moreover, the ecclesiastical jurisdiction being made a matter of historical discussion, no patriarch, no metropolitan, no bishop whatever is secured from some day witnessing a portion of his flock withdrawing from him, on account of some ancient document showing the primitive illegitimacy of some predecessor's jurisdiction. Finally, the principle so plainly and vigorously asserted in this book, that the Church of every State is entitled to make herself independent, necessarily puts the Oriental Orthodox Church on a level with civil societies, and causes ecclesiastical jurisdiction to be dependent on the success of arms and the cleverness of conspirators.

In fact people never stop at theory, as, should anyone doubt of it, recent events have too evidently proved. The good example thus set by Greece could not fail to find sincere appreciators and zealous imitators. Some years later Prince Couza[1] tried to do the same in Roumania, and, in more recent times, the Bulgarian Church, in alleging historical rights of independence on the Patriarchate of Constantinople did nothing else than reduce to practice the lessons she had been taught by the Archi-

αὐτὸ, ἡ ἐξαγγελτικὴ ἐπιστολὴ ἡ αὐτή, καὶ ἡ πρᾶξις τῆς ἐν Κωνσταντινουπόλει ἐκκλησίας πάντῃ διάφορος, καὶ ἡ ἀπάντησις ἄλλη καὶ ἄλλη !!! Διὰ τί; Διότι κ.τ.λ. Ὁ Συνοδικὸς Τόμος, pp. 596, 597.

[1] Striking observations of the Patriarch of Constantinople, the Synod of Russia, the Russian Government, and the Russian newspapers, upon Prince Couza's reforms in the Roumanian Church, are collected in the above-mentioned book of F. Gagarin, *Le Clergé russe*, p. 248 *et seq.*

mandrite Pharmakides in the second part of his book, Ὁ Συνοδικὸς Τόμος ἢ περὶ ἀληθείας, Chapter I. 'On Unity in the Church' (p. 161 *et seq.*), and Chapter V. 'On the Jurisdiction of the Archbishop of Constantinople over the Hellenic Church' (p. 219). Nay! the fate of the Oriental Orthodox Church will undoubtedly be in the future what it has been in the past: enslavement, with *revolutions*.

The chief independent authorities which actually share among themselves the government of the Oriental Orthodox Church are of *human* institution. Of human institution are the Tsar and the Synod of St. Petersburg; of human institution are the King of Greece and the Synod of Athens; of human institution is the present oligarchy formed by the four Oriental Patriarchates of Constantinople, Alexandria, Antioch, and Jerusalem. *Now, what men have made men can destroy.* Why should the canons of the Œcumenical Councils concerning the rights of the four Oriental Patriarchs deserve greater reverence and greater respect than many other canons *of the same Councils*, long since set aside? Or do the Synods of St. Petersburg and of Athens (not to speak of their sovereigns as 'heads of the Church') deserve more consideration than the rights of the former Patriarch of Moscow, and the Patriarch of Constantinople? The utility of such institutions for the welfare of the Church is only a matter of circumstance; let circumstances change, let political events suggest as more suitable to the condition of the Orthodox faithful other forms of ecclesiastical government, other partitions of the ecclesiastical jurisdiction, and the Oriental Orthodox Church will undoubtedly show herself no less pliable to circumstances in the future than she has done in the past. Why, again, if it be granted that Jesus Christ left to her the care of constituting herself in such a way as might best suit the interests of the faithful—why should she not be ready to pass through the most varying forms of government? In the patriarchates she is constituted into a monarchy, in the kingdom of Greece (not taking into account the King) she is governed by the half of her bishops, in Russia (to say nothing of the Tsar) the democratical element is already strongly represented, as of the seven members of the Synod two are not even bishops.

And might it not, moreover, become a duty for her to consult, in this respect, the tendencies of the different epochs, and to conform herself to them? Accordingly, why might she not, at the present day, form herself into a republic? *Is there a wider interval between a patriarchate and a Russian synod than between such a synod and a republic?* It would hardly be possible for her to act in future in greater opposition to her own doctrine than she has done in the past. Since WOMEN have ruled over her, since *laymen* have been entitled to exercise such an extensive and vexatious control over her bishops, why should the inferior clergy be excluded from sharing largely in the government of the Church? And should any one refuse to admit the possibility we are now pointing out, we need only refer him to what happened in the year 1833 in the kingdom of Greece, when Greece was about to carry into effect her plans of ecclesiastical independence. The subject was fairly discussed in the public papers, and many of them, says an historian, demanded 'that not only the bishops should be consulted, but also the archimandrites, and even representatives of the *hieromonachs and deacons.* Some papers, moreover, urged that the matter should *be discussed in a general national assembly.*'[1] Is there then

---

[1] 'Auch die öffentlichen Blätter endlich fingen an sich in diese Angelegenheiten zu mischen. Ein Blatt, der Χρόνος, das Blatt der sogenannten

a wide interval between a national assembly discussing matters of ecclesiastical jurisdiction, and the ecclesiastical republic we are alluding to?

But if an *Orthodox ecclesiastical republic* is not beyond the limits of possibility, what is equally within those limits is that the whole Orthodox Church should be constituted into a monarchy, with a *single visible head*, who, still as Vicar of Christ, should rule over her. Let only the cherished dream of Russian patriots be realised, and Russia have conquered all the countries of the Oriental Orthodox Creed, and another Tsar, like Peter, feel compelled *by his conscience* to apply also to the newly conquered portion of the Oriental Orthodox Church the 'Spiritual Regulation,' the Holy Synod, the Synod's Chief Procurator, and the 'Statute of the Ecclesiastical Consistories;'—would not, in this case, the whole Oriental Orthodox Church, *through the mere military successes of Russia*, be constituted into a monarchy? And would she not, moreover, then offer to the world the spectacle of a Church rejecting as a heresy the doctrine of a single *visible head of the Church*, and herself being at the same time ruled by such an one? And if such a lay Pope should ever become openly heretical or an active partisan of rationalism, or if he should be ever replaced by an irreligious oligarchy, or by an infidel republic, or even by an atheistic commune itself—which events are all

---

Capodistrianer, sprach ganz im Sinne des aus Russland und vom Berge Athos gekommenen Prälaten und Mönchs, gegen die zu ergreifenden Maassregeln. Die andere Blätter waren zwar dafür, nur wollten sie nicht allein die Berufung der Bischöfe, sondern auch noch der Archimandriten, *sogar die Berufung von Repräsentanten der Priester—Mönche und Diakone*. Sie verlangten ausserdem noch öffentliche Berathung. Manche sogar die *Berufung einer Nationalversammlung*, um über diesen hochwichtigen Gegenstand zu entscheiden.'—Maurer (von), *Das griechische Volk in öffentlicher kirchlicher und privat-rechtlicher Beziehung* (Heidelberg, 1835), Band ii. 157.

equally possible—at what a disadvantage would the Christian, not to say Orthodox minority, find itself, when it had to re-assert, against the *only existing* authority, the right of a Christian society to exist and to govern itself? What would be the ground to be taken, and by whom?

Let us, before concluding this chapter, point out another sad feature of the Oriental Orthodox Church. Not only is she unable to obviate such great revolutions as those to which we allude, but she is equally unable either finally to settle disputes of jurisdiction between bishops and bishops, or even effectually to prevent rebellions of the inferior clergy against their superiors. *Nowhere* in the Oriental Orthodox Church is there to be found an authority whose judgments in matters of *jurisdiction* necessarily bind, without *future* appeal, the conscience of the claimants. The limits of jurisdiction between bishops and bishops, and between bishops and their clergy, being a matter of ecclesiastical discipline and policy, contests must necessarily arise. Now unless some one be acknowledged as invested by God with the power of giving and withdrawing jurisdiction in such a way that what he gives or withdraws be incontestably (as to the *validity* of the sentence) given or withdrawn by God Himself, contests about ecclesiastical jurisdiction become of the same nature, and encounter the same fate, as any other contests for the possession of a real or asserted right. In other words, the only means by which the Oriental Orthodox Church is able to settle such disputes are mutual agreements or compromises—to be relied upon as far as human nature may warrant. Human nature cannot be bent by force; so long as persuasion is wanting, *virtue* or the force of *external circumstances* alone can prevent those who believe themselves unjustly robbed of a right, from exercising it. If a bishop of the Turkish empire, whose quarrel with a neighbour-bishop has been settled by a decree of the Patriarch, or a firman of the Sultan, is not convinced of the lawfulness of the judgment, who and what can bind his conscience to submit to the decision whenever he can safely attempt to regain his lost rights? And what we say of the quarrels between bishops and bishops may be equally applied to disputes about jurisdiction between bishops and their clergy. The removal of bishops *at pleasure* by the sovereigns, the occasional withdrawing of a portion of a bishop's flock from his jurisdiction because of mere political events which alone have changed the limits of his diocese, and above all the public and emphatic disregard shown, more than once, by rebellious subjects for the jurisdiction of their legitimate pastors, and subsequently sanctioned and made good by the pastors themselves—all this shows, without comment, what episcopal jurisdiction in the Oriental Orthodox Church is reduced to.

Nay, for this Church the alternative is *Catholicism or revolution*. Some years ago F. Gagarin, in a celebrated pamphlet, 'La Russie sera-t-elle catholique?'[1] stated that such is the dire dilemma in which Russia will soon find herself. Yet he spoke of a *political* revolution. We venture to put the same dilemma with reference to a *religious* revolution, and to extend it to the whole Oriental Orthodox Church—*Catholicism* or *revolution!* Of the last we have said enough; to Catholicism let us now turn our attention. Jesus Christ could not Himself have taught

---

[1] Paris, Douniol, 1856, in 8vo. One of the German translations of this work bears the following title: *Wird Russland's Kirche das Papstthum anerkennen!* with introduction and notes, by the celebrated Baron von Haxthausen (Münster, 1857). A Russian translation by F. J. Martinoff, S.J., appeared shortly afterwards in Paris, under this title:— О примиреніи Русской Церкви съ Римскою. (Paris, Frank. 1858.)

His Church a doctrine, concerning *her visible unity*, the mere application of which has had, and will constantly have, for its necessary result enslavement and *revolution*. Is it not in Catholicism that the true doctrine of Jesus Christ concerning the unity of the Church is to be found? Some words, as a conclusion of the whole work, will enable every one to answer this question for himself.

CHAPTER IV.

THE ROMAN PAPACY.

To Jesus Christ—to GOD—there cannot, without impiety, be ascribed a doctrine which, when reduced to practice, necessarily ends for the Church in enslavement and revolutions. The Church is more truly, and in a more perfect and specific sense, a society of God than other human societies are. Mankind comes from God, God being the common Creator and Father of all men; and in this sense it may well be said that all human societies are of God. But out of the immense number of created men, and from the numerous particular societies they form, God has gathered to Himself one society of privileged and more beloved sons. Master of His love, as He is master of His gifts, God has been pleased to bestow both more abundantly on a certain portion of mankind. This society of God's privileged and more beloved sons is the Church, and the blood of Jesus Christ was her price. A society conquered and bought at such a price well deserved that Jesus Christ, before leaving the earth, should not omit to prescribe for her such laws and institutions as should not only perpetuate her on earth, but enable her more perfectly to accomplish the mission given her, of leading men to eternal salvation. This Jesus Christ did not fail to do, and the Church was in fact provided by Him with rules and instructions for all her future necessities, and for whatever might concern, not only her existence, but also, so to speak, the details of her organisation. The sacraments, the ministry of the sacraments, and who are to be entrusted with the mission of teaching in the Church, all this has been pre-established and clearly prescribed by Jesus Christ.

Yet, according to the Oriental Orthodox Church, this very society of Jesus Christ exhibits to the world the strangest phenomenon ever presented by a society. The *Founder* of the Church, Jesus Christ, has omitted to tell her, with sufficient clearness, who is to be entrusted with the highest authority over her. Jesus Christ has taken care Himself to appoint the degrees of her hierarchy of order, the bishops, the priests, and even the deacons; but her hierarchy of jurisdiction, *i.e.* of *government*, He has left to the Church's care. GOD has founded *His* society with so little foresight as to omit, while giving it many other laws, just that one which was necessary to secure its existence, viz. the law of its government! In fact, since laymen and women have been empowered, in the Oriental Orthodox Church, to exercise jurisdiction over bishops, this plainly shows that she considers herself just as much mistress of the ecclesiastical jurisdiction *as if Jesus Christ had not given her any prescription whatever respecting it.*

Now, can we even suppose that Jesus Christ—GOD—has been that strange Founder? No, since the doctrine of the Oriental Orthodox Church necessarily results for her in enslavement and revolutions, let us rather acknowledge that Jesus Christ himself *must* have prescribed the form of Church government, and that the *Divine Founder* of the Church *must*, by the expression of His *divine will*, have prevented the perpetual contest which would else be produced by men's passions and self-will.

But how are we to know what is Jesus Christ's will concerning the government of the Church? To serious readers we need not remark that our enquiry would never obtain any result if we had previously to examine all the different forms of government in human societies, on the assumption that the best among them would necessarily be the very one given by Jesus Christ to his Church. If we mistake not, there is no other question that causes more irreconcileable differences of opinion among men than that as to the best form of government, and, very likely, many readers, taught by history and experience, have long since adopted on this matter the poet's opinion:—

> For forms of government let fools contest,
> Whate'er is best administer'd is best.[1]

Evidently we must follow some other way than that of a previous discussion of the best form of government. The Holy Scripture indeed and the tradition of the Church well answer the question, yet we do not purpose to speak of them. We beg rather to call the attention of the reader to a fact, patent, evident, inseparable from the very existence of the Oriental Orthodox Church, beginning from Jesus Christ, continuing down to the formation of the schism, and from that time again down to our day. It is this—*that never, since Jesus Christ, has a single bishop, either in Russia, or in the four Oriental Patriarchates, or in Greece, been bishop of his own diocese without being at the same time either subject to another bishop or himself superior to another.* The extent of such superiority of one bishop over another may indeed have varied according to epochs and countries; its exercise may have been confined to a few special cases; but still, never since Jesus Christ, has a bishop, either in Russia, or in the four Patriarchates, or in Greece, existed, who has not been related either by superiority or inferiority to another bishop. The appellations of archbishop, metropolitan, primate, patriarch, holy governing

[1] Alexander Pope, *Essay on Man*, 3rd epilogue, at the end.

synod, holy synod, have been granted to the bishop or bishops invested with the superiority we allude to; the titles also have varied, like the degrees of superiority attached to the titles; yet still, *never has the mere episcopal dignity been the supreme dignity in the Oriental Orthodox Church, never has a simple bishop constituted the highest degree in the hierarchy of the Oriental Orthodox Church.*

Now, unless it be admitted that a fact of such importance, which, being beyond any doubt, is admitted by all Orthodox and is inseparable from the very existence of the Oriental Orthodox Church, must be considered as a casualty, a mere result of circumstances, and by no means a hint of Providence, it evidently shows that there *must* be in the Church a *divinely instituted* authority superior to simple bishops. The doctrine that the bishop is the supreme and *independent* chief of his particular Church would be in such open opposition to the *practice* of the Oriental Orthodox Church, that we need only point out this opposition as the best argument by which the doctrine itself might be refuted.

Yet, where then is there to be found among the numberless authorities which, under the most various forms and names, have governed Oriental Orthodox bishops, or, at any rate, have possessed hierarchal pre-eminence over them, an authority to be relied upon as really appointed by Jesus Christ? History will answer the question. An authority appointed by Jesus Christ *must* necessarily have existed from the time of Jesus Christ down to our day. Let us first select the Œcumenical Patriarch of Constantinople. About three hundred years had already elapsed since the ascension of Our Lord, and the city of Constantine had only begun to be known to the world, when *its* Patriarch appeared. His first appearance in the world was therefore very late; he cannot have been appointed by Jesus Christ—the *Patriarchate* of Jerusalem is not of more ancient date than that of Constantinople; it cannot then have been instituted by Jesus Christ. Neither the Holy Governing Synod of St. Petersburg (1721) nor the Synod of Athens (1833) has been established by Jesus Christ, nor are they likely to advance the slightest pretension to such a claim. Two Patriarchates remain; they have not been directly instituted by Jesus Christ, but the history of their origin is inseparable from that of the holy Apostle to whom ALONE Jesus Christ said, '*Feed my lambs; feed my sheep.*' (John xxi. 15, 17.)

'St. Peter,' says Neale, 'founded the See of *Antioch*; and, on leaving it for Rome, ordained St. Euodius his first successor...'—'St. Peter,' says the same author, 'about the year 37, appears to have sent St. Mark into Egypt... St. Mark returned for a season to Jerusalem... From Palestine, St. Mark accompanied St. Peter to Rome. It was here that, under the direction of the Apostle, he wrote his Gospel... It was, apparently, towards the year 49, that St. Mark returned to Egypt; and there, till the time of his decease, he laboured with great success. And during this period the first church in *Alexandria* is said to have been built.'[1]

Now, as to the Patriarchate of Alexandria, it can advance no claim to a Divine institution except in virtue of St. Mark's having been sent there *by St. Peter*. St. Mark, it is well known, was not of the number of the Apostles upon whom St. Paul says that the Church has been built (Eph. ii. 20).[2] — With regard to the Patriarchate of Antioch, it has been directly founded by

[1] Neale (John Mason), *A History of the Holy Eastern Church*, General Introduction, i. chap. vi. p. 123, and vol. i. *The Patriarchate of Alexandria*, pp. 6, 7.

[2] It is worthy of remark that the liturgy of the Oriental Orthodox Church calls St. Peter not only *the foundation of the Church* (*by antonomasia*), (ἡ κρηπὶς τῆς Ἐκκλησίας, основаніе церкве), but also '*foundation of the Apostles*,' and, moreover, '*supreme foundation of the Apostles*' (ἡ κορυφαία

St. Peter. But, if the two Patriarchates of Antioch and Alexandria may lay some claim to a divine institution because of having been founded by Peter, that of Rome also may advance the same claim. 'There were,' says Neale again, 'many Christians both at Antioch and at Rome before St. Peter set foot in either place; *yet antiquity always considered him as the founder of the Churches in each.*' [1]

The simple fact of an *Apostolical origin*, however, may not be considered as decisive on the question with which we are now dealing. The conduct of the Church must also be attended to. The two Patriarchates of Antioch and Alexandria have not, even in the canons of the Œcumenical Councils, preserved their place of honour before that of Constantinople. Now, men cannot place what is *human* before what is of God, and the Church of Jesus Christ cannot even be supposed to have been guilty of that sin. Moreover, the Oriental Orthodox Church, let us remark again, has never so behaved with regard to those two Patriarchates as if there were any special will of Jesus Christ to interfere with her decisions concerning them. Finally, an authority confined to geographical limits cannot be the one we are looking for, since Jesus Christ could not, by the institution of such an authority, have been providing for a *catholic*, that is, for an *universal* Church.

Yes! an authority has *disappeared* from the Oriental Orthodox Church which was with her before the schism of Photius. It reappeared, and more than once, for a while, but in the eleventh century after Christ it finally disappeared. It is since its disappearance that enslavement

---

κρηπὶς τῶν 'Αποστόλων. верховное основаніе Апостоловъ. (See our publication: *La Primauté de saint Pierre prouvée par les titres que lui donne l'Église russe dans sa liturgie*, p. 10 (Paris, Palmé; London, Burns, Oates & Co. 1867).

[1] Neale, ibid. vol. i. p. 5.

and revolutions have formed the history of the Oriental Orthodox Church. This authority is the only one fit for a *catholic*, that is, an *universal* Church; this is the only one which leads us back to Jesus Christ; this is the only one which has been spoken of *in the Church* as coming from Him. Either *this* is from God, or God did not appoint any authority whatever for the government of that very Church which He has *conquered and bought with His blood.*

And this authority—the Pope—is the only one which is able to preserve the Church from enslavement and revolutions. More than eighteen centuries have elapsed since Jesus Christ, and the same answer of the Apostles to the chiefs of the Jews, 'If it be just in the sight of God to hear you rather than God, judge ye' (Acts iv. 19), is in the mouth of the successors of Peter. Thus far as to *enslavement:* moreover, *no one accuses the Catholic Church of being liable to be enslaved!*

Let us rather see if *revolutions* may threaten her. No revolution is possible in a Church whenever her chief is believed to have been personally appointed by God Himself; and this is the case with the Catholic Church. Her monarchical form of government, and the designation of the Bishop of Rome, as the *visible head of the Church,* constitute two articles of the Catholic faith; they cannot consequently be matter of dispute; all questions as to the Church's form of government and the choice of the persons to be entrusted with it are settled *for ever.* Discontent with the present government, desire for another, and, above all, the vulgar illusion of infirm minds that change should *necessarily* bring alleviation; these causes of revolution in civil societies and in the Oriental Orthodox Church, are not to be feared among Catholics. They accept the monarchical form of government of the Church and the designation of the Bishop of Rome as her head, as they accept any other points of their religious creed, even those less indulgent to human inclinations. Attempts to change the form of government of the Catholic Church, or to transfer the *supreme authority* from the Bishop of Rome to any other, are considered by Catholics just as sinful and senseless as attempts to change the form or matter of the sacraments; the very moment a man has made up his mind to overthrow the Papacy he has ceased to be a Catholic.

Further, in the Catholic Church alone can the jurisdiction of the bishops be *effectually* supported, the bishops themselves secured from becoming mere '*primi inter pares*' among their clergy, and quarrels of jurisdiction between bishops, or between bishops and their clergy settled for ever. And why so? Because in the Catholic Church alone exists an authority which not only is entitled to exercise full jurisdiction over the universal Church, but, moreover, is itself the *master* and *the source* of ecclesiastical jurisdiction. A jurisdiction not consented to by the Pope is no more jurisdiction, but usurpation, and any acts of such a jurisdiction are *null* and *void* before God as well as before men. In every question concerning ecclesiastical jurisdiction Catholics possess a sure standard and an infallible criterion for distinguishing the real and efficacious jurisdiction from the pretended and vain; namely, the conformity of the claims with the prescriptions of the Holy See. The Pope may pronounce a sentence depriving a bishop of a right of which the latter was the lawful possessor; the Pope may well be deceived as to the unjust claims of the pretender, he is even liable to indulge his personal inclinations and, in his sentence, to favour the usurper, but still from the very moment his sentence is made known to the claimants, the only lawful jurisdiction for them is that consented to by the Pope. Should the limits of the former jurisdiction be altered, and should the usurper be allowed to retain what he has usurped, and the innocent commanded not to lay claim any more to his former possession, what the Pope has commanded is ratified *as to its validity* by God himself. Until the Pope consents to a new trial, the jurisdiction originally usurped has become, and remains, the only real and legitimate one.[1]

Let us, on this important subject, take an illustration from what happens in civil societies. The civil and military functionaries of a State are appointed and dismissed by its chief—let it be a king—only too often for motives other than justice and merit. No one, however, calls in question the *validity* of the royal acts by which civil and military functionaries are appointed or dismissed; and no soldier, for instance, would dare to refuse obedience to his newly appointed general on the assumption that his nomination was owing to intrigue. Likewise when, in a case of quarrel as to the extent of civil or military jurisdiction, the king's sentence interferes, no one would presume either to contest its validity or declare the claimants entitled to act in opposition to it, or, finally, attach any value to the exercise of a civil and military jurisdiction not consented to by the king. And this doctrine as to the validity of the royal acts conferring, withdrawing, restraining, enlarging, or in any way modifying civil and military jurisdiction, is acknowledged and *felt* by every man, not only as the only one which may consist with the State's peace and prosperity, but even as the

---

[1] 'Quod si Papa in hoc ipso judicio erret nihilominus valebit actus; si enim Christus dispensandi facultatem ei non tribuisset nisi sub hac conditione, quod non erraret existimando adesse justam causam, haud sapienter egisset. *Cum enim in hisce particularibus negotiis infallibilitatis prerogativam Romano Pontifici non dederit,* numquam certum omnino foret validam esse (Episcopi) depositionem aut inviti translationem, quam faciendam duxisset Papa ex causa necessitatis aut utilitatis.'—D. Bouix, *De Jure Episcoporum* (Paris, 1852), vol. i. p. 373.

only one which causes a State to be really a State and not rather a coalition of intelligent beings.

Why, now, should it not be so in the Church? Why should not that which is the necessary *element* for every society's peace and prosperity be granted—in a more perfect way and *by a divine right*—to the society of Jesus Christ, to the Church? Let it consequently be supposed—as the case is not an impossible one—that the rights of a bishop should be violated by a neighbouring bishop, and the usurper refuse to respect them. In that case a sentence from the Pope annulling his acts settles the contest immediately and *finally*. The usurper's acts being declared by the Pope null and void, no Catholic will adhere to them, and should the usurper act in opposition to the sentence of the Pope, he is exposed to see himself deserted by anyone who desires to remain in the communion of the Catholic Church. The Fathers of the Vatican Council have consequently expressed but an elementary truth and a patent *fact* when they declared in the third chapter of the dogmatical Constitution ' de Ecclesia' that, ' So far is the power of the Supreme Pontiff from being any prejudice to the *ordinary* and *immediate* power of episcopal jurisdiction, by which bishops, who have been set by the Holy Ghost to succeed and hold the place of the Apostles,[1] feed and govern, each his own flock, as true Pastors, that this their episcopal authority is really *asserted, strengthened*, and *protected* by the supreme and universal Pastor; in accordance with the words of St. Gregory the Great: "My honour is the honour of the whole Church. My honour is the firm strength of my brethren. I am truly honoured when the honour due to each and all is not withheld." '—*Lett.* book viii. 30, vol. ii. p. 919, Benedictine edit. (Paris, 1705).[2]

[1] Conc. Trid. ch. iv. sess. xxiii: ' De ecclesiastica hierarchia et ordinatione.'
[2] Constit. dogm.: '*Pastor æternus*,' Jul. 18, 1870, chap. iii.

After having listened to this declaration of the Fathers of the Vatican Council, we are better enabled to enter into the subject of the limits to the Pope's authority and jurisdiction as well as of any possible abuse of his power. 'The Pope,' so reads the same Constitution 'de Ecclesia,' '*has full and supreme power of jurisdiction over the universal Church.*' No Catholic, however, well acquainted with the doctrine of his Church, ever did, or ever will, understand these words in the sense that the Pope is entitled to do in the Church '*whatever he likes.*' The Pope's power of jurisdiction has its limits, and they were traced centuries ago, with singular happiness of expression, by a man whom the Catholic Church honours and proclaims both as a saint and as one of her Doctors; we mean St. Bernard. In his treatise 'De Consideratione,' dedicated to his former disciple, the Pope Eugenius III., the Saint thus addresses the Pope: 'You preside, yet that you may be *useful.*[1] . . . You preside. Is it in order that you may take advantage of your subjects? No, but in order that these may take advantage from you.[2] Do you perhaps fancy that it is lawful to you to mutilate the Church in its members, to confuse order, to disturb limits your fathers fixed? . . . You err if you deem your apostolic power, as it is the highest, so also that it is the only one appointed by God. If so you think, you differ from Him who said, "There is no power but of God."[3] . . . You are

---

[1] Præsis ut provideas, ut consulas, ut procures, ut serves. *Præsis ut prosis*: præsis ut fidelis servus et prudens, quem constituit dominum super familiam suam. Ad quid? Ut des illis escam in tempore (Matt. xxiv. 45); hoc est, ut dispenses, non imperes. Hoc fac et dominari ne affectes hominum homo, ut non dominetur tui omnis injustitia.—Lib. iii. c. i. No. 2. ed. Migne (Paris, 1854), *Patrologiæ; cursus completus*, tom. 182, p. 759.

[2] Præes, et singulariter. Ad quid? Eget tibi dico, de consideratione. Numquid ut de subditis crescas? Nequaquam, sed ut ipsi de te.—Lib. iii. c. iii. No. 13. p. 764.

[3] Tunc, denique tibi licitum censeas, suis ecclesiis mutilare membris, confundere ordinem, perturbare terminos, quos posuerunt patres tui? Si

"stewards to edification, not to destruction." " Stewards must be faithful." . . . Their utility is common not personal . . . else not faithful administration but cruel dissipation.'¹

Therefore, according to the doctrine of St. Bernard, the Pope is bound to consult in all his actions the welfare of the Church, and *on that condition* he is entitled to do whatever, before God, he deems the best. Does, perhaps, this power appear to be excessive?—But is not this equally the case with every sovereign, yet with this considerable difference that catholic faith, always inseparable from a Pope, lays far more restraints on the jurisdiction of a Pope *than the mere conscience of kings does on theirs?* It belongs to the very nature of all human laws, however useful and wise at first, to become, under particular circumstances, an obstacle to the welfare of society; and no society whatever can last, unless on condition of possessing an authority entitled to abrogate existing laws whenever they have ceased to be useful. Why, we ask therefore again, should that be denied to the Church, the society of God, which is granted to every society of men—which is, moreover, considered as necessary to the very existence of every human society?

Here, however, we meet the objection which leads us to speak of the Pope's abuse of power. Who can assure

---

justitiæ est jus cuique servare suum; auferre cuiquam sua, justo quomodo poterit convenire? Erras, si ut summam, ita et solam institutam a Deo vestram apostolicam potestatem existimas. Si hoc sentis ab eo dissentis qui ait: '*Non est potestas nisi a Deo.*'—Ibid. No. 17. p. 768.

¹ Non sum tam rudis ut ignorem positos vos dispensatores, sed in ædificationem, non in destructionem (2 Cor. xiii. 10). Denique quæritur inter dispensatores ut fidelis quis inveniatur (1 Cor. iv. 2). Ubi necessitas urget, excusabilis dispensatio est; ubi utilitas provocat, dispensatio laudabilis est. Utilitas, dico, communis, non propria. Nam cum nihil horum est, non plane fidelis dispensatio, sed crudelis dissipatio est.'—Ibid. No. 18, p. 769.

us, we are told, that the Popes would always conform themselves to the doctrine of St. Bernard? How did the Popes behave in many cases? The very language of the holy Doctor to the Pope Eugenius III. shows that there is no security in practice against their abuse of power. Is it to be presumed that an authority which, in many cases, has proved to be what St. Bernard says, '*in destructionem*,' has been really appointed by God? Is it not rather to be presumed that God has preferred dividing or sharing the government of the Church among many, in order to prevent the incalculable evils which may impend on the whole Church from a single Pope's malice or incapacity? Such is, in all its strength, the objection. Let us examine it.

First of all, should we take history as a standard for deciding whether monarchy is the form of government more convenient to the Church or not, the answer is evidently enough unfavourable to the assumption that many rulers diminish the evils of the Church. The increased number of rulers has, too often, for its principal effect that of increasing the amount of human passions preventing the right exercise of the supreme authority in society; at any rate the question, if seriously discussed, would lead us again to the poet's above-quoted opinion on forms of government. Should we, moreover, take a glance at the history of the Oriental Orthodox Church, her fortunes are not likely to create any strong persuasion of its being an advantage that the government of the Church should be shared among many, rather than concentrated in the hands of a single Pope.

Setting aside, however, the lessons of history, we prefer answering the objection in a better way. We fairly recognise and plainly admit that abuses of power on the side of the Popes are possible. Baronius' 'Annales Ecclesiastici' bear, should evidence be required, a sad yet undeniable evidence to that possibility. Besides, Saints have acknowledged and Popes have confessed them. Let us, before proceeding, quote an instance proving at once both assertions, as, at a time when the Popes' *doctrinal infallibility, when speaking ex cathedrâ,* is, even by learned men, so often confused with his *impeccability*, it is useful, if not even necessary, to point out, on every occasion, how distinct and separate the two things are.

Since St. Bernard, whose words we have quoted above, a long series of saints, both men and women, have acknowledged, like the holy Doctor, the possibility of a Pope's bad administration and abuse of power. Passing by many of them, we shall confine ourselves to quoting an Italian, we mean St. Leonard da Porto-Maurizio (*d.* 1751). We purposely choose St. Leonard, as he was proclaimed saint by the present Pope, Pius IX. It is Pius IX. who has recently canonised a man who, once preaching in *Rome*, on the subject of the universal judgment, coming to the separation the angels of God will then make of the elect from the reprobate, did not fail to make the angels begin their separation with the Popes. 'All the Popes,' said St. Leonard, with a liberty which might perhaps be termed rudeness, 'have been called "Holy Father;" all the Popes have been deservedly honoured with prostrations and the title of *Most Blessed;* but it is indeed a great weight to be answerable for the souls of the whole world; no wonder, therefore, if among many, some Popes, men as they are, will go to the bottom and be declared *most unhappy.* What shame for that poor Pope!...'[1]

We should be happy to find that the same freedom of

---

[1] 'Questa separazione non è invenzione capricciosa dei predicatori, è Vangelo. *Exibunt Angeli et separabunt.* Si porterà l'Angelo separatore al luogo dei Papi, *et separabit.* Tutti i Pontefici furono chiamati padri santi, tutti furono inchinati col titolo di beatissimi meritamente; ma quell'

language has been allowed to Russian orthodox preachers, in reference to the chief of their Church.¹

Having now stated that Saints have acknowledged and Popes confessed the possibility of abuse of power in a Pope, let us go on to state that *no one on earth has*

avere a render conto di tutte le anime d' un mondo è pure un gran peso; nè sarà maraviglia se fra tanti, alcuni come uomini anderanno al fondo, e saranno dichiarati sfortunatissimi. Che confusione di quel povero papa, eh!...'—*Raccolta delle opere sacro-morali del B. Leonardo da Porto-Maurizio.* Venezia, Gius. Antonelli, 1839. T. i. 'Lunedì dopo la prima domen. di Quaresima,' p. 106. 'Del Giudizio universale,' p. 114.

¹ Among the advices given to preachers in the *Spiritual Regulation*, there is one reminding them that they must not speak of the sins of those who govern. The Russian expression говорить о грѣхахъ властительскихъ cannot be translated otherwise. Полн. Собр. 1 ser. tom. vi. Дух. Регл. p. 338, No. 5.

After having quoted the words of St. Leonard da Porto-Maurizio, we cannot indeed refrain from quoting the following ones, dictated by a filial devotion to the Holy Father, as well as by the calm and conscientious conviction of a superior mind. The writer is not an Italian. 'I cannot shut my eyes to the fact,' says Fath. Newman, 'that the Sovereign Pontiffs have a gift, proper to themselves, of understanding what is good for the Church, and what Catholic interests require. And, in the next place, I find that this gift exercises itself in absolute independence of secular politics, and a detachment from every earthly and temporal advantage, and pursues its end by uncommon courses, and by unlikely instruments, and by methods of its own.'— *On Universities*, p. 222. And again: 'In his (the Pope's) administration of Christ's kingdom, in his religious acts, we must never oppose his will, or dispute his word, or criticise his policy, or shrink from his side.... We must never murmur at that absolute rule which the Sovereign Pontiff has over us, because it is given him by Christ, and in obeying him we are obeying Our Lord. We must never suffer ourselves to doubt that, in his government of the Church, he is guided by an intelligence more than human .... Even in secular matters it is ever safe to be on his side, dangerous to be on the side of his enemies. Our duty is, not indeed *to mix up Christ's Vicar with this or that party of men*, because he, in his high station, is above all parties; but to look at his acts, to follow him whither he goeth, and never to desert him, however he may be tried; but to defend him at all hazards, and against all comers, as a son would a father, and as a wife a husband, knowing that his cause is the cause of God.'—*The Pope and the Revolution*, in the *Sermons preached on various occasions*. London: Burns, Oates & Co., serm. xiv. p. 268.

more constantly and more effectually protested against them than the Popes themselves. And how so? In very many ways, but above all, by what the Popes constantly did in order to maintain, propagate, and increase the worship and love of Jesus Christ. What more eloquent protest against the asserted or supposed abuses of power of the Vicars of Christ than the thought and the sight of our crucified Redeemer? The Popes did not act like that strange reformer of Wittemberg, who, after having, in order to *purify* the religion of Jesus Christ, abolished confession, religious vows, *virginity*, fast-days, abstinence, necessity of good works—whatever, in a word, could mortify the corrupted passions of men—abolished also the images, among them the CRUCIFIX[1]—that visible and expressive compendium of the essence of the Gospel;—then proceeding still further, mutilated, so to speak, Jesus Christ himself, by almost exclusively representing him as a Redeemer, too little as a *Model*. Jesus Christ is both, and the Popes have constantly kept him *entire*, and constantly presented him *entire* to the adoration of the world.

This consideration alone (and we pass over many others) might well disarm the passionate and bitter zeal of many adversaries of the Popes. Even to an enemy, if he acknowledges and confesses the injustice of his behaviour, we feel ashamed to say, 'You were wrong.' Why should not a similar feeling prevail in our hearts with regard to the Popes; since, even when experiencing the misery and infirmity of our nature, they never cease to say to the world, 'Your model is Jesus Christ,—on the cross, naked, bleeding, His head crowned with thorns!'

---

[1] St. Paul found some utility in the *representation*, by words at least, of the crucifix, when he said, 'O senseless Galatians, who hath bewitched you, that you should not obey the truth, *before whose eyes Jesus Christ hath been set forth* (προεγράφη), *crucified among you?* (GALAT. iii. 1.)

Nay, in such circumstances, we need not be afraid of any Pope's abuses of power. They are permitted—they will remain in history as an undeniable argument that *it is not to men* the Catholic Church is indebted for her existence and triumphs, but to Jesus Christ himself. No Pope, should he even aim at it, would ever be able to cause any real harm to her. And why? Because the Church is the Society of God, and nothing—no man and no angel—can prevail against God. What Jesus Christ was able to say shortly before His passion: 'Father, those that thou gavest me I have kept' (John xvii. 12) Jesus Christ will, beyond any doubt, be able to say again at the end of the world, when *His* Church, the *price* of *His* blood, shall have accomplished the same mission He accomplished during His earthly life. What St. Augustine says with regard to the law of Providence in the general government of the world, that 'God has preferred to draw good out of evil, rather than to prevent evil,' is specially true with regard to the law of Providence in the government of the Church. Nay, God is far more interested than men are, or ever can be, in the welfare of *His* Church; he has far more at heart than men have, or ever can have, the salvation of souls. Hence, what is good for the present existence of the Church is *what happens to-day*; what is good for her existence to-morrow is *what will happen to-morrow*; what is good for the whole existence of the Church is *what happens, has happened, and will happen* to her, down to the end of the world.

And this is as far from *fatalism* as an ignoble apathy and a selfish indifference for whatever may happen in the world, is far from a filial confidence in the omnipotence and goodness of that FATHER who is in Heaven,—this filial confidence, in fact, does not dispense with the *strict* obligation in us of loving the Church as our mother, of rejoicing with her and weeping with her—with the obligation, above all, of contributing by all means in our power, at least by our *prayers* and *example*, to the welfare of the Church, and, whenever and wherever there is need of it, even to the *reform* of the Church. Yes, even to her *reform*. We do not refrain from using this word, as we are well aware that not all Catholics are holy, not all priests, nor all religious; not all bishops are saints; just as not all Popes have been saints. Until this work of sanctification is *completed*, there will always be some need of reform in the Catholic Church. To all who undertake to co-operate in *such* reform of the Church, we, as Catholics, owe, and shall always feel, the greatest gratitude, and the more so because we seek—because our soul longs for—the return of the Oriental Orthodox Church to Catholic unity,[1] and by nothing can this return be more effectually promoted than *by increasing the sanctity of all Catholics*. Yes, let us, with the utmost zeal, promote *this* reform of the Church,

---

[1] An *Association of Prayers* for the return of the Oriental Orthodox Church, and especially of Russia, to Catholic unity, was the dearest wish of an illustrious Russian convert, Count Gregory Schouvaloff (*d.* Apr. 2, 1859), after he had joined the Congregation of the Barnabites. His brethren in religion have kept up the same idea, and are most desirous of spreading everywhere this association of prayers, which has obtained a special blessing of the Holy Father (Briefs, Sept. 2, 1862; June 11, 1869) and the cordial approbation of many bishops; among others, of the present Archbishop of Westminster and the late lamented Bishop of Southwark. What the Barnabite Fathers most desire is to obtain a celebration of masses on certain days, as is already practised in Paris in the Church of the Congregation the first Saturday of every month.

F. Schouvaloff used to say—and he has left the same words written in his account of his own conversion and vocation: 'It will not be without a result that the Russians have preserved amongst the treasures of their faith an intense devotion to Mary. Yes, Mary will be the bond which shall unite the two Churches, and she will make of all those who love her a family of brothers, under the common father, the Vicar of Jesus Christ.'— *Ma Conversion et ma Vocation* (Paris, Douniol, 1859 and 1864), part ii. § ix.

as hardly any other work can be more glorious to God, more useful to the Church, and more salutary to souls.

Now, in the interest of such a holy work, *and in that of the return of the Oriental Orthodox Church to Catholic unity*, we beg, before concluding, to suggest the most sure and powerful means for bringing about the most perfect reform in the Catholic Church. It is to *imitate the Popes* in maintaining, propagating, and increasing the worship and love of our crucified Redeemer, Jesus Christ. This means has immense advantages over every other. First of all, the very speaking of Jesus Christ to the hearts of sinners—let them be laymen or persons consecrated to God—will ensure a marvellous efficacy to our sermons and our tracts. Moreover, in putting forward Jesus Christ, and in asking the conversion of sinners for Jesus's sake, we are not exposed to counteract by our simple presence, or generally by our conduct, the good effect produced by our words, letters, or books. Then, by using this means, we are sure of obtaining abundant encouragements, blessings, and *briefs* from the Holy See. Finally, *and above all*, by using this means we are secured from becoming guilty of one of the greatest crimes before God, that of dividing the ONE Church of Jesus Christ, by raising in her dissensions and schisms. Alas! the history of many a pretended reformer of the Church but too clearly contains a hint of Providence, a terrible lesson. St. Paul expressed his fear: '*Ne cum aliis prædicaverim, ipse reprobus efficiar*' (1 Cor. ix. 27): 'Lest when he had preached to others he himself should become a reprobate.' Whence is it that many pretended reformers (let the world call them so) have become 'reprobate'? Their intentions, in the beginning at least, perhaps, were good; the Catholic Church really wanted reform; some of them were even men of self-denial; yet, after having preached to others, they became reprobate! Why? Because no reform can be truly so which is accomplished in the Church by disregarding the *hierarchy* given by Jesus Christ to *His* Church. That is not reform which is accomplished by the subversion in the Church of the *legitimate* powers and the destruction of her order. Whatever reform cannot be obtained but by the illegitimate way of a revolution must be left to God alone; the Church is *His*. He knows her necessities and how to provide for them, and he is far more willing to do so than men are. The impossibility of men accomplishing such reform without revolution, shows either that the time is not yet come—and God is *master* of *His* Church—or that God Himself will directly provide by some miracle, no more difficult for Him than the creation of the world.

But *never*, under any circumstances, can man be allowed to bring about a reform in the Church by which a *divine* hierarchy should be disregarded, and the powers appointed by God subverted.—' It is for *Truth*,' they will perhaps answer, 'that we are fighting, and for *Truth's* sake even the scandal must be encountered. So we are taught by a true Father and true Doctor of the Catholic Church, St. Jerome.'[1] Well, it is indeed so, and even the author of the 'Ὁ Συνοδικὸs τόμος ἢ περὶ ἀληθείας ('The Holy Volume, or On Truth') did not fail to put this sentence on the first page of his work. It is so indeed, and we subscribe to it. Yet, what is *Truth*?

Some one, more than eighteen centuries ago, put the same question to Jesus Christ. He did not await the answer, but almost immediately afterwards condemned Jesus Christ to death (John xviii. 38).

What is Truth? Some asserted reformer of the Church has, perhaps, also asked Jesus Christ, ' What is Truth?'

---

[1] 'Si ex voritate nascitur scandalum, utilius permittitur nasci scandalum quam veritas amittatur.'

It was an inspiration from Heaven. But he also did not wait for the answer of Jesus Christ. . . .

What is Truth? Truth is something different from our conceptions, from our ideas, from our delusions. Truth is what is true in itself, and *not* what we fancy or believe to be true;[1] it is something distinct and separate from our opinion or conviction, something apart and totally independent of the phenomena of the clearness or dulness of our vision; of the shadows which darken its brightness to our eyes, and of the clouds of passion starting up from the heart and enveloping the mind.

No! to these reformers must be applied the words of the Scripture: ' There was a great overthrow of the people, because they did not hearken to Judas and his brethren, thinking that they should do manfully; *but they were not of the seed of those men by whom salvation was brought to Israel*' (1 Mach. v. 61, 62).

And if any such exist now in the Church, we beg, with the greatest respect for immortal souls, to lay before them this question: How can you presume to pronounce what is the best for the Church? Are the secrets of souls known to you? and do you know all the effects which are being produced on them by the events now passing in the Church? Or do you forget that the Church has a life which lasts beyond our own, and that events passing to-day in her may be ordained for the salvation of the *last* generation of men?

---

[1] Of the just-quoted Doctor are the following words, which well deserve a serious consideration: '*Animales* reor esse philosophos qui proprios cogitatus putant esse sapientiam, de quibus recte dicitur: *Animalis autem homo non recipit ea quæ sunt spiritus. Stultitia quippe est ei* . . . . Quod si (anima) proprio crediderit cogitatui, et absque gratia Spiritus Sancti invenire se æstimaverit veritatem, quasi aurum sordidum *animalis hominis* appellatione signatur.'— *Comment. in Epist. ad Galat.* lib. iii. cap. v. 17; Migne, *Patrolog. curs. compl.* ser. i. tom. xxvi; *Scti. Hieronymi*, tom. vii. pp. 411-412.

POSTSCRIPT.

As we are concluding this book, we are irresistibly struck by the analogy, as to their form of government, which exists between the Anglican Church and the different branches of the Oriental Orthodox Church, especially the State Church of Russia. In England, too, the bishops are not the supreme authority of the Church; the Church of England, too, is constituted into a Papacy like that of Russia, with this difference, however, that of the three powers possessed by the Pope of Rome—that of order, the doctrinal power, and the power of jurisdiction—the chief of the Church of England has exercised the *two* last, whilst the Tsar has as yet exercised only the last. The Church of England, too, is liable to enslavement and revolutions.

Besides, the declaration of His Majesty King James I. concerning the Thirty-nine 'Articles agreed upon by the Archbishops and Bishops of both provinces, and the whole clergy, in the convocation holden at London in the year 1562, for the avoiding of diversities of opinions, and for the establishing of consent touching true religion,' reprinted by His Majesty's *commandment*, with his royal declaration, and prefixed to the said Articles in the Book of Common Prayer, has features strikingly analogous to Peter the Great's ukase of January 25, 1721, for the establishment of the Synod. And the ratification by Her Majesty Queen Elizabeth of the Thirty-nine Articles reads almost literally like Peter the Great's ratification of the 'Spiritual Regulation.'

After this one might imagine, from the additional circumstance of our having written this book in English, that we have had in view the State Church of England rather than the Oriental Orthodox Church.

For this we are not answerable.

By the same Author.

1ST ÉTUDE SUR LA QUESTION RELIGIEUSE DE RUSSIE.

LA PRIMAUTÉ DE ST. PIERRE PROUVÉE PAR LES TITRES QUE LUI DONNE L'ÉGLISE RUSSE DANS SA LITURGIE.

Price 2s. 6d.

Paris (1867): PALMÉ. London: BURNS, OATES, & CO.

In preparation,

LE RÈGLEMENT ECCLÉSIASTIQUE ('SPIRITUAL REGULATION') DE PIERRE-LE-GRAND;

Viz.:—The Statutes of the Holy Synod of St. Petersburg, translated from the original Russian into French, with Introduction and Notes, together with the re-impression of the Latin translation printed at St. Petersburg in 1785.

This important publication is undertaken by the PARIS SOCIÉTÉ BIBLIOGRAPHIQUE (77 Rue du Bac). For information concerning the advantages offered by this Society to persons engaged in serious studies, in order to facilitate their researches, apply to M. G. DE BEAUCOURT, Président de la Société Bibliographique, 44 Rue de Bellechasse, Paris; or to the Agent of the Society, M. G. DE GRAËT, 77 Rue du Bac, Paris.

[A Committee of the Society is likely to be formed also in London.]

[SEPTEMBER 1871.]

GENERAL LIST OF WORKS

PUBLISHED BY

MESSRS. LONGMANS, GREEN, AND CO.

PATERNOSTER ROW, LONDON.

History, Politics, Historical Memoirs, &c.

The HISTORY of ENGLAND from the Fall of Wolsey to the Defeat of the Spanish Armada. By JAMES ANTHONY FROUDE, M.A. late Fellow of Exeter College, Oxford.
LIBRARY EDITION, 12 VOLS. 8vo. price £8 18s.
CABINET EDITION, in 12 vols. crown 8vo. price 72s.

The HISTORY of ENGLAND from the Accession of James II. By Lord MACAULAY.
STUDENT'S EDITION, 2 vols. crown 8vo. 12s.
PEOPLE'S EDITION, 4 vols. crown 8vo. 16s.
CABINET EDITION, 8 vols. post 8vo. 48s.
LIBRARY EDITION, 5 vols. 8vo. £4.

LORD MACAULAY'S WORKS. Complete and Uniform Library Edition. Edited by his Sister, Lady TREVELYAN. 8 vols. 8vo. with Portrait, price £5 5s. cloth, or £8 8s. bound in tree-calf by Rivière.

VARIETIES of VICE-REGAL LIFE. By Sir WILLIAM DENISON, K.C.B. late Governor-General of the Australian Colonies, and Governor of Madras. With Two Maps. 2 vols. 8vo. 28s.

On PARLIAMENTARY GOVERNMENT in ENGLAND: Its Origin, Development, and Practical Operation. By ALPHEUS TODD, Librarian of the Legislative Assembly of Canada. 2 vols. 8vo. price £1 17s.

A HISTORICAL ACCOUNT of the NEUTRALITY of GREAT BRITAIN DURING the AMERICAN CIVIL WAR. By MOUNTAGUE BERNARD, M.A. Chichele Professor of International Law and Diplomacy in the University of Oxford. Royal 8vo. 16s.

The CONSTITUTIONAL HISTORY of ENGLAND, since the Accession of George III. 1760—1860. By Sir THOMAS ERSKINE MAY, C.B. Second Edition. Cabinet Edition, thoroughly revised. 3 vols. crown 8vo. price 18s.

The HISTORY of ENGLAND, from the Earliest Times to the Year 1865. By C. D. YONGE, Regius Professor of Modern History in Queen's College, Belfast. New Edition. Crown 8vo. price 7s. 6d.

A

The **OXFORD REFORMERS**—John Colet, Erasmus, and Thomas More; being a History of their Fellow-work. By FREDERIC SEEBOHM. Second Edition, enlarged. 8vo. 14s.

LECTURES on the **HISTORY** of **ENGLAND**, from the earliest Times to the Death of King Edward II. By WILLIAM LONGMAN. With Maps and Illustrations. 8vo. 15s.

The **HISTORY** of the **LIFE** and **TIMES** of **EDWARD** the **THIRD**. By WILLIAM LONGMAN. With 9 Maps, 8 Plates, and 16 Woodcuts. 2 vols. 8vo. 28s.

The **OVERTHROW** of the **GERMANIC CONFEDERATION** by PRUSSIA in 1866. By Sir ALEXANDER MALET, Bart. K.C.B. With 5 Maps. 8vo. 18s.

The **MILITARY RESOURCES** of **PRUSSIA** and **FRANCE**, and **RECENT CHANGES** in the **ART** of **WAR**. By Lieut.-Col. CHESNEY, R.E. and HENRY REEVE, D.C.L. Crown 8vo. price 7s. 6d.

WATERLOO LECTURES; a Study of the Campaign of 1815. By Colonel CHARLES C. CHESNEY, R.E. late Professor of Military Art and History in the Staff College. New Edition. 8vo. with Map, 10s. 6d.

DEMOCRACY in **AMERICA**. By ALEXIS DE TOCQUEVILLE. Translated by HENRY REEVE. 2 vols. 8vo. 21s.

HISTORY of the **REFORMATION** in **EUROPE** in the Time of Calvin. By J. H. MERLE D'AUBIGNÉ, D.D. Vols. I. and II. 8vo. 28s. VOL. III. 12s. VOL. IV. 16s. VOL. V. price 16s.

CHAPTERS from **FRENCH HISTORY**; St. Louis, Joan of Arc, Henri IV. with Sketches of the Intermediate Periods. By J. H. GURNEY, M.A. New Edition. Fcp. 8vo. 6s. 6d.

MEMOIR of **POPE SIXTUS** the **FIFTH**. By Baron HUBNER. Translated from the Original in French, with the Author's sanction, by HUBERT E. H. JERNINGHAM. 2 vols. 8vo. [In preparation.

IGNATIUS LOYOLA and the **EARLY JESUITS**. By STEWART ROSE. New Edition, revised. 8vo. with Portrait, price 16s.

The **HISTORY** of **GREECE**. By C. THIRLWALL, D.D. Lord Bishop of St. David's. 8 vols. fcp. 8vo. price 28s.

GREEK HISTORY from Themistocles to Alexander, in a Series of Lives from Plutarch. Revised and arranged by A. H. CLOUGH. New Edition. Fcp. with 44 Woodcuts, 6s.

CRITICAL HISTORY of the **LANGUAGE** and **LITERATURE** of Ancient Greece. By WILLIAM MURE, of Caldwell. 5 vols. 8vo. £3 9s.

The **TALE** of the **GREAT PERSIAN WAR**, from the Histories of Herodotus. By GEORGE W. COX, M.A. New Edition. Fcp. 3s. 6d.

HISTORY of the **LITERATURE** of **ANCIENT GREECE**. By Professor K. O. MÜLLER. Translated by the Right Hon. Sir GEORGE CORNEWALL LEWIS, Bart. and by J. W. DONALDSON, D.D. 3 vols. 8vo. 21s.

HISTORY of the **CITY** of **ROME** from its Foundation to the Sixteenth Century of the Christian Era. By THOMAS H. DYER, LL.D. 8vo. with 2 Maps, 15s.

The **HISTORY** of **ROME**. By WILLIAM IHNE. English Edition, translated and revised by the Author. Vols. I. and II. 8vo. price 30s.

HISTORY of the ROMANS under the EMPIRE. By the Very Rev. C. MERIVALE, D.C.L. Dean of Ely. 8 vols. post 8vo. 48s.

The FALL of the ROMAN REPUBLIC; a Short History of the Last Century of the Commonwealth. By the same Author. 12mo. 7s. 6d.

A STUDENT'S MANUAL of the HISTORY of INDIA, from the Earliest Period to the Present. By Colonel MEADOWS TAYLOR, M.R.A.S. M.R.I.A. Crown 8vo. with Maps, 7s. 6d.

The HISTORY of INDIA, from the Earliest Period to the close of Lord Dalhousie's Administration. By JOHN CLARK MARSHMAN. 3 vols. crown 8vo. 22s. 6d.

INDIAN POLITY: a View of the System of Administration in India. By Lieutenant-Colonel GEORGE CHESNEY, Fellow of the University of Calcutta. New Edition, revised; with Map. 8vo. price 21s.

HOME POLITICS; being a consideration of the Causes of the Growth of Trade in relation to Labour, Pauperism, and Emigration. By DANIEL GRANT. 8vo. 7s.

REALITIES of IRISH LIFE. By W. STEUART TRENCH, Land Agent in Ireland to the Marquess of Lansdowne, the Marquess of Bath, and Lord Digby. Fifth Edition. Crown 8vo. price 6s.

The STUDENT'S MANUAL of the HISTORY of IRELAND. By MARY F. CUSACK, Author of 'The Illustrated History of Ireland, from the Earliest Period to the Year of Catholic Emancipation.' Crown 8vo. price 6s.

CRITICAL and HISTORICAL ESSAYS contributed to the *Edinburgh Review*. By the Right Hon. LORD MACAULAY.

CABINET EDITION, 4 vols. post 8vo. 24s. | LIBRARY EDITION, 3 vols. 8vo. 36s.
PEOPLE'S EDITION, 2 vols. crown 8vo. 8s. | STUDENT'S EDITION, 1 vol. cr. 8vo. 6s.

SAINT-SIMON and SAINT-SIMONISM; a chapter in the History of Socialism in France. By ARTHUR J. BOOTH, M.A. Crown 8vo. price 7s. 6d.

HISTORY of EUROPEAN MORALS, from Augustus to Charlemagne. By W. E. H. LECKY, M.A. Second Edition. 2 vols. 8vo. price 28s.

HISTORY of the RISE and INFLUENCE of the SPIRIT of RATIONALISM in EUROPE. By W. E. H. LECKY, M.A. Cabinet Edition, being the Fourth. 2 vols. crown 8vo. price 16s.

GOD in HISTORY; or, the Progress of Man's Faith in the Moral Order of the World. By Baron BUNSEN. Translated by SUSANNA WINKWORTH; with a Preface by Dean STANLEY. 3 vols. 8vo. price 42s.

The HISTORY of PHILOSOPHY, from Thales to Comte. By GEORGE HENRY LEWES. Fourth Edition. 2 vols. 8vo. 32s.

An HISTORICAL VIEW of LITERATURE and ART in GREAT BRITAIN from the Accession of the House of Hanover to the Reign of Queen Victoria. By J. MURRAY GRAHAM, M.A. 8vo. price 14s.

The MYTHOLOGY of the ARYAN NATIONS. By GEORGE W. COX, M.A. late Scholar of Trinity College, Oxford, Joint-Editor, with the late Professor Brande, of the Fourth Edition of 'The Dictionary of Science, Literature, and Art,' Author of 'Tales of Ancient Greece,' &c. 2 vols. 8vo. 28s.

HISTORY of CIVILISATION in England and France, Spain and Scotland. By HENRY THOMAS BUCKLE. New Edition of the entire Work with a complete INDEX. 3 vols. crown 8vo. 24s.

A 2

HISTORY of the CHRISTIAN CHURCH, from the Ascension of Christ to the Conversion of Constantine. By E. BURTON, D.D. late Prof. of Divinity in the Univ. of Oxford. New Edition. Fcp. 3s. 6d.

SKETCH of the HISTORY of the CHURCH of ENGLAND to the Revolution of 1688. By the Right Rev. T. V. SHORT, D.D. Lord Bishop of St. Asaph. Eighth Edition. Crown 8vo. 7s. 6d.

HISTORY of the EARLY CHURCH, from the First Preaching of the Gospel to the Council of Nicæa, A.D. 325. By ELIZABETH M. SEWELL, Author of 'Amy Herbert.' New Edition, with Questions. Fcp. 4s. 6d.

The ENGLISH REFORMATION. By F. C. MASSINGBERD, M.A. Chancellor of Lincoln and Rector of South Ormsby. Fourth Edition, revised. Fcp. 8vo. 7s. 6d.

MAUNDER'S HISTORICAL TREASURY; comprising a General Introductory Outline of Universal History, and a series of Separate Histories. Latest Edition, revised and brought down to the Present Time by the Rev. GEORGE WILLIAM COX, M.A. Fcp. 6s. cloth, or 9s. 6d. calf.

HISTORICAL and CHRONOLOGICAL ENCYCLOPÆDIA; comprising Chronological Notices of all the Great Events of Universal History: Treaties, Alliances, Wars, Battles, &c.; Incidents in the Lives of Eminent Men and their Works, Scientific and Geographical Discoveries, Mechanical Inventions, and Social, Domestic, and Economical Improvements. By B. R. WOODWARD, B.A. and W. L. R. CATES. 1 vol. 8vo. [*In the press.*

Biographical Works.

A MEMOIR of DANIEL MACLISE, R.A. By W. JUSTIN O'DRISCOLL, M.R.I.A. Barrister-at-Law. With Portrait and Woodcuts. Post 8vo. price 7s. 6d.

MEMOIRS of the MARQUIS of POMBAL; with Extracts from his Writings and from Despatches in the State Papers Office. By the CONDE DA CARNOTA. New Edition. 8vo. price 7s.

REMINISCENCES of FIFTY YEARS. By MARK BOYD. Post 8vo. price 10s. 6d.

The LIFE of ISAMBARD KINGDOM BRUNEL, Civil Engineer. By ISAMBARD BRUNEL, B.C.L. of Lincoln's Inn; Chancellor of the Diocese of Ely. With Portrait, Plates, and Woodcuts. 8vo. 21s.

The LIFE and LETTERS of FARADAY. By Dr. BENCE JONES, Secretary of the Royal Institution. Second Edition, thoroughly revised. 2 vols. 8vo. with Portrait, and Eight Engravings on Wood, price 28s.

FARADAY as a DISCOVERER. By JOHN TYNDALL, LL.D. F.R.S. Professor of Natural Philosophy in the Royal Institution. New and Cheaper Edition, with Two Portraits. Fcp. 8vo. 3s. 6d.

The LIFE and LETTERS of the Rev. SYDNEY SMITH. Edited by his Daughter, Lady HOLLAND, and Mrs. AUSTIN. New Edition, complete in One Volume. Crown 8vo. price 6s.

SOME MEMORIALS of R. D. HAMPDEN, Bishop of Hereford. Edited by his Daughter, HENRIETTA HAMPDEN. With Portrait. 8vo. price 12s.

The LIFE and TRAVELS of GEORGE WHITEFIELD, M.A. By JAMES PATERSON GLEDSTONE. 8vo. price 14s.

LIVES of the LORD CHANCELLORS and KEEPERS of the GREAT SEAL of IRELAND, from the Earliest Times to the Reign of Queen Victoria. By J. R. O'FLANAGAN, M.R.I.A. Barrister-at-Law. 2 vols. 8vo. 30s.

DICTIONARY of GENERAL BIOGRAPHY; containing Concise Memoirs and Notices of the most Eminent Persons of all Countries, from the Earliest Ages to the Present Time. Edited by W. L. R. CATES. 8vo. 21s.

LIVES of the QUEENS of ENGLAND. By AGNES STRICKLAND. Library Edition, newly revised; with Portraits of every Queen, Autographs, and Vignettes. 8 vols. post 8vo. 7s. 6d. each.

LIFE of the DUKE of WELLINGTON. By the Rev. G. R. GLEIG, M.A. Popular Edition, carefully revised; with copious Additions. Crown 8vo. with Portrait, 5s.

HISTORY of MY RELIGIOUS OPINIONS. By J. H. NEWMAN, D.D. Being the Substance of Apologia pro Vitâ Suâ. Post 8vo. 6s.

The PONTIFICATE of PIUS the NINTH; being the Third Edition of 'Rome and its Ruler,' continued to the latest moment and greatly enlarged. By J. F. MAGUIRE, M.P. Post 8vo. with Portrait, 12s. 6d.

FATHER MATHEW: a Biography. By JOHN FRANCIS MAGUIRE, M.P. for Cork. Popular Edition, with Portrait. Crown 8vo. 3s. 6d.

FELIX MENDELSSOHN'S LETTERS from *Italy and Switzerland*, and *Letters from 1833 to 1847*, translated by Lady WALLACE. New Edition, with Portrait. 2 vols. crown 8vo. 5s. each.

MEMOIRS of SIR HENRY HAVELOCK, K.C.B. By JOHN CLARK MARSHMAN. Cabinet Edition, with Portrait. Crown 8vo. price 3s. 6d.

VICISSITUDES of FAMILIES. By Sir J. BERNARD BURKE, C.B. Ulster King of Arms. New Edition, remodelled and enlarged. 2 vols. crown 8vo. 21s.

ESSAYS in ECCLESIASTICAL BIOGRAPHY. By the Right Hon. Sir J. STEPHEN, LL.D. Cabinet Edition, being the Fifth. Crown 8vo. 7s. 6d.

MAUNDER'S BIOGRAPHICAL TREASURY. Thirteenth Edition, reconstructed, thoroughly revised, and in great part rewritten; with about 1,000 additional Memoirs and Notices, by W. L. R. CATES. Fcp. 6s.

LETTERS and LIFE of FRANCIS BACON, including all his Occasional Works. Collected and edited, with a Commentary, by J. SPEDDING, Trin. Coll. Cantab. VOLS. I. and II. 8vo. 24s. VOLS. III. and IV. 24s. VOL. V. price 12s.

Criticism, Philosophy, Polity, &c.

The INSTITUTES of JUSTINIAN; with English Introduction, Translation, and Notes. By T. C. SANDARS, M.A. Barrister, late Fellow of Oriel Coll. Oxon. New Edition. 8vo. 15s.

SOCRATES and the SOCRATIC SCHOOLS. Translated from the German of Dr. E. Zeller, with the Author's approval, by the Rev. Oswald J. Reichel, B.C.L. and M.A. Crown 8vo. 8s. 6d.

The STOICS, EPICUREANS, and SCEPTICS. Translated from the German of Dr. E. Zeller, with the Author's approval, by Oswald J. Reichel, B.C.L. and M.A. Crown 8vo. price 14s.

The ETHICS of ARISTOTLE, illustrated with Essays and Notes. By Sir A. Grant, Bart. M.A. LL.D. Second Edition, revised and completed. 2 vols. 8vo. price 28s.

The NICOMACHEAN ETHICS of ARISTOTLE newly translated into English. By R. Williams, B.A. Fellow and late Lecturer of Merton College, and sometime Student of Christ Church, Oxford. 8vo. 12s.

ELEMENTS of LOGIC. By R. Whately, D.D. late Archbishop of Dublin. New Edition. 8vo. 10s. 6d. crown 8vo. 4s. 6d.

Elements of Rhetoric. By the same Author. New Edition. 8vo. 10s. 6d. crown 8vo. 4s. 6d.

English Synonymes. By E. Jane Whately. Edited by Archbishop Whately. 5th Edition. Fcp. 3s.

BACON'S ESSAYS with ANNOTATIONS. By R. Whately, D.D. late Archbishop of Dublin. Sixth Edition. 8vo. 10s. 6d.

LORD BACON'S WORKS, collected and edited by J. Spedding, M.A. R. L. Ellis, M.A. and D. D. Heath. New and Cheaper Edition. 7 vols. 8vo. price £3 13s. 6d.

The SUBJECTION of WOMEN. By John Stuart Mill. New Edition. Post 8vo. 5s.

On REPRESENTATIVE GOVERNMENT. By John Stuart Mill. Third Edition. 8vo. 9s. Crown 8vo. 2s.

On LIBERTY. By John Stuart Mill. Fourth Edition. Post 8vo. 7s. 6d. Crown 8vo. 1s. 4d.

PRINCIPLES of POLITICAL ECONOMY. By the same Author. Eighth Edition. 2 vols. 8vo. 30s. Or in 1 vol. crown 8vo. 5s.

A SYSTEM of LOGIC, RATIOCINATIVE and INDUCTIVE. By the same Author. Seventh Edition. Two vols. 8vo. 25s.

ANALYSIS of Mr. MILL'S SYSTEM of LOGIC. By W. Stebbing, M.A. Fellow of Worcester College, Oxford. New Edition. 12mo. 3s. 6d.

UTILITARIANISM. By John Stuart Mill. Fourth Edition. 8vo. 5s.

DISSERTATIONS and DISCUSSIONS, POLITICAL, PHILOSOPHICAL, and HISTORICAL. By John Stuart Mill. Second Edition, revised. 3 vols. 8vo. 36s.

EXAMINATION of Sir W. HAMILTON'S PHILOSOPHY, and of the Principal Philosophical Questions discussed in his Writings. By John Stuart Mill. Third Edition. 8vo. 16s.

An OUTLINE of the NECESSARY LAWS of THOUGHT: a Treatise on Pure and Applied Logic. By the Most Rev. William, Lord Archbishop of York, D.D. F.R.S. Ninth Thousand. Crown 8vo. 5s. 6d.

The **ELEMENTS** of POLITICAL ECONOMY. By HENRY DUNNING
MACLEOD, M.A. Barrister-at-Law. 8vo. 16s.

A **Dictionary** of Political Economy; Biographical, Bibliographical, Historical, and Practical. By the same Author. Vol. I. royal 8vo. 30s.

The **ELECTION** of **REPRESENTATIVES**, Parliamentary and Municipal; a Treatise. By THOMAS HARE, Barrister-at-Law. Third Edition, with Additions. Crown 8vo. 6s.

SPEECHES of the RIGHT HON. LORD MACAULAY, corrected by Himself. People's Edition, crown 8vo. 3s. 6d.

Lord Macaulay's Speeches on Parliamentary Reform in 1831 and 1832. 16mo. 1s.

INAUGURAL ADDRESS delivered to the University of St. Andrews. By JOHN STUART MILL. 8vo. 5s. People's Edition, crown 8vo. 1s.

A **DICTIONARY** of the **ENGLISH LANGUAGE**. By R. G. LATHAM, M.A. M.D. F.R.S. Founded on the Dictionary of Dr. SAMUEL JOHNSON, as edited by the Rev. H. J. TODD, with numerous Emendations and Additions. In Four Volumes, 4to. price £7.

THESAURUS of **ENGLISH WORDS** and **PHRASES**, classified and arranged so as to facilitate the Expression of Ideas, and assist in Literary Composition. By P. M. ROGET, M.D. New Edition. Crown 8vo. 10s. 6d.

LECTURES on the **SCIENCE** of **LANGUAGE**. By F. MAX MÜLLER, M.A. &c. Foreign Member of the French Institute. Sixth Edition. 2 vols. crown 8vo. price 16s.

CHAPTERS on LANGUAGE. By FREDERIC W. FARRAR, F.R.S. Head Master of Marlborough College. Crown 8vo. 8s. 6d.

The **DEBATER**; a Series of Complete Debates, Outlines of Debates, and Questions for Discussion. By F. ROWTON. Fcp. 6s.

MANUAL of **ENGLISH LITERATURE**, Historical and Critical. By THOMAS ARNOLD, M.A. Second Edition. Crown 8vo. price 7s. 6d.

SOUTHEY'S DOCTOR, complete in One Volume. Edited by the Rev. J. W. WARTER, B.D. Square crown 8vo. 12s. 6d.

HISTORICAL and **CRITICAL COMMENTARY** on the OLD TESTAMENT; with a New Translation. By M. M. KALISCH, Ph.D. VOL. I. *Genesis*, 8vo. 18s. or adapted for the General Reader, 12s. VOL. II. *Exodus*, 15s. or adapted for the General Reader, 12s. VOL. III. *Leviticus*, PART I. 15s. or adapted for the General Reader, 8s.

A **HEBREW GRAMMAR**, with **EXERCISES**. By M. M. KALISCH, Ph.D. PART I. *Outlines with Exercises*, 8vo. 12s. 6d. KEY, 5s. PART II. *Exceptional Forms and Constructions*, 12s. 6d.

A **LATIN-ENGLISH DICTIONARY**. By JOHN T. WHITE, D.D. Oxon. and J. E. RIDDLE, M.A. Oxon. Third Edition, revised. 2 vols. 4to. pp. 2,128, price 42s. cloth.

White's College Latin-English Dictionary (Intermediate Size), abridged for the use of University Students from the Parent Work (as above). Medium 8vo. pp. 1,048, price 18s. cloth.

White's Junior Student's Complete Latin-English and English-Latin Dictionary. New Edition. Square 12mo. pp. 1,058, price 12s.

Separately { The ENGLISH-LATIN DICTIONARY, price 5s. 6d.
The LATIN-ENGLISH DICTIONARY, price 7s. 6d.

An **ENGLISH-GREEK LEXICON**, containing all the Greek Words used by Writers of good authority. By C. D. YONGE, B.A. New Edition. 4to. 21s.

Mr. **YONGE'S NEW LEXICON**, English and Greek, abridged from his larger work (as above). Revised Edition. Square 12mo. 8s. 6d.

A **GREEK-ENGLISH LEXICON**. Compiled by H. G. LIDDELL, D.D. Dean of Christ Church, and R. SCOTT, D.D. Dean of Rochester. Sixth Edition. Crown 4to. price 36s.

A Lexicon, Greek and English, abridged from LIDDELL and SCOTT'S *Greek-English Lexicon*. Twelfth Edition. Square 12mo. 7s. 6d.

A **SANSKRIT-ENGLISH DICTIONARY**, the Sanskrit words printed both in the original Devanagari and in Roman Letters. Compiled by T. BENFEY, Prof. in the Univ. of Göttingen. 8vo. 52s. 6d.

WALKER'S PRONOUNCING DICTIONARY of the **ENGLISH LANGUAGE**. Thoroughly revised Editions, by B. H. SMART. 8vo. 12s. 16mo. 6s.

A **PRACTICAL DICTIONARY** of the **FRENCH** and **ENGLISH LANGUAGES**. By L. CONTANSEAU. Fourteenth Edition. Post 8vo. 10s. 6d.

Contanseau's Pocket Dictionary, French and English, abridged from the above by the Author. New Edition, revised. Square 18mo. 3s. 6d.

NEW PRACTICAL DICTIONARY of the **GERMAN LANGUAGE**; German-English and English-German. By the Rev. W. L. BLACKLEY, M.A. and Dr. CARL MARTIN FRIEDLÄNDER. Post 8vo. 7s. 6d.

The **MASTERY of LANGUAGES**; or, the Art of Speaking Foreign Tongues Idiomatically. By THOMAS PRENDERGAST, late of the Civil Service at Madras. Second Edition. 8vo. 6s.

Miscellaneous Works and *Popular Metaphysics.*

The **ESSAYS and CONTRIBUTIONS** of A. K. H. B., Author of 'The Recreations of a Country Parson.' Uniform Editions:—

Recreations of a Country Parson. By A. K. H. B. FIRST and SECOND SERIES, crown 8vo. 3s. 6d. each.

The **COMMON-PLACE PHILOSOPHER** in **TOWN** and **COUNTRY**. By A. K. H. B. Crown 8vo. price 3s. 6d.

Leisure Hours in Town; Essays Consolatory, Æsthetical, Moral, Social, and Domestic. By A. K. H. B. Crown 8vo. 3s. 6d.

The Autumn Holidays of a Country Parson; Essays contributed to *Fraser's Magazine* and to *Good Words*. By A. K. H. B. Crown 8vo. 3s. 6d.

The Graver Thoughts of a Country Parson. By A. K. H. B. FIRST and SECOND SERIES, crown 8vo. 3s. 6d. each.

Critical Essays of a Country Parson, selected from Essays contributed to *Fraser's Magazine*. By A. K. H. B. Crown 8vo. 3s. 6d.

Sunday Afternoons at the Parish Church of a Scottish University City. By A. K. H. B. Crown 8vo. 3s. 6d.

LESSONS of MIDDLE AGE; with some Account of various Cities and Men. By A. K. H. B. Crown 8vo. 9s. 6d.

Counsel and Comfort spoken from a City Pulpit. By A. K. H. B. Crown 8vo. price 3s. 6d.

Changed Aspects of Unchanged Truths; Memorials of St. Andrews Sundays. By A. K. H. B. Crown 8vo. 3s. 6d.

Present-day Thoughts; Memorials of St. Andrews Sundays. By A. K. H. B. Crown 8vo. 3s. 6d.

SHORT STUDIES on GREAT SUBJECTS. By JAMES ANTHONY FROUDE, M.A. late Fellow of Exeter Coll. Oxford. Third Edition. 8vo. 12s. SECOND SERIES. 8vo. price 12s.

LORD MACAULAY'S MISCELLANEOUS WRITINGS:—
  LIBRARY EDITION. 2 vols. 8vo. Portrait, 21s.
  PEOPLE's EDITION. 1 vol. crown 8vo. 4s. 6d.

LORD MACAULAY'S MISCELLANEOUS WRITINGS and SPEECHES. STUDENT's EDITION, in crown 8vo. price 6s.

The REV. SYDNEY SMITH'S MISCELLANEOUS WORKS; including his Contributions to the *Edinburgh Review*. Crown 8vo. 6s.

The Wit and Wisdom of the Rev. Sydney Smith; a Selection of the most memorable Passages in his Writings and Conversation. 16mo. 3s. 6d.

The ECLIPSE of FAITH; or, a Visit to a Religious Sceptic. By HENRY ROGERS. Twelfth Edition. Fcp. 5s.

Defence of the Eclipse of Faith, by its Author; a rejoinder to Dr. Newman's *Reply*. Third Edition. Fcp. 3s. 6d.

Selections from the Correspondence of R. E. H. Greyson. By the same Author. Third Edition. Crown 8vo. 7s. 6d.

FAMILIES of SPEECH, Four Lectures delivered at the Royal Institution of Great Britain. By the Rev. F. W. FARRAR, M.A. F.R.S. Head Master of Marlborough College. Post 8vo. with Two Maps, 5s. 6d.

CHIPS from a GERMAN WORKSHOP; being Essays on the Science of Religion, and on Mythology, Traditions, and Customs. By F. MAX MÜLLER, M.A. &c. Foreign Member of the French Institute. 3 vols. 8vo. 42s.

UEBERWEG'S SYSTEM of LOGIC and HISTORY of LOGICAL DOCTRINES. Translated, with Notes and Appendices, by T. M. LINDSAY, M.A. F.R.S.E. Examiner in Philosophy to the University of Edinburgh. 8vo. price 16s.

ANALYSIS of the PHENOMENA of the HUMAN MIND. By JAMES MILL. A New Edition, with Notes, Illustrative and Critical, by ALEXANDER BAIN, ANDREW FINDLATER, and GEORGE GROTE. Edited, with additional Notes, by JOHN STUART MILL. 2 vols. 8vo. price 28s.

An INTRODUCTION to MENTAL PHILOSOPHY, on the Inductive Method. By J. D. MORELL, M.A. LL.D. 8vo. 12s.

ELEMENTS of PSYCHOLOGY, containing the Analysis of the Intellectual Powers. By the same Author. Post 8vo. 7s. 6d.

The SECRET of HEGEL: being the Hegelian System in Origin, Principle, Form, and Matter. By J. H. STIRLING. 2 vols. 8vo. 28s.

SIR WILLIAM HAMILTON; being the Philosophy of Perception: an Analysis. By J. H. STIRLING. 8vo. 5s.

The SENSES and the INTELLECT. By ALEXANDER BAIN, M.D. Professor of Logic in the University of Aberdeen. Third Edition. 8vo. 15s.

MENTAL and MORAL SCIENCE: a Compendium of Psychology and Ethics. By the same Author. Second Edition. Crown 8vo. 10s. 6d.

LOGIC, DEDUCTIVE and INDUCTIVE. By the same Author. In TWO PARTS, crown 8vo. 10s. 6d. Each Part may be had separately:—
PART I. *Deduction*, 4s. PART II. *Induction*, 6s. 6d.

TIME and SPACE; a Metaphysical Essay. By SHADWORTH H. HODGSON. (This work covers the whole ground of Speculative Philosophy.) 8vo. price 16s.

The Theory of Practice; an Ethical Inquiry. By the same Author. (This work, in conjunction with the foregoing, completes a system of Philosophy.) 2 vols. 8vo. price 24s.

The PHILOSOPHY of NECESSITY; or, Natural Law as applicable to Mental, Moral, and Social Science. By CHARLES BRAY. Second Edition. 8vo. 9s.

The Education of the Feelings and Affections. By the same Author. Third Edition. 8vo. 3s. 6d.

On Force, its Mental and Moral Correlates. By the same Author. 8vo. 5s.

A TREATISE on HUMAN NATURE; being an Attempt to Introduce the Experimental Method of Reasoning into Moral Subjects. By DAVID HUME. Edited, with Notes, &c. by T. H. GREEN, Fellow, and T. H. GROSE, late Scholar, of Balliol College, Oxford. [*In the press.*

ESSAYS MORAL, POLITICAL, and LITERARY. By DAVID HUME. By the same Editors. [*In the press.*

Astronomy, Meteorology, Popular Geography, &c.

OUTLINES of ASTRONOMY. By Sir J. F. W. HERSCHEL, Bart. Eleventh Edition, with Plates and Woodcuts. Square crown 8vo. 12s.

The SUN; RULER, LIGHT, FIRE, and LIFE of the PLANETARY SYSTEM. By RICHARD A. PROCTOR, B.A. F.R.A.S. With 10 Plates (7 coloured) and 107 Figures on Wood. Crown 8vo. 14s.

OTHER WORLDS THAN OURS; the Plurality of Worlds Studied under the Light of Recent Scientific Researches. By the same Author. Second Edition, with 14 Illustrations. Crown 8vo. 10s. 6d.

SATURN and its SYSTEM. By the same Author. 8vo. with 14 Plates, 14s.

SCHALLEN'S SPECTRUM ANALYSIS, in its application to Terrestrial Substances and the Physical Constitution of the Heavenly Bodies. Translated by JANE and C. LASSELL; edited by W. HUGGINS, LL.D. F.R.S. Crown 8vo. with Illustrations. [*Nearly ready.*

CELESTIAL OBJECTS for COMMON TELESCOPES. By the Rev. T. W. WEBB, M.A. F.R.A.S. Second Edition, revised, with a large Map of the Moon, and several Woodcuts. 16mo. 7s. 6d.

NAVIGATION and NAUTICAL ASTRONOMY (Practical, Theoretical, Scientific) for the use of Students and Practical Men. By J. MERRIFIELD, F.R.A.S and H. EVERS. 8vo. 14s.

DOVE'S LAW of STORMS, considered in connexion with the Ordinary Movements of the Atmosphere. Translated by R. H. SCOTT, M.A. T.C.D. 8vo. 10s. 6d.

The CANADIAN DOMINION. By CHARLES MARSHALL. With 6 Illustrations on Wood. 8vo. price 12s. 6d.

A GENERAL DICTIONARY of GEOGRAPHY, Descriptive, Physical, Statistical, and Historical: forming a complete Gazetteer of the World. By A. KEITH JOHNSTON, LL.D. F.R.G.S. Revised Edition. 8vo. 31s. 6d.

A MANUAL of GEOGRAPHY, Physical, Industrial, and Political. By W. HUGHES, F.R.G.S. With 6 Maps. Fcp. 7s. 6d.

MAUNDER'S TREASURY of GEOGRAPHY, Physical, Historical, Descriptive, and Political. Edited by W. HUGHES, F.R.G.S. Revised Edition, with 7 Maps and 16 Plates. Fcp. 6s. cloth, or 9s. 6d. bound in calf.

The PUBLIC SCHOOLS ATLAS of MODERN GEOGRAPHY. In 31 Maps, exhibiting clearly the more important Physical Features of the Countries delineated, and Noting all the Chief Places of Historical, Commercial, or Social Interest. Edited, with an Introduction, by the Rev. G. BUTLER, M.A. Imp. 4to. price 3s. 6d. sewed, or 5s. cloth. [*Nearly ready.*

Natural History and *Popular Science.*

ELEMENTARY TREATISE on PHYSICS, Experimental and Applied. Translated and edited from GANOT's *Éléments de Physique* (with the Author's sanction) by E. ATKINSON, Ph.D. F.C.S. New Edition, revised and enlarged, with a Coloured Plate and 620 Woodcuts. Post 8vo. 15s.

The ELEMENTS of PHYSICS or NATURAL PHILOSOPHY. By NEIL ARNOTT, M.D. F.R.S. Physician Extraordinary to the Queen. Sixth Edition, rewritten and completed. Two Parts. 8vo. 21s.

SOUND: a Course of Eight Lectures delivered at the Royal Institution of Great Britain. By JOHN TYNDALL, LL.D. F.R.S. New Edition, crown 8vo. with Portrait of *M. Chladni* and 169 Woodcuts, price 9s.

HEAT a MODE of MOTION. By Professor JOHN TYNDALL, LL.D. F.R.S. Fourth Edition. Crown 8vo. with Woodcuts, 10s. 6d.

RESEARCHES on DIAMAGNETISM and MAGNE-CRYSTALLIC ACTION; including the Question of Diamagnetic Polarity. By the same Author. With 6 Plates and many Woodcuts. 8vo. price 14s.

PROFESSOR TYNDALL'S ESSAYS on the USE and LIMIT of the IMAGINATION in SCIENCE. Being the Second Edition, with Additions, of his Discourse on the Scientific Use of the Imagination. 8vo. 3s.

NOTES of a COURSE of SEVEN LECTURES on ELECTRICAL PHENOMENA and **THEORIES**, delivered at the Royal Institution, A.D. 1870. By Professor TYNDALL. Crown 8vo. 1s. sewed, or 1s. 6d. cloth.

NOTES of a COURSE of NINE LECTURES on LIGHT delivered at the Royal Institution, A.D. 1869. By the same Author. Crown 8vo. price 1s. sewed, or 1s. 6d. cloth.

FRAGMENTS of SCIENCE for UNSCIENTIFIC PEOPLE; a Series of detached Essays, Lectures, and Reviews. By JOHN TYNDALL, LL.D. F.R.S. Second Edition. 8vo. price 14s.

LIGHT SCIENCE for LEISURE HOURS; a Series of Familiar Essays on Scientific Subjects, Natural Phenomena, &c. By R. A. PROCTOR, B.A. F.R.A.S. Crown 8vo. price 7s. 6d.

LIGHT: Its Influence on Life and Health. By FORBES WINSLOW, M.D. D.C.L. Oxon. (Hon.). Fcp. 8vo. 6s.

A TREATISE on ELECTRICITY, in Theory and Practice. By A. DE LA RIVE, Prof. in the Academy of Geneva. Translated by C. V. WALKER, F.R.S. 3 vols. 8vo. with Woodcuts, £3 13s.

The BEGINNING: its When and its How. By MUNGO PONTON, F.R.S.E. Post 8vo. with very numerous Illustrations, price 18s.

The CORRELATION of PHYSICAL FORCES. By W. R. GROVE, Q.C. V.P.R.S. Fifth Edition, revised, and followed by a Discourse on Continuity. 8vo. 10s. 6d. The *Discourse on Continuity*, separately, 2s. 6d.

MANUAL of GEOLOGY. By S. HAUGHTON, M.D. F.R.S. Revised Edition, with 66 Woodcuts. Fcp. 7s. 6d.

VAN DER HOEVEN'S HANDBOOK of ZOOLOGY. Translated from the Second Dutch Edition by the Rev. W. CLARK, M.D. F.R.S. 2 vols. 8vo. with 24 Plates of Figures, 60s.

Professor OWEN'S LECTURES on the COMPARATIVE ANATOMY and Physiology of the Invertebrate Animals. Second Edition, with 235 Woodcuts. 8vo. 21s.

The COMPARATIVE ANATOMY and PHYSIOLOGY of the VERTEbrate Animals. By RICHARD OWEN, F.R.S. D.C.L. With 1,472 Woodcuts. 3 vols. 8vo. £3 13s. 6d.

The ORIGIN of CIVILISATION and the PRIMITIVE CONDITION of MAN; Mental and Social Condition of Savages. By Sir JOHN LUBBOCK, Bart. M.P. F.R.S. Second Edition, with 25 Woodcuts. 8vo. price 16s.

The PRIMITIVE INHABITANTS of SCANDINAVIA: containing a Description of the Implements, Dwellings, Tombs, and Mode of Living of the Savages in the North of Europe during the Stone Age. By SVEN NILSSON. With 16 Plates of Figures and 3 Woodcuts. 8vo. 18s.

BIBLE ANIMALS; being a Description of every Living Creature mentioned in the Scriptures, from the Ape to the Coral. By the Rev. J. G. WOOD, M.A. F.L.S. With about 100 Vignettes on Wood. 8vo. 21s.

HOMES WITHOUT HANDS: a Description of the Habitations of Animals, classed according to their Principle of Construction. By Rev. J. G. WOOD, M.A. F.L.S. With about 140 Vignettes on Wood. 8vo. 21s.

INSECTS AT HOME. By the Rev. J. G. WOOD, M.A. F.L.S. With a Frontispiece in Colours, 21 full-page Illustrations, and about 700 smaller Illustrations from original designs engraved on Wood by G. Pearson. 8vo. price 21s.

STRANGE DWELLINGS; being a description of the Habitations of Animals, abridged from 'Homes without Hands.' By J. G. WOOD, M.A. F.L.S. With a New Frontispiece and about 60 other Woodcut Illustrations. Crown 8vo. price 7s. 6d.

A FAMILIAR HISTORY of BIRDS. By E. STANLEY, D.D. F.R.S. late Lord Bishop of Norwich. Seventh Edition, with Woodcuts. Fcp. 3s. 6d.

The HARMONIES of NATURE and UNITY of CREATION. By Dr. GEORGE HARTWIG. 8vo. with numerous Illustrations, 18s.

The SEA and its LIVING WONDERS. By the same Author. Third (English) Edition. 8vo. with many Illustrations, 21s.

The TROPICAL WORLD. By Dr. GEO. HARTWIG. With 8 Chromo-xylographs and 172 Woodcuts. 8vo. 21s.

The SUBTERRANEAN WORLD. By Dr. GEORGE HARTWIG. With 3 Maps and about 80 Woodcuts, including 8 full size of page. 8vo. price 21s.

The POLAR WORLD; a Popular Description of Man and Nature in the Arctic and Antarctic Regions of the Globe. By Dr. GEORGE HARTWIG. With 8 Chromoxylographs, 3 Maps, and 85 Woodcuts. 8vo. 21s.

KIRBY and SPENCE'S INTRODUCTION to ENTOMOLOGY, or Elements of the Natural History of Insects. 7th Edition. Crown 8vo. 5s.

MAUNDER'S TREASURY of NATURAL HISTORY, or Popular Dictionary of Zoology. Revised and corrected by T. S. COBBOLD, M.D. Fcp. with 900 Woodcuts, 6s. cloth, or 9s. 6d. bound in calf.

The TREASURY of BOTANY, or Popular Dictionary of the Vegetable Kingdom; including a Glossary of Botanical Terms. Edited by J. LINDLEY, F.R.S. and T. MOORE, F.L.S. assisted by eminent Contributors. With 274 Woodcuts and 20 Steel Plates. Two Parts, fcp. 12s. cloth, or 19s. calf.

The ELEMENTS of BOTANY for FAMILIES and SCHOOLS. Tenth Edition, revised by THOMAS MOORE, F.L.S. Fcp. with 154 Woodcuts. 2s. 6d.

The ROSE AMATEUR'S GUIDE. By THOMAS RIVERS. Ninth Edition. Fcp. 4s.

LOUDON'S ENCYCLOPÆDIA of PLANTS; comprising the Specific Character, Description, Culture, History, &c. of all the Plants found in Great Britain. With upwards of 12,000 Woodcuts. 8vo. 42s.

MAUNDER'S SCIENTIFIC and LITERARY TREASURY. New Edition, thoroughly revised and in great part re-written, with above 1,000 new Articles, by J. Y. JOHNSON, Corr. M.Z.S. Fcp. 6s. cloth, or 9s. 6d. calf.

A DICTIONARY of SCIENCE, LITERATURE, and ART. Fourth Edition, re-edited by W. T. BRANDE (the original Author), and GEORGE W. COX, M.A. assisted by contributors of eminent Scientific and Literary Acquirements. 3 vols. medium 8vo. price 63s. cloth.

Chemistry, Medicine, Surgery, and the Allied Sciences.

A DICTIONARY of CHEMISTRY; and the Allied Branches of other Sciences. By HENRY WATTS, F.R.S. assisted by eminent Contributors. Complete in 5 vols. medium 8vo. £7 3s.

ELEMENTS of CHEMISTRY, Theoretical and Practical. By W. ALLEN MILLER, M.D. late Prof. of Chemistry, King's Coll. London. Fourth Edition. 3 vols. 8vo. £3. PART I. CHEMICAL PHYSICS, 15s. PART II. INORGANIC CHEMISTRY, 21s. PART III. ORGANIC CHEMISTRY, 24s.

A MANUAL of CHEMISTRY, Descriptive and Theoretical. By WILLIAM ODLING, M.B. F.R.S. PART I. 8vo. 9s. PART II. *just ready.*

OUTLINES of CHEMISTRY; or, Brief Notes of Chemical Facts. By WILLIAM ODLING, M.B. F.R.S. Crown 8vo. 7s. 6d.

A Course of Practical Chemistry, for the use of Medical Students. By the same Author. New Edition, with 70 Woodcuts. Crown 8vo, 7s. 6d.

Lectures on Animal Chemistry, delivered at the Royal College of Physicians in 1865. By the same Author. Crown 8vo. 4s. 6d.

Lectures on the Chemical Changes of Carbon. Delivered at the Royal Institution of Great Britain. By the same Author. Crown 8vo. price 4s. 6d.

SELECT METHODS in CHEMICAL ANALYSIS, chiefly INORGANIC. By WILLIAM CROOKES, F.R.S. With 22 Woodcuts. Crown 8vo. price 12s. 6d.

A TREATISE on MEDICAL ELECTRICITY, THEORETICAL and PRACTICAL; and its Use in the Treatment of Paralysis, Neuralgia, and other Diseases. By JULIUS ALTHAUS, M.D. &c. Second Edition, revised and partly re-written. Post 8vo. with Plate and 2 Woodcuts, price 15s.

The DIAGNOSIS, PATHOLOGY, and TREATMENT of DISEASES of Women; including the Diagnosis of Pregnancy. By GRAILY HEWITT, M.D. Second Edition, enlarged; with 116 Woodcut Illustrations. 8vo. 24s.

On SOME DISORDERS of the NERVOUS SYSTEM in CHILDHOOD; being the Lumleian Lectures delivered before the Royal College of Physicians in March 1871. By CHARLES WEST, M.D. Crown 8vo. price 5s.

LECTURES on the DISEASES of INFANCY and CHILDHOOD. By CHARLES WEST, M.D. &c. Fifth Edition, revised and enlarged. 8vo. 16s.

A SYSTEM of SURGERY, Theoretical and Practical. In Treatises by Various Authors. Edited by T. HOLMES, M.A. &c. Surgeon and Lecturer on Surgery at St. George's Hospital, and Surgeon-in-Chief to the Metropolitan Police. Second Edition, thoroughly revised, with numerous Illustrations. 5 vols. 8vo. £5 5s.

The SURGICAL TREATMENT of CHILDREN'S DISEASES. By T. HOLMES, M.A. &c. late Surgeon to the Hospital for Sick Children. Second Edition, with 9 Plates and 112 Woodcuts. 8vo. 21s.

LECTURES on the PRINCIPLES and PRACTICE of PHYSIC. By Sir THOMAS WATSON, Bart. M.D. Fifth Edition, thoroughly revised. 2 vols. 8vo. price 36s.

LECTURES on SURGICAL PATHOLOGY. By Sir JAMES PAGET, Bart. F.R.S. Third Edition, revised and re-edited by the Author and Professor W. TURNER, M.B. 8vo. with 131 Woodcuts, 21s.

COOPER'S DICTIONARY of PRACTICAL SURGERY and Encyclopædia of Surgical Science. New Edition, brought down to the present time. By S. A. LANE, Surgeon to St. Mary's Hospital, assisted by various Eminent Surgeons. VOL. II. 8vo. completing the work. [*In the press.*

On CHRONIC BRONCHITIS, especially as connected with GOUT, EMPHYSEMA, and DISEASES of the HEART. By E. HEADLAM GREENHOW, M.D. F.R.C.P. &c. 8vo. 7s. 6d.

The CLIMATE of the SOUTH of FRANCE as SUITED to INVALIDS; with Notices of Mediterranean and other Winter Stations. By C. T. WILLIAMS, M.A. M.D. Oxon. Assistant-Physician to the Hospital for Consumption at Brompton. Second Edition. Crown 8vo. 6s.

REPORTS on the PROGRESS of PRACTICAL and SCIENTIFIC MEDICINE in Different Parts of the World. Edited by HORACE DOBELL, M.D. assisted by numerous and distinguished Coadjutors. Vols. I. and II. 8vo. 18s. each.

PULMONARY CONSUMPTION; its Nature, Varieties, and Treatment: with an Analysis of One Thousand Cases to exemplify its Duration. By C. J. B. WILLIAMS, M.D. F.R.S. and C. T. WILLIAMS, M.A. M.D. Oxon. Post 8vo. price 10s. 6d.

CLINICAL LECTURES on DISEASES of the LIVER, JAUNDICE, and ABDOMINAL DROPSY. By CHARLES MURCHISON, M.D. Post 8vo. with 25 Woodcuts, 10s. 6d.

ANATOMY, DESCRIPTIVE and SURGICAL. By HENRY GRAY, F.R.S. With about 400 Woodcuts from Dissections. Fifth Edition, by T. HOLMES, M.A. Cantab. with a new Introduction by the Editor. Royal 8vo. 28s.

CLINICAL NOTES on DISEASES of the LARYNX, investigated and treated with the assistance of the Laryngoscope. By W. MARCET, M.D. F.R.S. Crown 8vo. with 5 Lithographs, 6s.

OUTLINES of PHYSIOLOGY, Human and Comparative. By JOHN MARSHALL, F.R.C.S. Surgeon to the University College Hospital. 2 vols. crown 8vo. with 122 Woodcuts, 32s.

PHYSIOLOGICAL ANATOMY and PHYSIOLOGY of MAN. By the late R. B. TODD, M.D. F.R.S. and W. BOWMAN, F.R.S. of King's College. With numerous Illustrations. VOL. II. 8vo. 25s.
VOL. I. New Edition by Dr. LIONEL S. BEALE, F.R.S. in course of publication, with many Illustrations. PARTS I. and II. price 7s. 6d. each.

COPLAND'S DICTIONARY of PRACTICAL MEDICINE, abridged from the larger work and throughout brought down to the present State of Medical Science. 8vo. 36s.

REIMANN'S HANDBOOK of ANILINE and its DERIVATIVES; a Treatise on the Manufacture of Aniline and Aniline Colours. Edited by WILLIAM CROOKES, F.R.S. With 5 Woodcuts. 8vo. 10s. 6d.

On the MANUFACTURE of BEET-ROOT SUGAR in ENGLAND and IRELAND. By WILLIAM CROOKES, F.R.S. Crown 8vo. with 11 Woodcuts, 8s. 6d.

A MANUAL of MATERIA MEDICA and THERAPEUTICS, abridged from Dr. PEREIRA's *Elements* by F. J. FARRE, M.D. assisted by R. BENTLEY, M.R.C.S. and by R. WARINGTON, F.R.S. 8vo. with 90 Woodcuts, 21s.

THOMSON'S CONSPECTUS of the BRITISH PHARMACOPŒIA. 25th Edition, corrected by E. LLOYD BIRKETT, M.D. 18mo. price 6s.

The Fine Arts, and *Illustrated Editions*.

IN FAIRYLAND; Pictures from the Elf-World. By RICHARD DOYLE. With a Poem by W. ALLINGHAM. With Sixteen Plates, containing Thirty-six Designs printed in Colours. Folio, 31s. 6d.

LIFE of JOHN GIBSON, R.A. SCULPTOR. Edited by Lady EASTLAKE. 8vo. 10s. 6d.

MATERIALS for a HISTORY of OIL PAINTING. By Sir CHARLES LOCKE EASTLAKE, sometime President of the Royal Academy. 2 vols. 8vo. price 30s.

HALF-HOUR LECTURES on the HISTORY and PRACTICE of the Fine and Ornamental Arts. By WILLIAM B. SCOTT. New Edition, revised by the Author; with 50 Woodcuts. Crown 8vo. 8s. 6d.

ALBERT DURER, HIS LIFE and WORKS; including Autobiographical Papers and Complete Catalogues. By WILLIAM B. SCOTT. With Six Etchings by the Author, and other Illustrations. 8vo. 16s.

SIX LECTURES on HARMONY, delivered at the Royal Institution of Great Britain in the Year 1867. By G. A. MACFARREN. With numerous engraved Musical Examples and Specimens. 8vo. 10s. 6d.

The CHORALE BOOK for ENGLAND: the Hymns translated by Miss C. WINKWORTH; the Tunes arranged by Prof. W. S. BENNETT and OTTO GOLDSCHMIDT. Fcp. 4to. 12s. 6d.

The NEW TESTAMENT, illustrated with Wood Engravings after the Early Masters, chiefly of the Italian School. Crown 4to. 63s. cloth, gilt top; or £5 5s. elegantly bound in morocco.

LYRA GERMANICA; the Christian Year. Translated by CATHERINE WINKWORTH; with 125 Illustrations on Wood drawn by J. LEIGHTON, F.S.A. 4to. 21s.

LYRA GERMANICA; the Christian Life. Translated by CATHERINE WINKWORTH; with about 200 Woodcut Illustrations by J. LEIGHTON, F.S.A. and other Artists. 4to. 21s.

The LIFE of MAN SYMBOLISED by the MONTHS of the YEAR. Text selected by R. PIGOT; Illustrations on Wood from Original Designs by J. LEIGHTON, F.S.A. 4to. 42s.

CATS' and FARLIE'S MORAL EMBLEMS; with Aphorisms, Adages, and Proverbs of all Nations. 121 Illustrations on Wood by J. LEIGHTON, F.S.A. Text selected by R. PIGOT. Imperial 8vo. 31s. 6d.

SACRED and LEGENDARY ART. By Mrs. JAMESON.

Legends of the Saints and Martyrs. Fifth Edition, with 19 Etchings and 187 Woodcuts. 2 vols. square crown 8vo. 31s. 6d.

Legends of the Monastic Orders. Third Edition, with 11 Etchings and 83 Woodcuts. 1 vol. square crown 8vo. 21s.

Legends of the Madonna. Third Edition, with 27 Etchings and 165 Woodcuts. 1 vol. square crown 8vo. 21s.

The History of Our Lord, with that of his Types and Precursors. Completed by Lady EASTLAKE. Revised Edition, with 31 Etchings and 281 Woodcuts. 2 vols. square crown 8vo. 42s.

The Useful Arts, Manufactures, &c.

HISTORY of the GOTHIC REVIVAL; an Attempt to shew how far the taste for Mediæval Architecture was retained in England during the last two centuries, and has been re-developed in the present. By CHARLES L. EASTLAKE, Architect. With many Illustrations. Imp. 8vo. price 31s. 6d.

GWILT'S ENCYCLOPÆDIA of ARCHITECTURE, with above 1,600 Engravings on Wood. Fifth Edition, revised and enlarged by WYATT PAPWORTH. 8vo. 52s. 6d.

A MANUAL of ARCHITECTURE: being a Concise History and Explanation of the principal Styles of European Architecture, Ancient, Mediæval, and Renaissance; with a Glossary of Technical Terms. By THOMAS MITCHELL. Crown 8vo. with 150 Woodcuts, 10s. 6d.

ITALIAN SCULPTORS; being a History of Sculpture in Northern, Southern, and Eastern Italy. By C. C. PERKINS. With 30 Etchings and 13 Wood Engravings. Imperial 8vo. 42s.

TUSCAN SCULPTORS, their Lives, Works, and Times. With 45 Etchings and 28 Woodcuts from Original Drawings and Photographs. By the same Author. 2 vols. imperial 8vo. 63s.

HINTS on HOUSEHOLD TASTE in FURNITURE, UPHOLSTERY, and other Details. By CHARLES L. EASTLAKE, Architect. Second Edition, with about 90 Illustrations. Square crown 8vo. 18s.

The ENGINEER'S HANDBOOK; explaining the Principles which should guide the Young Engineer in the Construction of Machinery. By C. S. LOWNDES. Post 8vo. 5s.

PRINCIPLES of MECHANISM, designed for the Use of Students in the Universities, and for Engineering Students generally. By R. WILLIS, M.A. F.R.S. &c. Jacksonian Professor in the University of Cambridge. Second Edition, enlarged; with 374 Woodcuts. 8vo. 18s.

LATHES and TURNING, Simple, Mechanical, and ORNAMENTAL. By W. HENRY NORTHCOTT. With about 240 Illustrations on Steel and Wood. 8vo. 18s.

URE'S DICTIONARY of ARTS, MANUFACTURES, and MINES. Sixth Edition, chiefly rewritten and greatly enlarged by ROBERT HUNT, F.R.S. assisted by numerous Contributors eminent in Science and the Arts, and familiar with Manufactures. With above 2,000 Woodcuts, 3 vols. medium 8vo. price £4 14s. 6d.

HANDBOOK of PRACTICAL TELEGRAPHY. By R. S. CULLEY, Memb. Inst. C.E. Engineer-in-Chief of Telegraphs to the Post Office. Fifth Edition, with 118 Woodcuts and 9 Plates. 8vo. price 14s.

ENCYCLOPÆDIA of CIVIL ENGINEERING, Historical, Theoretical, and Practical. By E. CRESY, C.E. With above 3,000 Woodcuts. 8vo. 42s.

TREATISE on MILLS and MILLWORK. By Sir W. FAIRBAIRN, Bart. F.R.S. New Edition, with 18 Plates and 322 Woodcuts. 2 vols. 8vo. 32s.

USEFUL INFORMATION for ENGINEERS. By the same Author. FIRST, SECOND, and THIRD SERIES, with many Plates and Woodcuts, 3 vols. crown 8vo. 10s. 6d. each.

The APPLICATION of CAST and WROUGHT IRON to Building Purposes. By Sir W. FAIRBAIRN, Bart. F.R.S. Fourth Edition, enlarged; with 6 Plates and 118 Woodcuts. 8vo. price 16s.

IRON SHIP BUILDING, its History and Progress, as comprised in a Series of Experimental Researches. By the same Author. With 4 Plates and 130 Woodcuts. 8vo. 18s.

A TREATISE on the STEAM ENGINE, in its various Applications to Mines, Mills, Steam Navigation, Railways and Agriculture. By J. BOURNE, C.E. Eighth Edition; with Portrait, 37 Plates, and 546 Woodcuts. 4to. 42s.

CATECHISM of the STEAM ENGINE, in its various Applications to Mines, Mills, Steam Navigation, Railways, and Agriculture. By the same Author. With 89 Woodcuts. Fcp. 6s.

HANDBOOK of the STEAM ENGINE. By the same Author, forming a KEY to the Catechism of the Steam Engine, with 67 Woodcuts. Fcp. 9s.

BOURNE'S RECENT IMPROVEMENTS in the STEAM ENGINE in its various applications to Mines, Mills, Steam Navigation, Railways, and Agriculture. Being a Supplement to the Author's 'Catechism of the Steam Engine.' By JOHN BOURNE, C.E. New Edition, including many New Examples; with 124 Woodcuts. Fcp. 8vo. 6s.

A TREATISE on the SCREW PROPELLER, SCREW VESSELS, and Screw Engines, as adapted for purposes of Peace and War; with Notices of other Methods of Propulsion, Tables of the Dimensions and Performance of Screw Steamers, and detailed Specifications of Ships and Engines. By J. BOURNE, C.E. New Edition, with 54 Plates and 287 Woodcuts. 4to. 63s.

EXAMPLES of MODERN STEAM, AIR, and GAS ENGINES of the most Approved Types, as employed for Pumping, for Driving Machinery, for Locomotion, and for Agriculture, minutely and practically described. By JOHN BOURNE, C.E. In course of publication in 24 Parts, price 2s. 6d. each, forming One volume 4to. with about 50 Plates and 400 Woodcuts.

A HISTORY of the MACHINE-WROUGHT HOSIERY and LACE Manufactures. By WILLIAM FELKIN, F.L.S. F.S.S. Royal 8vo. 21s.

PRACTICAL TREATISE on METALLURGY, adapted from the last German Edition of Professor KERL's *Metallurgy* by W. CROOKES, F.R.S. &c. and E. RÖHRIG, Ph.D. M.E. With 625 Woodcuts. 3 vols. 8vo. price £4 19s.

MITCHELL'S MANUAL of PRACTICAL ASSAYING. Third Edition, for the most part re-written, with all the recent Discoveries incorporated, by W. CROOKES, F.R.S. With 188 Woodcuts. 8vo. 28s.

The **ART of PERFUMERY**; the History and Theory of Odours, and the Methods of Extracting the Aromas of Plants. By Dr. PIESSE, F.C.S. Third Edition, with 53 Woodcuts. Crown 8vo. 10s. 6d.

Chemical, Natural, and Physical Magic, for Juveniles during the Holidays. By the same Author. Third Edition, with 38 Woodcuts. Fcp. 6s.

LOUDON'S ENCYCLOPÆDIA of AGRICULTURE: comprising the Laying-out, Improvement, and Management of Landed Property, and the Cultivation and Economy of the Productions of Agriculture. With 1,100 Woodcuts. 8vo. 21s.

Loudon's Encyclopædia of Gardening: comprising the Theory and Practice of Horticulture, Floriculture, Arboriculture, and Landscape Gardening. With 1,000 Woodcuts. 8vo. 21s.

BAYLDON'S ART of VALUING RENTS and TILLAGES, and Claims of Tenants upon Quitting Farms, both at Michaelmas and Lady-Day. Eighth Edition, revised by J. C. MORTON. 8vo. 10s. 6d.

Religious and *Moral Works.*

OLD TESTAMENT SYNONYMS, their BEARING on CHRISTIAN FAITH and PRACTICE. By the Rev. R. B. GIRDLESTONE, M.A. 8vo. [*Nearly ready.*

An INTRODUCTION to the THEOLOGY of the CHURCH of ENGLAND, in an Exposition of the Thirty-nine Articles. By the Rev. T. P. BOULTBEE, M.A. Fcp. 8vo. price 6s.

FUNDAMENTALS; or, Bases of Belief concerning MAN and GOD: a Handbook of Mental, Moral, and Religious Philosophy. By the Rev. T. GRIFFITH, M.A. 8vo. price 10s. 6d.

PRAYERS SELECTED from the COLLECTION of the late BARON BUNSEN, and Translated by CATHERINE WINKWORTH. PART I. For the Family. PART II. Prayers and Meditations for Private Use. Fcp. 8vo. price 3s. 6d.

The STUDENT'S COMPENDIUM of the BOOK of COMMON PRAYER; being Notes Historical and Explanatory of the Liturgy of the Church of England. By the Rev. H. ALLDEN NASH. Fcp. 8vo. price 2s. 6d.

The BIBLE and POPULAR THEOLOGY; a Re-statement of Truths and Principles, with special reference to recent works of Dr. Liddon, Lord Hatherley, and the Right Hon. W. E. Gladstone. By G. VANCE SMITH, B.A. Ph.D. 8vo. price 7s. 6d.

The TRUTH of the BIBLE: Evidence from the Mosaic and other Records of Creation; the Origin and Antiquity of Man; the Science of Scripture; and from the Archæology of Different Nations of the Earth. By the Rev. B. W. SAVILE, M.A. Crown 8vo. price 7s. 6d.

CHURCHES and their CREEDS. By the Rev. Sir PHILIP PERRING, Bart. late Scholar of Trin. Coll. Cambridge, and University Medallist. Crown 8vo. price 10s. 6d.

CONSIDERATIONS on the REVISION of the ENGLISH NEW TESTAMENT. By C. J. ELLICOTT, D.D. Lord Bishop of Gloucester and Bristol. Post 8vo. price 5s. 6d.

An EXPOSITION of the 39 ARTICLES, Historical and Doctrinal. By E. HAROLD BROWNE, D.D. Lord Bishop of Ely. Ninth Edit. 8vo. 16s.

The **LIFE** and **EPISTLES** of **ST. PAUL**. By the Rev. W. J.
CONYBEARE, M.A., and the Very Rev. J. S. HOWSON, D.D. Dean of Chester:—
LIBRARY EDITION, with all the Original Illustrations, Maps, Landscapes
on Steel, Woodcuts, &c. 2 vols. 4to. 48s.
INTERMEDIATE EDITION, with a Selection of Maps, Plates, and Woodcuts.
2 vols. square crown 8vo. 31s. 6d.
STUDENT'S EDITION, revised and condensed, with 46 Illustrations and
Maps. 1 vol. crown 8vo. price 9s.

The **VOYAGE** and **SHIPWRECK** of **ST. PAUL**; with Dissertations
on the Life and Writings of St. Luke and the Ships and Navigation of the
Ancients. By JAMES SMITH, F.R.S. Third Edition. Crown 8vo. 10s. 6d.

A **CRITICAL** and **GRAMMATICAL COMMENTARY** on **ST. PAUL'S**
Epistles. By C. J. ELLICOTT, D.D. Lord Bishop of Gloucester & Bristol. 8vo.

Galatians, Fourth Edition, 8s. 6d.

Ephesians, Fourth Edition, 8s. 6d.

Pastoral Epistles, Fourth Edition, 10s. 6d.

Philippians, Colossians, and Philemon, Third Edition, 10s. 6d.

Thessalonians, Third Edition, 7s. 6d.

HISTORICAL LECTURES on the **LIFE** of **OUR LORD JESUS**
CHRIST; being the Hulsean Lectures for 1859. By C. J. ELLICOTT, D.D.
Lord Bishop of Gloucester and Bristol. Fifth Edition. 8vo. price 12s.

EVIDENCE of the **TRUTH** of the **CHRISTIAN RELIGION** derived
from the Literal Fulfilment of Prophecy. By ALEXANDER KEITH, D.D.
37th Edition, with numerous Plates, in square 8vo. 12s. 6d.; also the 39th
Edition, in post 8vo. with 5 Plates, 6s.

History and Destiny of the World and Church, according to
Scripture. By the same Author. Square 8vo. with 40 Illustrations, 10s.

An **INTRODUCTION** to the **STUDY** of the **NEW TESTAMENT**,
Critical, Exegetical, and Theological. By the Rev. S. DAVIDSON, D.D.
LL.D. 2 vols. 8vo. 30s.

HARTWELL HORNE'S INTRODUCTION to the **CRITICAL STUDY**
and Knowledge of the Holy Scriptures, as last revised; with 4 Maps and
22 Woodcuts and Facsimiles. 4 vols. 8vo. 42s.

Horne's Compendious Introduction to the Study of the Bible. Re-
edited by the Rev. JOHN AYRE, M.A. With Maps, &c. Post 8vo. 6s.

EWALD'S HISTORY of **ISRAEL** to the **DEATH** of **MOSES**. Translated from the German. Edited, with a Preface and an Appendix, by RUSSELL
MARTINEAU, M.A. Second Edition. 2 vols. 8vo. 24s.

The **HISTORY** and **LITERATURE** of the **ISRAELITES**, according
to the Old Testament and the Apocrypha. By C. DE ROTHSCHILD and
A. DE ROTHSCHILD. Second Edition, revised. 2 vols. post 8vo. with Two
Maps, price 12s. 6d.

The **SEE** of **ROME** in the **MIDDLE AGES**. By the Rev. OSWALD
J. REICHEL, B.C.L. and M.A. 8vo. price 18s.

The **TREASURY** of **BIBLE KNOWLEDGE**; being a Dictionary of the
Books, Persons, Places, Events, and other matters of which mention is made
in Holy Scripture. By Rev. J. AYRE, M.A. With Maps, 15 Plates, and
numerous Woodcuts. Fcp. 8vo. price 6s. cloth, or 9s. 6d. neatly bound in calf.

The **GREEK TESTAMENT**; with Notes, Grammatical and Exegetical. By the Rev. W. WEBSTER, M.A. and the Rev. W. F. WILKINSON, M.A. 2 vols. 8vo. £2 4s.

EVERY-DAY SCRIPTURE DIFFICULTIES explained and illustrated. By J. E. PRESCOTT, M.A. VOL. I. *Matthew* and *Mark*; VOL. II. *Luke* and *John*. 2 vols. 8vo. 9s. each.

The **PENTATEUCH** and **BOOK** of **JOSHUA CRITICALLY EXAMINED**. By the Right Rev. J. W. COLENSO, D.D. Lord Bishop of Natal. People's Edition, in 1 vol. crown 8vo. 6s.

SIX SERMONS on the **FOUR CARDINAL VIRTUES** in relation to the Public and Private Life of Catholics. By the Rev. ORBY SHIPLEY, M.A. Crown 8vo. with Frontispiece, price 7s. 6d.

The **FORMATION** of **CHRISTENDOM**. By T. W. ALLIES. PARTS I. and II. 8vo. price 12s. each Part.

ENGLAND and **CHRISTENDOM**. By ARCHBISHOP MANNING, D.D. Post 8vo. price 10s. 6d.

CHRISTENDOM'S DIVISIONS, PART I. a Philosophical Sketch of the Divisions of the Christian Family in East and West. By EDMUND S. FFOULKES. Post 8vo. price 7s. 6d.

Christendom's Divisions, PART II. Greeks and Latins, being a History of their Dissensions and Overtures for Peace down to the Reformation. By the same Author. Post 8vo. 15s.

A VIEW of the **SCRIPTURE REVELATIONS CONCERNING** a **FUTURE STATE**. By RICHARD WHATELY, D.D. late Archbishop of Dublin. Ninth Edition. Fcp. 8vo. 5s.

THOUGHTS for the **AGE**. By ELIZABETH M. SEWELL, Author of 'Amy Herbert' &c. New Edition, revised. Fcp. 8vo. price 5s.

Passing Thoughts on Religion. By the same Author. Fcp. 8vo. 5s.

Self-Examination before Confirmation. By the same Author. 32mo. price 1s. 6d.

Readings for a Month Preparatory to Confirmation, from Writers of the Early and English Church. By the same Author. Fcp. 4s.

Readings for Every Day in Lent, compiled from the Writings of Bishop JEREMY TAYLOR. By the same Author. Fcp. 5s.

Preparation for the Holy Communion; the Devotions chiefly from the works of JEREMY TAYLOR. By the same Author. 32mo. 3s.

THOUGHTS for the **HOLY WEEK** for Young Persons. By the Author of 'Amy Herbert.' New Edition. Fcp. 8vo. 2s.

PRINCIPLES of **EDUCATION** Drawn from Nature and Revelation, and applied to Female Education in the Upper Classes. By the Author of 'Amy Herbert.' 2 vols. fcp. 12s. 6d.

SINGERS and **SONGS** of the **CHURCH**: being Biographical Sketches of the Hymn-Writers in all the principal Collections; with Notes on their Psalms and Hymns. By JOSIAH MILLER, M.A. Post 8vo. price 10s. 6d.

LYRA GERMANICA, translated from the German by Miss C. WINKWORTH. FIRST SERIES, Hymns for the Sundays and Chief Festivals. SECOND SERIES, the Christian Life. Fcp. 3s. 6d. each SERIES.

'SPIRITUAL SONGS' for the SUNDAYS and HOLIDAYS throughout the Year. By J. S. B. MONSELL, LL.D. Vicar of Egham and Rural Dean. Fourth Edition, Sixth Thousand. Fcp. 4s. 6d.

The BEATITUDES: Abasement before God; Sorrow for Sin; Meekness of Spirit; Desire for Holiness; Gentleness; Purity of Heart; the Peacemakers; Sufferings for Christ. By the same. Third Edition. Fcp. 3s. 6d.

His PRESENCE—not his MEMORY, 1855. By the same Author, in Memory of his Son. Sixth Edition. 16mo. 1s.

LYRA EUCHARISTICA; Hymns and Verses on the Holy Communion, Ancient and Modern: with other Poems. Edited by the Rev. ORBY SHIPLEY, M.A. Second Edition. Fcp. 5s.

Lyra Messianica; Hymns and Verses on the Life of Christ, Ancient and Modern; with other Poems. By the same Editor. Second Edition, altered and enlarged. Fcp. 5s.

Lyra Mystica; Hymns and Verses on Sacred Subjects, Ancient and Modern. By the same Editor. Fcp. 5s.

ENDEAVOURS after the CHRISTIAN LIFE: Discourses. By JAMES MARTINEAU. Fourth Edition, carefully revised. Post 8vo. 7s. 6d.

INVOCATION of SAINTS and ANGELS, for the use of Members of the English Church. Edited by the Rev. ORBY SHIPLEY. 24mo. 3s. 6d.

WHATELY'S INTRODUCTORY LESSONS on the CHRISTIAN Evidences. 18mo. 6d.

FOUR DISCOURSES of CHRYSOSTOM, chiefly on the Parable of the Rich Man and Lazarus. Translated by F. ALLEN, B.A. Crown 8vo. 3s. 6d.

BISHOP JEREMY TAYLOR'S ENTIRE WORKS. With Life by BISHOP HEBER. Revised and corrected by the Rev. C. P. EDEN, 10 vols. price £5 5s.

Travels, Voyages, &c.

HOW to SEE NORWAY. By Captain J. R. CAMPBELL. With Map and 5 Woodcuts. Fcp. 8vo. price 5s.

PAU and the PYRENEES. By Count HENRY RUSSELL, Member of the Alpine Club, &c. With 2 Maps. Fcp. 8vo. price 5s.

SCENES in the SUNNY SOUTH; including the Atlas Mountains and the Oases of the Sahara in Algeria. By Lieut.-Col. the Hon. C. S. VEREKER, M.A. Commandant of the Limerick Artillery Militia. 2 vols. post 8vo. price 21s.

The PLAYGROUND of EUROPE. By LESLIE STEPHEN, late President of the Alpine Club. With 4 Illustrations engraved on Wood by E. Whymper. Crown 8vo. price 10s. 6d.

CADORE; or, TITIAN'S COUNTRY. By JOSIAH GILBERT, one of the Authors of 'The Dolomite Mountains.' With Map, Facsimile, and 40 Illustrations. Imperial 8vo. 31s. 6d.

HOURS of EXERCISE in the ALPS. By JOHN TYNDALL, LL.D. F.R.S. Second Edition, with 7 Woodcuts by E. WHYMPER. Crown 8vo. price 12s. 6d.

TRAVELS in the CENTRAL CAUCASUS and BASHAN. Including Visits to Ararat and Tabreez and Ascents of Kasbek and Elbruz. By D. W. FRESHFIELD. Square crown 8vo. with Maps, &c. 18s.

PICTURES in TYROL and Elsewhere. From a Family Sketch-Book. By the Authoress of 'A Voyage en Zigzag,' &c. Second Edition. Small 4to. with numerous Illustrations, 21s.

HOW WE SPENT the SUMMER; or, a Voyage en Zigzag in Switzerland and Tyrol with some Members of the ALPINE CLUB. From the Sketch-Book of one of the Party. In oblong 4to. with 300 Illustrations, 15s.

BEATEN TRACKS; or, Pen and Pencil Sketches in Italy. By the Authoress of 'A Voyage en Zigzag.' With 42 Plates, containing about 200 Sketches from Drawings made on the Spot. 8vo. 16s.

MAP of the CHAIN of MONT BLANC, from an actual Survey in 1863—1864. By A. ADAMS-REILLY, F.R.G.S. M.A.C. Published under the Authority of the Alpine Club. In Chromolithography on extra stout drawing-paper 28in. × 17in. price 10s. or mounted on canvas in a folding case, 12s. 6d.

WESTWARD by RAIL; the New Route to the East. By W. F. RAE. With Map shewing the Lines of Rail between the Atlantic and the Pacific and Sections of the Railway. Second Edition, enlarged. Post 8vo. 10s. 6d.

HISTORY of DISCOVERY in our AUSTRALASIAN COLONIES, Australia, Tasmania, and New Zealand, from the Earliest Date to the Present Day. By WILLIAM HOWITT. 2 vols. 8vo. with 3 Maps, 20s.

The CAPITAL of the TYCOON; a Narrative of a Three Years' Residence in Japan. By Sir RUTHERFORD ALCOCK, K.C.B. 2 vols. 8vo. with numerous Illustrations, 42s.

ZIGZAGGING AMONGST DOLOMITES. By the Author of 'How we Spent the Summer, or a Voyage en Zigzag in Switzerland and Tyrol.' With upwards of 300 Illustrations by the Author. Oblong 4to. price 15s.

The DOLOMITE MOUNTAINS; Excursions through Tyrol, Carinthia, Carniola, and Friuli, 1861-1863. By J. GILBERT and G. C. CHURCHILL, F.R.GS. With numerous Illustrations. Square crown 8vo. 21s.

GUIDE to the PYRENEES, for the use of Mountaineers. By CHARLES PACKE. 2nd Edition, with Map and Illustrations. Cr. 8vo. 7s. 6d.

The ALPINE GUIDE. By JOHN BALL, M.R.I.A. late President of the Alpine Club. Thoroughly Revised Editions, in Three Volumes, post 8vo. with Maps and other Illustrations:—

GUIDE to the WESTERN ALPS, including Mont Blanc, Monte Rosa, Zermatt, &c. Price 6s. 6d.

GUIDE to the CENTRAL ALPS, including all the Oberland District. Price 7s. 6d.

GUIDE to the EASTERN ALPS, price 10s. 6d.

Introduction on Alpine Travelling in General, and on the Geology of the Alps, price 1s. Each of the Three Volumes or Parts of the Alpine Guide may be had with this INTRODUCTION prefixed, price 1s. extra.

The NORTHERN HEIGHTS of LONDON; or, Historical Associations of Hampstead, Highgate, Muswell Hill, Hornsey, and Islington. By WILLIAM HOWITT. With about 40 Woodcuts. Square crown 8vo. 21s.

VISITS to REMARKABLE PLACES: Old Halls, Battle-Fields, and Scenes Illustrative of Striking Passages in English History and Poetry. By WILLIAM HOWITT. 2 vols. square crown 8vo. with Woodcuts, 25s.

The **RURAL LIFE** of **ENGLAND**. By the same Author. With Woodcuts by Bewick and Williams. Medium 8vo. 12s. 6d.

PILGRIMAGES in the **PYRENEES** and **LANDES**. By DENYS SHYNE LAWLOR. Crown 8vo. with Frontispiece and Vignette, price 15s.

Works of Fiction.

NOVELS and TALES. By the Right Hon. B. DISRAELI, M.P. Cabinet Edition, complete in Ten Volumes, crown 8vo. price 6s. each, as follows:—

LOTHAIR, 6s.	HENRIETTA TEMPLE, 6s.
CONINGSBY, 6s.	CONTARINI FLEMING, &c. 6s.
SYBIL, 6s.	ALROY, IXION, &c. 6s.
TANCRED, 6s.	The YOUNG DUKE, &c. 6s.
VENETIA, 6s.	VIVIAN GREY, 6s.

The **MODERN NOVELIST'S LIBRARY**. Each Work, in crown 8vo. complete in a Single Volume:—
 MELVILLE'S GLADIATORS, 2s. boards; 2s. 6d. cloth.
 ———— GOOD FOR NOTHING, 2s. boards; 2s. 6d. cloth.
 ———— HOLMBY HOUSE, 2s. boards; 2s. 6d. cloth.
 ———— INTERPRETER, 2s. boards; 2s. 6d. cloth.
 ———— KATE COVENTRY, 2s. boards; 2s. 6d. cloth.
 ———— QUEEN'S MARIES, 2s. boards; 2s. 6d. cloth.
 TROLLOPE'S WARDEN, 1s. 6d. boards; 2s. cloth.
 ———— BARCHESTER TOWERS, 2s. boards; 2s. 6d. cloth.
 BRAMLEY-MOORE'S SIX SISTERS of the VALLEYS, 2s. boards; 2s. 6d. cloth.

IERNE; a Tale. By W. STEUART TRENCH, Author of 'Realities of Irish Life.' Second Edition. 2 vols. post 8vo. price 21s.

The **HOME** at **HEATHERBRAE**; a Tale. By the Author of 'Everley.' Fcp. 8vo. price 5s.

CABINET EDITION of STORIES and TALES by Miss SEWELL:—

AMY HERBERT, 2s. 6d.	IVORS, 2s. 6d.
GERTRUDE, 2s. 6d.	KATHARINE ASHTON, 2s. 6d.
The EARL'S DAUGHTER, 2s. 6d.	MARGARET PERCIVAL, 5s.
EXPERIENCE of LIFE, 2s. 6d.	LANETON PARSONAGE, 4s. 6d.
CLEVE HALL, 2s. 6d.	URSULA, 4s. 6d.

STORIES and TALES. By E. M. SEWELL. Comprising:—Amy Herbert; Gertrude; The Earl's Daughter; The Experience of Life; Cleve Hall; Ivors; Katharine Ashton; Margaret Percival; Laneton Parsonage; and Ursula. The Ten Works, complete in Eight Volumes, crown 8vo. bound in leather, and contained in a Box, price 42s.

A Glimpse of the World. By the Author of 'Amy Herbert.' Fcp. 7s. 6d.

The Journal of a Home Life. By the same Author. Post 8vo. 9s. 6d.

After Life; a Sequel to 'The Journal of a Home Life.' Price 10s. 6d.

UNCLE PETER'S FAIRY TALE for the **NINETEENTH CENTURY**. Edited by E. M. SEWELL, Author of 'Amy Herbert,' &c. Fcp. 8vo. 7s. 6d.

THE GIANT; A Witch's Story for English Boys. By the same Author and Editor. Fcp. 8vo. price 5s.

WONDERFUL STORIES from NORWAY, SWEDEN, and ICELAND. Adapted and arranged by JULIA GODDARD. With an Introductory Essay by the Rev. G. W. COX, M.A. and Six Woodcuts. Square post 8vo. 6s.

A VISIT to MY DISCONTENTED COUSIN. Reprinted, with some Additions, from *Fraser's Magazine*. Crown 8vo. price 7s. 6d.

BECKER'S GALLUS; or, Roman Scenes of the Time of Augustus: with Notes and Excursuses. New Edition. Post 8vo. 7s. 6d.

BECKER'S CHARICLES; a Tale illustrative of Private Life among the Ancient Greeks: with Notes and Excursuses. New Edition. Post 8vo. 7s. 6d.

CABINET EDITION of NOVELS and TALES by G. J. WHYTE MELVILLE:—

The GLADIATORS, 5s.	HOLMBY HOUSE, 5s.
DIGBY GRAND, 5s.	GOOD for NOTHING, 6s.
KATE COVENTRY, 5s.	The QUEEN'S MARIES, 6s.
GENERAL BOUNCE, 5s.	The INTERPRETER, 5s.

TALES of ANCIENT GREECE. By GEORGE W. COX, M.A. late Scholar of Trin. Coll. Oxon. Crown 8vo. price 6s. 6d.

A MANUAL of MYTHOLOGY, in the form of Question and Answer. By the same Author. Fcp. 3s.

OUR CHILDREN'S STORY, by one of their Gossips. By the Author of 'Voyage en Zigzag,' 'Pictures in Tyrol,' &c. Small 4to. with Sixty Illustrations by the Author. price 10s. 6d.

Poetry and *The Drama.*

THOMAS MOORE'S POETICAL WORKS, the only Editions containing the Author's last Copyright Additions:—
CABINET EDITION, 10 vols. fcp. 8vo. price 35s.
SHAMROCK EDITION, crown 8vo. price 3s. 6d.
RUBY EDITION, crown 8vo. with Portrait, price 6s.
LIBRARY EDITION, medium 8vo. Portrait and Vignette, 14s.
PEOPLE'S EDITION, square crown 8vo. with Portrait, &c. 10s. 6d.

MOORE'S IRISH MELODIES, Maclise's Edition, with 161 Steel Plates from Original Drawings. Super-royal 8vo. 31s. 6d.

Miniature Edition of Moore's Irish Melodies with Maclise's Designs (as above) reduced in Lithography. Imp. 16mo. 10s. 6d.

MOORE'S LALLA ROOKH. Tenniel's Edition, with 68 Wood Engravings from original Drawings and other Illustrations. Fcp. 4to. 21s.

SOUTHEY'S POETICAL WORKS, with the Author's last Corrections and copyright Additions. Library Edition, in 1 vol. medium 8vo. with Portrait and Vignette, 14s.

LAYS of ANCIENT ROME; with *Ivry* and the *Armada*. By the Right Hon. LORD MACAULAY. 16mo. 4s. 6d.

Lord Macaulay's Lays of Ancient Rome. With 90 Illustrations on Wood, from the Antique, from Drawings by G. SCHARF. Fcp. 4to. 21s.

Miniature Edition of Lord Macaulay's Lays of Ancient Rome, with the Illustrations (as above) reduced in Lithography. Imp. 16mo. 10s. 6d.

GOLDSMITH'S POETICAL WORKS, with Wood Engravings from Designs by Members of the ETCHING CLUB. Imperial 16mo. 7s. 6d.

JOHN JERNINGHAM'S JOURNAL. Fcp. 8vo. price 3s. 6d.

POEMS OF BYGONE YEARS. Edited by the Author of 'Amy Herbert,' &c. Fcp. 8vo. price 5s.

POEMS. By JEAN INGELOW. Fifteenth Edition. Fcp. 8vo. 5s.

EUCHARIS; a Poem. By F. REGINALD STATHAM (Francis Reynolds), Author of 'Alice Rushton, and other Poems' and 'Glaphyra, and other Poems.' Fcp. 8vo. price 3s. 6d.

POEMS by Jean Ingelow. With nearly 100 Illustrations by Eminent Artists, engraved on Wood by the Brothers DALZIEL. Fcp. 4to. 21s.

The MAD WAR PLANET, and other POEMS. By WILLIAM HOWITT, Author of 'Visits to Remarkable Places,' &c. Fcp. 8vo. price 5s.

MOPSA the FAIRY. By JEAN INGELOW. Pp. 256, with Eight Illustrations engraved on Wood. Fcp. 8vo. 6s.

A STORY of DOOM, and other Poems. By JEAN INGELOW. Third Edition. Fcp. 5s.

WORKS by EDWARD YARDLEY:—
    FANTASTIC STORIES. Fcp. 3s. 6d.
    MELUSINE and OTHER POEMS. Fcp. 5s.
    HORACE'S ODES, *translated into* English Verse. Crown 8vo. 6s.
    SUPPLEMENTARY STORIES *and* POEMS. Fcp. 3s. 6d.

BOWDLER'S FAMILY SHAKSPEARE, cheaper Genuine Editions. Medium 8vo. large type, with 36 WOODCUTS, price 14s. Cabinet Edition, with the same ILLUSTRATIONS, 6 vols. fcp. 3s. 6d. each.

HORATII OPERA, Pocket Edition, with carefully corrected Text, Marginal References, and Introduction. Edited by the Rev. J. E. YONGE, M.A. Square 18mo. 4s. 6d.

HORATII OPERA. Library Edition, with Marginal References and English Notes. Edited by the Rev. J. E. YONGE. 8vo. 21s.

The ÆNEID of VIRGIL Translated into English Verse. By JOHN CONINGTON, M.A. New Edition. Crown 8vo. 9s.

ARUNDINES CAMI, sive Musarum Cantabrigiensium Lusus canori. Collegit atque edidit H. DRURY, M.A. Editio Sexta, curavit H. J. HODGSON, M.A. Crown 8vo. 7s. 6d.

HUNTING SONGS and MISCELLANEOUS VERSES. By R. E. EGERTON WARBURTON. Second Edition. Fcp. 8vo. 5s.

Rural Sports, &c.

ENCYCLOPÆDIA of RURAL SPORTS; a complete Account, Historical, Practical, and Descriptive, of Hunting, Shooting, Fishing, Racing, and all other Rural and Athletic Sports and Pastimes. By D. P. BLAINE. With above 600 Woodcuts (20 from Designs by JOHN LEECH). 8vo. 21s.

The DEAD SHOT, or Sportsman's Complete Guide; a Treatise on the Use of the Gun, Dog-breaking, Pigeon-shooting, &c. By MARKSMAN. Revised Edition. Fcp. 8vo. with Plates, 5s.

The FLY-FISHER'S ENTOMOLOGY. By ALFRED RONALDS. With coloured Representations of the Natural and Artificial Insect. Sixth Edition; with 20 coloured Plates. 8vo. 14s.

A BOOK on ANGLING; a complete Treatise on the Art of Angling in every branch. By FRANCIS FRANCIS. Second Edition, with Portrait and 15 other Plates, plain and coloured. Post 8vo. 15s.

The BOOK of the ROACH. By GREVILLE FENNELL, of 'The Field.' Fcp. 8vo. price 2s. 6d.

WILCOCKS'S SEA-FISHERMAN; comprising the Chief Methods of Hook and Line Fishing in the British and other Seas, a Glance at Nets, and Remarks on Boats and Boating. Second Edition, enlarged; with 80 Woodcuts. Post 8vo. 12s. 6d.

HORSES and STABLES. By Colonel F. FITZWYGRAM, XV. the King's Hussars. With Twenty-four Plates of Illustrations, containing very numerous Figures engraved on Wood. 8vo. 15s.

The HORSE'S FOOT, and HOW to KEEP IT SOUND. By W. MILES, Esq. Ninth Edition, with Illustrations. Imperial 8vo. 12s. 6d.

A PLAIN TREATISE on HORSE-SHOEING. By the same Author. Sixth Edition. Post 8vo. with Illustrations, 2s. 6d.

STABLES and STABLE-FITTINGS. By the same. Imp. 8vo. with 13 Plates, 15s.

REMARKS on HORSES' TEETH, addressed to Purchasers. By the same. Post 8vo. 1s. 6d.

ROBBINS'S CAVALRY CATECHISM, or Instructions on Cavalry Exercise and Field Movements, Brigade Movements, Out-post Duty, Cavalry supporting Artillery, Artillery attached to Cavalry. 18mo. 5s.

BLAINE'S VETERINARY ART; a Treatise on the Anatomy, Physiology, and Curative Treatment of the Diseases of the Horse, Neat Cattle and Sheep. Seventh Edition, revised and enlarged by C. STEEL, M.R.C.V.S.L. 8vo. with Plates and Woodcuts, 18s.

The HORSE; with a Treatise on Draught. By WILLIAM YOUATT. New Edition, revised and enlarged. 8vo. with numerous Woodcuts, 12s. 6d.

The DOG. By the same Author. 8vo. with numerous Woodcuts, 6s.

The DOG in HEALTH and DISEASE. By STONEHENGE. With 70 Wood Engravings. Square crown 8vo. 10s. 6d.

The GREYHOUND. By STONEHENGE. Revised Edition, with 24 Portraits of Greyhounds. Square crown 8vo. 10s. 6d.

The OX; his Diseases and their Treatment: with an Essay on Parturition in the Cow. By J. R. DOBSON. Crown 8vo. with Illustrations. 7s. 6d.

Works of Utility and General Information.

The THEORY and PRACTICE of BANKING. By H. D. MACLEOD, M.A. Barrister-at-Law. Second Edition, entirely remodelled, 2 vols. 8vo. 30s.

A **DICTIONARY**, Practical, Theoretical, and Historical, of Commerce and Commercial Navigation. By J. R. M'CULLOCH. New and thoroughly revised Edition. 8vo. price 63s. cloth, or 70s. half-bd. in russia.

The **LAW of NATIONS** Considered as Independent Political Communities. By Sir TRAVERS TWISS, D.C.L. 2 vols. 8vo. 30s.; or separately, PART I. *Peace*, 12s. PART II. *War*, 18s.

The **CABINET LAWYER**; a Popular Digest of the Laws of England, Civil, Criminal, and Constitutional; intended for Practical Use and General Information. Twenty-third Edition. Fcp. 8vo. price 7s. 6d.

PEWTNER'S COMPREHENSIVE SPECIFIER; A Guide to the Practical Specification of every kind of Building-Artificers' Work; with Forms of Building Conditions and Agreements, an Appendix, Foot-Notes, and a copious Index. Edited by W. YOUNG, Architect. Crown 8vo. price 6s.

The **LAW RELATING to BENEFIT BUILDING SOCIETIES**; with Practical Observations on the Act and all the Cases decided thereon; also a Form of Rules and Forms of Mortgages. By W. TIDD PRATT, Barrister. Second Edition. Fcp. 3s. 6d.

COLLIERIES and COLLIERS: a Handbook of the Law and Leading Cases relating thereto. By J. C. FOWLER, of the Inner Temple, Barrister. Second Edition. Fcp. 8vo. 7s. 6d.

The **MATERNAL MANAGEMENT of CHILDREN in HEALTH and** Disease. By THOMAS BULL, M.D. Fcp. 5s.

HINTS to MOTHERS on the MANAGEMENT of their HEALTH during the Period of Pregnancy and in the Lying-in Room. By the late THOMAS BULL, M.D. Fcp. 5s.

HOW to NURSE SICK CHILDREN; containing Directions which may be found of service to all who have charge of the Young. By CHARLES WEST, M.D. Second Edition. Fcp. 8vo. 1s. 6d.

NOTES on LYING-IN INSTITUTIONS; with a Proposal for Organising an Institution for Training Midwives and Midwifery Nurses. By FLORENCE NIGHTINGALE. With several Illustrations. 8vo. price 7s. 6d.

NOTES on HOSPITALS. By FLORENCE NIGHTINGALE. Third Edition, enlarged; with 13 Plans. Post 4to. 18s.

CHESS OPENINGS. By F. W. LONGMAN, Balliol College, Oxford. Fcp. 8vo. 2s. 6d.

A **PRACTICAL TREATISE on BREWING**; with Formulæ for Public Brewers, and Instructions for Private Families. By W. BLACK. 8vo. 10s. 6d.

MODERN COOKERY for PRIVATE FAMILIES, reduced to a System of Easy Practice in a Series of carefully-tested Receipts. By ELIZA ACTON. Newly revised and enlarged Edition; with 8 Plates of Figures and 150 Woodcuts. Fcp. 6s.

WILLICH'S POPULAR TABLES, for ascertaining, according to the Carlisle Table of Mortality, the value of Lifehold, Leasehold, and Church Property, Renewal Fines, Reversions, &c. Seventh Edition, edited by MONTAGUE MARRIOTT, Barrister-at-Law. Post 8vo. price 10s.

MAUNDER'S TREASURY of KNOWLEDGE and LIBRARY of Reference: comprising an English Dictionary and Grammar, Universal Gazetteer, Classical Dictionary, Chronology, Law Dictionary, a Synopsis of the Peerage, useful Tables, &c. Revised Edition. Fcp. 8vo. price 6s.

INDEX.

ACTON's Modern Cookery 23
ALCOCK's Residence in Japan 22
ALLEN's Four Discourses of Chrysostom .. 22
ALLIES on Formation of Christendom 21
Alpine Guide (The) 22
ALTHAUS on Medical Electricity 14
ARNOLD's Manual of English Literature .. 7
ARNOTT's Elements of Physics 11
Arundines Cami 25
Autumn Holidays of a Country Parson ... 8
AYRE's Treasury of Bible Knowledge..... 20

BACON's Essays, by WHATELY 6
——— Life and Letters, by SPEDDING .. 5
——— Works, edited by SPEDDING 5
BAIN's Logic, Deductive and Inductive ... 10
——— Mental and Moral Science 10
——— on the Senses and Intellect..... 10
BALL's Alpine Guide 22
BAYLDON's Rents and Tillages 19
Beaten Tracks 22
BECKER's Charicles and Gallus 25
BENFEY's Sanskrit Dictionary 8
BERNARD on British Neutrality 1
BLACK's Treatise on Brewing 20
BLACKLEY's German-English Dictionary... 8
BLAINE's Rural Sports 25
——— Veterinary Art 27
BOOTH's Saint-Simon 3
BOULTBEE on 39 Articles 19
BOURNE on Screw Propeller 15
BOURNE's Catechism of the Steam Engine. 15
——— Handbook of Steam Engine 15
——— Improvements in the Steam Engine ....
——— Treatise on the Steam Engine .. 15
——— Examples of Modern Engines ... 15
BOWDLER's Family SHAKSPEARE 25
BOYD's Reminiscences 4
BRAMLEY-MOORE's Six Sisters of the Valleys 24
BRANDE's Dictionary of Science, Literature, and Art ....
BRAY's (C.) Education of the Feelings ... 10
——— Philosophy of Necessity 10
——— on Force 10
BROWNE's Exposition of the 39 Articles... 19
BRUNEL's Life of BRUNEL 4
BUCKLE's History of Civilisation 3
BULL's Hints to Mothers 23
——— Maternal Management of Children 23
BUNSEN's God in History 3
——— Prayers 19
BUNSEN's Vicissitudes of Families 4
BURTON's Christian Church 4

Cabinet Lawyer 26
CAMPBELL's Norway 22

CARNOTA's Memoirs of Pombal 4
CATES's Biographical Dictionary 5
CATS' and FARLIE's Moral Emblems 16
Changed Aspects of Unchanged Truths 9
CHESNEY's Indian Polity 2
——— Waterloo Campaign 2
——— and REEVE's Military Essays ... 2
Chorale Book for England 16
CLOUGH's Lives from Plutarch 3
COLENSO (Bishop) on Pentateuch 21
Commonplace Philosopher 8
CONINGTON's Translation of the Æneid... 25
CONTANSEAU's French-English Dictionaries 8
CONYBEARE and HOWSON's St. Paul 20
COTTON's (Bishop) Life 5
COOPER's Surgical Dictionary 13
COPLAND's Dictionary of Practical Medicine 13
Counsel and Comfort from a City Pulpit.. 9
COX's Aryan Mythology 3
——— Manual of Mythology 22
——— Tale of the Great Persian War ... 3
——— Tales of Ancient Greece........ 22
CRESY's Encyclopædia of Civil Engineering 16
Critical Essays of a Country Parson 8
CROOKES on Beet-Root Sugar 15
——— 's Chemical Analysis 14
CULLEY's Handbook of Telegraphy....... 16
CUSACK's History of Ireland 3

D'AUBIGNÉ's History of the Reformation
  in the time of CALVIN 3
DAVIDSON's Introduction to New Testament 20
Dead Shot (The), by MARKSMAN 27
DE LA RIVE's Treatise on Electricity .. 12
DENISON's Vice-Regal Life 1
DE TOCQUEVILLE's Democracy in America . 3
DISRAELI's Lothair 24
——— Novels and Tales 24
DORELL's Medical Reports 13
DOBSON on the Ox 27
DOVE on Storms 11
DOYLE's Fairyland 16
DYER's City of Rome 2

EASTLAKE's Hints on Household Taste ... 17
——— History of Oil Painting 16
——— Gothic Revival 17
——— Life of Gibson 16
Elements of Botany 12
ELLICOTT on the Revision of the English
  New Testament 19
——— Commentary on Ephesians 20
——— Commentary on Galatians 20
——— Pastoral Epist. 20
——— Philippians, &c. 20
——— Thessalonians 20
——— Lectures on the Life of Christ. 20

NEW WORKS PUBLISHED BY LONGMANS AND CO.

Essays and Contributions of A. K. H. B. 6
EWALD'S History of Israel 20

FAIRBAIRN on Iron Shipbuilding 16
——— 's Applications of Iron 16
——— Information for Engineers .. 16
——— Mills and Millwork 16
FARADAY'S Life and Letters 4
FARRAR'S Families of Speech 9
——— Chapters on Language 7
FELKIN on Hosiery and Lace Manufactures 16
FFRENCH'S Book of the Roach 27
FFOULKES'S Christendom's Divisions 21
FITZWYGRAM on Horses and Stables 27
FOWLER'S Collieries and Colliers 23
FRANCIS'S Fishing Book 27
FREEHFIELD'S Travels in the Caucasus 23
FROUDE'S History of England 1
——— Short Studies on Great Subjects ... 9

GANOT'S Elementary Physics 11
GILBERT'S Cadore, or Titian's Country 23
GILBERT and CHURCHILL'S Dolomites 23
GIRDLESTONE'S Bible Synonymes 19
GLADSTONE'S Life of WHITEFIELD 3
GODDARD'S Wonderful Stories 23
GOLDSMITH'S Poems, Illustrated 25
GRAHAM'S View of Literature and Art 8
GRANT'S Home Politics 3
——— Ethics of Aristotle 6
Graver Thoughts of a Country Parson 8
GRAY'S Anatomy 15
GRINDROW on Bronchitis 15
GRIFFITH'S Fundamentals 19
GROVE on Correlation of Physical Forces .. 12
GURNEY'S Chapters of French History 2
GWILT'S Encyclopædia of Architecture 17

HAMPDEN'S (Bishop) Memorials 4
HARE on Election of Representatives 7
HARTWIG'S Harmonies of Nature 13
——— Polar World 13
——— Sea and its Living Wonders .. 13
——— Subterranean World 13
——— Tropical World 13
HAUGHTON'S Manual of Geology 12
HERSCHEL'S Outlines of Astronomy 10
HEWITT on Diseases of Women 14
HODGSON'S Theory of Practice 10
——— Time and Space 10
HOLMES'S System of Surgery 14
——— Surgical Diseases of Infancy .. 14
Home (The) at Heatherbrae 24
HORNE'S Introduction to the Scriptures .. 20
——— Compendium of ditto 20
How we Spent the Summer 23
HOWITT'S Australian Discovery 22
——— Mad War Planet 26
——— Northern Heights of London ... 23
——— Rural Life of England 24
——— Visits to Remarkable Places 24

HÜBNER'S Memoir of Sixtus V. 2
HUGHES'S (W.) Manual of Geography 11
HUME'S Essays 10
——— Treatise on Human Nature 10

INMAN'S Roman History 2
INGELOW'S Poems 25
——— Story of Doom 25
——— Mopsa 25

JAMESON'S Saints and Martyrs 17
——— Legends of the Madonna 17
——— Monastic Orders 17
JAMESON and EASTLAKE'S Saviour 17
John Jerningham's Journal 25
JOHNSTON'S Geographical Dictionary 11

KALISCH'S Commentary on the Bible 7
——— Hebrew Grammar 7
KEITH on Fulfilment of Prophecy 20
——— Destiny of the World 20
KERL'S Metallurgy 16
BOHRIG 16
KIRBY and SPENCE'S Entomology 13

LATHAM'S English Dictionary ....
LAWLOR'S Pilgrimages in the Pyrenees 24
LECKY'S History of European Morals 3
——— Rationalism 3
Leisure Hours in Town 9
Lessons of Middle Age 9
LEWES' History of Philosophy 3
LIDDELL and SCOTT'S Two Lexicons 8
Life of Man Symbolised 16
LINDLEY and MOORE'S Treasury of Botany 12
LONGMAN'S Edward the Third 3
——— Lectures on the History of England 2
——— Chess Openings 26
LOUDON'S Agriculture 19
——— Gardening 19
——— Plants 12
LOWNDES'S Engineer's Handbook 17
LUBBOCK on Origin of Civilisation 12
Lyra Eucharistica 22
——— Germanica 16, 21
——— Messianica 22
——— Mystica 22

MACAULAY'S (Lord) Essays 2
——— History of England .. 1
——— Lays of Ancient Rome 25
——— Miscellaneous Writings 9
——— Speeches 7
——— Complete Works 1
MACFARREN'S Lectures on Harmony 16
MACLEOD'S Elements of Political Economy 7
——— Dictionary of Political Economy 7
——— Theory and Practice of Banking 17
MCCULLOCH'S Dictionary of Commerce 25

MAGUIRE's Life of Father Mathew 6
——— Pope Pius IX 5
MALET's Overthrow of the Germanic Confederation by Prussia 3
MANNING's England and Christendom 21
MARCET on the Larynx 15
MARSHALL's Canadian Dominion 11
——— Physiology 15
MARSHMAN's Life of Havelock 3
——— History of India 2
MASSINGBERD's Christian Life 22
MASSINGBERD's History of the Reformation 4
MAUNDER's Biographical Treasury 5
——— Geographical Treasury 11
——— Historical Treasury 4
——— Scientific and Literary Treasury 13
——— Treasury of Knowledge 20
——— Treasury of Natural History 15
MAY's Constitutional History of England . 1
MELVILLE's Novels and Tales .... 24 & 25
MENDELSSOHN's Letters 6
MERIVALE's Fall of the Roman Republic .. 2
——— Romans under the Empire . 2
MERRIFIELD and EVERS's Navigation 11
MILES on Horse's Foot and Horseshoeing .. 27
——— Horses' Teeth and Stables 27
MILL (J.) on the Mind 8
MILL (J. S.) on Liberty 5
——— on Representative Government 5
——— on Utilitarianism 5
MILL's (J. S.) Dissertations and Discussions 5
——— Political Economy 5
——— System of Logic 8
——— Hamilton's Philosophy 8
——— Inaugural Address 8
——— Subjection of Women 7
MILLER's Elements of Chemistry 14
——— Hymn-Writers 21
MITCHELL's Manual of Architecture 17
——— Manual of Assaying 26
MONSELL's Beatitudes 22
——— His Presence not his Memory 22
——— 'Spiritual Songs' 22
MOORE's Irish Melodies 25
——— Lalla Rookh 25
——— Poetical Works 25
MORELL's Elements of Psychology 9
——— Mental Philosophy 9
MÜLLER's (MAX) Chips from a German Workshop 9
——— Lectures on Language 7
——— (K. O.) Literature of Ancient Greece 3
MURCHISON on Liver Complaints 15
MURE's Language and Literature of Greece 3

NASH's Compendium of the Prayer Book .. 19
New Testament, Illustrated Edition 15
NEWMAN's History of his Religious Opinions 5
NIGHTINGALE's Notes on Hospitals 20
——— Lying-In Institutions 20
NILSSON's Scandinavia 13

NORTHCOTT's Lathes and Turning 17

ODLING's Animal Chemistry 14
——— Course of Practical Chemistry .. 14
——— Manual of Chemistry 14
——— Lectures on Carbon 14
——— Outlines of Chemistry 14
O'DRISCOLL's Memoirs of MACLISE 4
O'FLANAGAN's Irish Chancellors 5
Our Children's Story 25
OWEN's Lectures on the Invertebrata 12
——— Comparative Anatomy and Physiology of Vertebrate Animals 12

PACKE's Guide to the Pyrenees 23
PAGET's Lectures on Surgical Pathology .. 15
PEREIRA's Manual of Materia Medica 16
PERKIN's Italian and Tuscan Sculptors.... 17
PERRING's Churches and Creeds 10
PEWTNER's Comprehensive Specifier 22
Pictures in Tyrol 23
PIESSE's Art of Perfumery 19
——— Natural Magic 19
POSTON's Beginning 12
PRATT's Law of Building Societies 22
PRENDERGAST's Mastery of Languages.... 5
PRESCOTT's Scripture Difficulties 21
Present-Day Thoughts 9
PROCTOR on Plurality of Worlds 10
——— Saturn and its System 10
——— The Sun 10
——— 's Scientific Essays 13
Public Schools Atlas (The) 11

RAE's Westward by Rail 23
Recreations of a Country Parson 8
REICHEL's See of Rome 22
REILLY's Map of Mont Blanc 23
REIMANN on Aniline Dyes 15
RIVERS' Rose Amateur's Guide 19
ROBBINS's Cavalry Catechism 27
ROGERS's Correspondence of Greyson 9
——— Eclipse of Faith 9
——— Defence of ditto 9
ROGET's English Words and Phrases 7
RONALD's Fly-Fisher's Entomology 27
ROSS's Ignatius Loyola 2
ROTHSCHILD's Israelites 20
ROWTON's Debater 7
RUSSELL's Pau and the Pyrenees 23

SANDARS's Justinian's Institutes 5
SAVILE on the Truth of the Bible 19
SCHELLEN's Spectrum Analysis 11
SCOTT's Lectures on the Fine Arts 16
——— Albert Durer 16
SHIRLEY's Oxford Reformers of 1498 2
SEWELL's After Life 24
——— Amy Herbert 24
——— Cleve Hall 24
——— Earl's Daughter 24
——— Examination for Confirmation .. 21

SEWELL's Experience of Life 24
——— Gertrude..................... 24
——— Giant 25
——— Glimpse of the World 24
——— History of the Early Church 3
——— Ivors........................ 24
——— Journal of a Home Life........ 24
——— Katharine Ashton............. 24
——— Laneton Parsonage........... 24
——— Margaret Percival 24
——— Passing Thoughts on Religion .. 17
——— Poems of Bygone Years 22
——— Preparations for Communion ... 17
——— Principles of Education....... 17
——— Readings for Confirmation 17
——— Readings for Lent............ 17
——— Tales and Stories 21
——— Thoughts for the Age 17
——— Ursula...................... 22
——— Thoughts for the Holy Week... 21
SHIPLEY's Four Cardinal Virtues........ 21
——— Invocation of Saints 22
SHORT's Church History................ 4
SHART's WALKER's Dictionary 6
SMITH's (V.) Bible and Popular Theology 19
——— (J.) Paul's Voyage and Shipwreck 20
——— (SYDNEY) Miscellaneous Works. 9
——— Wit and Wisdom 9
——— Life and Letters......... 4
SOUTHEY's Doctor 7
——— Poetical Works 20
STANLEY's History of British Birds 13
STATHAM's Eucharis 18
STEBBING's Analysis of MILL's Logic 6
STEPHEN's Ecclesiastical Biography 4
——— Playground of Europe..... 22
STIRLING's Secret of Hegel 9
——— Sir WILLIAM HAMILTON 10
STONEHENGE on the Dog 27
——— on the Greyhound........... 27
STRICKLAND's Queens of England........ 8
Sunday Afternoons at the Parish Church of
a Scottish University City (St. Andrews).. 8

TAYLOR's History of India 3
——— (Jeremy) Works, edited by EDEN 22
THIRLWALL's History of Greece............ 3
THOMPSON's (Archbishop) Laws of Thought 6
——— (A. T.) Conspectus........ 16
TODD (A.) on Parliamentary Government 1
TODD and BOWMAN's Anatomy and Physiology of Man.............................. 15
TRENCH's Ierne, a Tale 24
TRENCH's Realities of Irish Life 8
TROLLOPE's Barchester Towers 24
——— Warden 24
TWISS's Law of Nations................. 22
TYNDALL on Diamagnetism................ 11
——— Electricity.................. 12

TYNDALL on Heat....................... 11
——— Imagination in Science ... 12
——— Sound 11
——— 's Faraday as a Discoverer .. 4
——— Fragments of Science 12
——— Hours of Exercise in the Alps.. 22
——— Lectures on Light........... 12

UEBERWEG's System of Logic............ 9
UNCLE PETER's Fairy Tale 24
URE's Arts, Manufactures, and Mines....... 17

VAN DER HOEVEN's Handbook of Zoology 12
VEREKER's Sunny South 22
Visit to my Discontented Cousin 25

WARBURTON's Hunting Songs 28
WATSON's Principles and Practice of Physic 14
WATTS's Dictionary of Chemistry 14
WEBB's Objects for Common Telescopes .. 11
WEBSTER and WILKINSON's Greek Testament 21
WELLINGTON's Life, by GLEIG 5
WEST on Children's Diseases........... 14
——— Nursing Sick Children....... 22
——— 's Lumleian Lectures 14
WHATELY's English Synonymes 6
——— Logic 6
——— Rhetoric 6
WHATELY on a Future State 21
——— Truth of Christianity 3
WHITE's Latin-English Dictionaries 7
WILCOCK's Sea Fisherman.............. 27
WILLIAMS's Aristotle's Ethics 6
WILLIAMS on Climate of South of France 15
——— Consumption............. 15
WILLICH's Popular Tables 28
WILLIS's Principles of Mechanism 17
WINSLOW on Light.................... 12
WOOD's Bible Animals 12
——— Homes without Hands 12
——— Insects at Home 12
——— Strange Dwellings 12
WOODWARD and CATES's Encyclopaedia.. 4

YARDLEY's Poetical Works............... 28
YONGE's English-Greek Lexicons 8
——— Two Editions of Horace............ 28
——— History of England 1
YOUATT on the Dog 27
——— on the Horse 27

ZELLER's Socrates...................... 6
——— Stoics, Epicureans, and Sceptics.. 6
Zigzagging amongst Dolomites 22

Spottiswoode & Co., Printers, New-street Square, London.

This book is a preservation photocopy.
It is made in compliance with copyright law
and produced on acid-free archival
60# book weight paper
which meets the requirements of
ANSI/NISO Z39.48-1992 (permanence of paper)

Preservation photocopying and binding
by
Acme Bookbinding
Charlestown, Massachusetts

2000

www.ingramcontent.com/pod-product-compliance
Lightning Source LLC
Chambersburg PA
CBHW021821230426
43669CB00008B/827